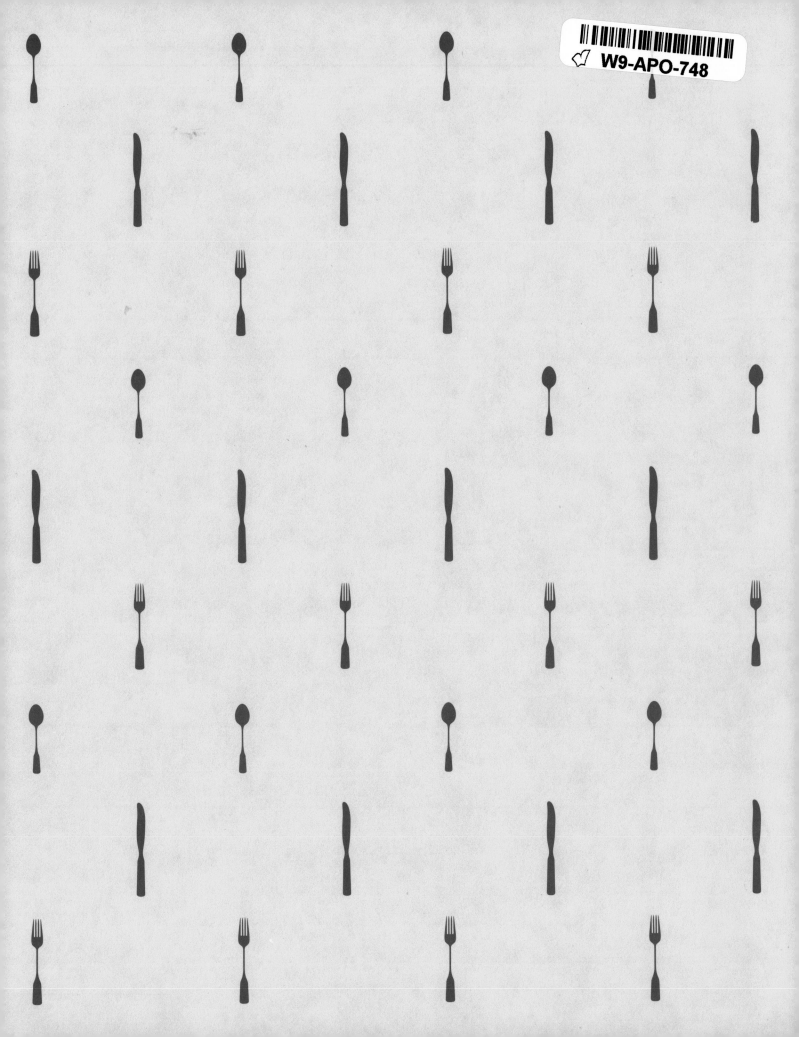

Fresh Ways
with Vegetarian Dishes

Time-Life Books Inc.
is a wholly owned subsidiary of
TIME INCORPORATED

FOUNDER: Henry R. Luce 1898-1967

Editor-in-Chief: Jason McManus
Chairman and Chief Executive Officer: J. Richard Munro
President and Chief Operating Officer: N. J. Nicholas, Jr.
Editorial Director: Ray Cave
Executive Vice President, Books: Kelso F. Sutton
Vice President, Books: Paul V. McLaughlin

COVER
Spinach, onions, potatoes, and sweet red pepper make a colorful filling for these light vegetarian pancakes (recipe, page 28). Because only the white of the egg is used in the batter, the pancakes are low in cholesterol and saturated fat, allowing the addition of a crusty topping of low-fat cheese.

TIME-LIFE BOOKS INC.

EDITOR: George Constable
Executive Editor: Ellen Phillips
Director of Design: Louis Klein
Director of Editorial Resources: Phyllis K. Wise
Editorial Board: Russell B. Adams, Jr., Dale M. Brown, Roberta Conlan, Thomas H. Flaherty, Lee Hassig, Donia Ann Steele, Rosalind Stubenberg
Director of Photography and Research: John Conrad Weiser
Assistant Director of Editorial Resources: Elise Ritter Gibson

EUROPEAN EXECUTIVE EDITOR: Gillian Moore
Design Director: Ed Skyner
Assistant Design Director: Mary Staples
Chief of Research: Vanessa Kramer
Chief Sub-Editor: Ilse Gray

PRESIDENT: Christopher T. Linen
Chief Operating Officer: John M. Fahey, Jr.
Senior Vice Presidents: Robert M. DeSena, James L. Mercer, Paul R. Stewart
Vice Presidents: Stephen L. Bair, Ralph J. Cuomo, Neal Goff, Stephen L. Goldstein, Juanita T. James, Hallett Johnson III, Carol Kaplan, Susan J. Maruyama, Robert H. Smith, Joseph J. Ward
Director of Production Services: Robert J. Passantino
Supervisor of Quality Control: James King

Library of Congress Cataloging in Publication Data
Fresh ways with vegetarian dishes / by the editors of Time-Life Books.
      p.   cm. — (Healthy home cooking)
Includes index.
ISBN 0-8094-6075-0 — ISBN 0-8094-6076-9 (lib. bdg.)
1. Vegetarian cookery. I. Time-Life Books.
TX837.F69 1989   641.5'636—dc19   88-38891
                                   CIP

For information on and a full description of any Time-Life Books series, please call 1-800-621-7026 or write:
Reader Information
Time-Life Customer Service
P.O. Box C-32068
Richmond, Virginia 23261-2068

HEALTHY HOME COOKING

SERIES DIRECTOR: Jackie Matthews
Studio Stylist: Liz Hodgson

Editorial Staff for *Fresh Ways with Vegetarian Dishes:*
Editor: Frances Dixon
Researcher: Eva Reynolds
Designer: Paul Reeves
Sub-Editors: Christine Noble, Eugénie Romer
Indexer: Myra Clark

Picture Department:
Administrator: Patricia Murray
Picture Coordinator: Amanda Hindley

Editorial Production:
Chief: Maureen Kelly
Assistant: Samantha Hill
Editorial Department: Theresa John, Debra Lelliott

U.S. Edition:
Assistant Editor: Barbara Fairchild Quarmby
Copy Coordinators: Marfé Ferguson Delano, Ann Lee Bruen
Picture Coordinator: Betty H. Weatherley

Editorial Operations
Copy Chief: Diane Ullius
Production: Celia Beattie
Library: Louise D. Forstall

Correspondents: Elisabeth Kraemer-Singh (Bonn); Maria Vincenza Aloisi (Paris); Ann Natanson (Rome).

THE CONTRIBUTORS

LISA CHERKASKY has worked as a chef at numerous restaurants in Washington, D.C., and in Madison, Wisconsin, including nationally known Le Pavillon and Le Lion d'Or. A graduate of The Culinary Institute of America at Hyde Park, New York, she has also taught classes in French cooking technique.

SILVIJA DAVIDSON studied at Leith's School of Food and Wine in London and specializes in the development of recipes from Latvia, as well as other international cuisines.

JOANNA FARROW is a home economist and recipe writer who contributes to food magazines. Her books include *Creative Cake Decorating* and *Novelty Cakes for Children.*

ANTONY KWOK has won several awards for his Asian-inspired style of cooking and was the *London Standard* Gastronomic Seafish cook of 1986.

COLIN SPENCER is a well-known author on vegetarian cuisine. His books include *Gourmet Cooking for Vegetarians, Cordon Vert,* and *The New Vegetarian.*

JANE SUTHERING is a food writer and home economist who concentrates on vegetarian dishes. She is consultant to a major health-food restaurant chain.

The following people also have contributed recipes to this volume: Pat Alburey, Cordelia Banks, Joanna Blythman, Maddalena Bonino, Jo Chalmers, Gail Duff, Anne Gains, Yvonne Hamlett, Carole Handslip, Cristine MacKie, Roselyne Masselin, Susie Theodorou, Nicole Veillard, Rosemary Wadey, and Steven Wheeler.

THE COOKS

The recipes in this book were prepared for photographing by Pat Alburey, Jackie Baxter, Allyson Birch, Jane Bird, Jill Eggleton, Joanna Farrow, Anne Gains, Carole Handslip, Antony Kwok, Lesley Sendall, Jane Suthering, Rosemary Wadey, and Steven Wheeler. *Studio Assistant:* Rita Walters.

THE CONSULTANT

PAT ALBUREY is a home economist with a wide experience in preparing foods for photography, teaching cooking, and creating recipes. She has written a number of cookbooks, and she was the studio consultant for the Time-Life Books series The Good Cook. She has created a number of the recipes in this volume.

THE NUTRITION CONSULTANT

PATRICIA JUDD trained as a dietician and worked in hospital nutrition before returning to college to earn her M.Sc. and Ph.D. degrees. She has since lectured in Nutrition and Dietetics at London University.

Nutritional analyses for *Fresh Ways with Vegetarian Dishes* were derived from McCance and Widdowson's *The Composition of Food* by A. A. Paul and D. A. T. Southgate, and other current data.

Fresh Ways
with Vegetarian Dishes

BY

THE EDITORS OF TIME-LIFE BOOKS

TIME-LIFE BOOKS / ALEXANDRIA, VIRGINIA

Contents

The Vegetarian Alternative...6

The Key to Better Eating.......................8
Vegetable Stock 9

1 *A Wealth of Vegetables* 10

Zucchini Tian..12
Spanish Omelette..................................13
Ratatouille Terrine.................................14
Peeling and Seeding a Tomato..........14
Eggplant and Mozzarella
Ramekins..15
Eggplant Rolls with a Ricotta-Raisin
Filling 16
Eggplant Fans.......................................17
Squash Soufflé 19
Spring Vegetables in Watercress
Crepes 20
Peeling Sweet Peppers........................21
Asparagus Mousse with Goat
Cheese Sauce 21
Baked Fennel in Roquefort
Sauce 22
Belgian Endive and Pistachio-
Stuffed Tomatoes 23
Stuffed Leeks with Gruyère
Sauce 24
Spicy Mold of Leeks, Zucchini, and
Cabbage...25
Chili Peppers—A Cautionary Note....25
Chestnuts and Brussels Sprouts with
Red Cabbage and Caraway Potatoes....26
Spiced Red Cabbage 27

Asparagus Mousse with Goat Cheese Sauce

Lacy Pancakes with Spinach
Filling 28
Spinach, Stilton, and Tomato
Roulade 29
Spinach and Pine Nut Layered
Terrine 30
Kohlrabi and Zucchini Gratin 31

Spinach, Stilton, and Tomato Roulade

Stuffed Mushrooms.............................32
Celeriac Rolls with Mustard Sauce 33
Salsify with Pepper and Onion
Relish 34
Boiled Yams with Hot-Pepper Sauce....35
Chestnut-Stuffed Sweet Potatoes
with Chili Sauce...................................36
Peeling Chestnuts...............................37
Sweet Potato Timbales with Two
Paprika Sauces.....................................37
Saffron and Potato Stew with
Rouille 38
Potato, Carrot, and Celeriac Rösti.....39
Baked Potatoes with an Onion
and Chive Filling..................................40
Scandinavian Salad 41
Jerusalem Artichoke and Walnut
Soufflés 42
Curried Rutabaga Soup 43
Mixed Root Vegetables in Orange
Sauce 44
Stir-Fried Vegetables in a
Sweet-and-Sour Sauce........................45
Lohans' Feast......................................46

Okra and Sweet Pepper Stew...........48
Vegetable Curry with Coconut.........49
Mexican Sweet Potato Stew 50
Hot-and-Sour Potato and Turnip
Casserole...51

2 *Treasures from the Store Cupboard* 52

Salad of Avocado, Flageolets,
Almonds, and Brown Rice.................54
Caribbean Spiced Rice 55
Basmati and Wild Rice Molds with
Braised Artichokes 56
Gâteau of Crepes with Wild Rice
and Mushrooms...................................56
Wild and Brown Rice Pilaf with
Mushroom Ragout 58
Pumpkin and Pecorino Risotto..........60
Pea and Mushroom Risotto...............61
Eight Treasures in Lotus Leaves 62
Shaping a Lotus-Leaf Parcel..............63
Rice Cakes with Onion Relish 64
Buckwheat and Lentil Pilaf................65
Semolina Gnocchi with Julienned
Vegetables...66
Chili Beans with Cornbread
Topping..67

Polenta Pizza

Polenta Pizza......................................68
Polenta Ring with Pine Nuts and
Mozzarella 69

Provençal Casserole 70
Tandoori Patties 71
Gingered Black Beans with Saffron
Rice 72

Butter Bean Succotash

Tuscan-Style Beans 73
Lima Beans Baked with an Herbed
Crust..74
Butter Bean Succotash 75
Cabbage Stuffed with Black-Eyed
Peas and Mushrooms..........................76
Hollowing a Whole Cabbage..............76
Chickpea and Okra Casserole with
Couscous...77
Chickpea and Bulgur Kofta 78
Chickpea Salad in Artichoke Cups....78
Preparing Artichokes for Stuffing......79
Indonesian Vegetable Stew................80
Lentils with Spinach and
Carrots...81
Lentil and Potato Cakes with
Mustard Pickle..................................82
Lentils with Cumin and Onion..........83
Lentil Soufflés Baked in Sweet
Pepper Cases.....................................84
Sichuan Tofu with Sweet Pepper
and Peanuts......................................84
Storing and Draining Tofu..............85
Tofu and Vegetable Dumplings........86

Tofu and Vegetable Stir-Fry with
Noodles 87
Tofu, Zucchini, and Mushroom
Kabobs 88

Barley and Mushroom Broth with
Smoked Tofu 89

3 A Sustaining Trio.........90

Ricotta and Zucchini
Tortellini with Mint Yogurt Sauce 92

*Goat Cheese and
Parsley Ravioli*

Shaping Tortellini................................93
Vegetable Lasagna 94
Penne with Celery and Ricotta
Cheese..95
Goat Cheese and Parsley Ravioli 96
Making Ravioli..................................97
Spaghetti with Omelette Strips and
Stir-Fried Vegetables 97
Saffron Fettuccine with Hazelnut
and Tarragon Sauce 98
Summer Beans with Fresh
Fettuccine and Basil..........................99
Nut and Avocado Dumplings with
a Citrus Sauce 100
Herbed Spring Rolls with Peanut
Sauce 101
Carrot and Broccoli
Tortes..102
Asparagus and Morel Tart...............103
Savory Pumpkin Pie 104
Mustard-Cauliflower Quiche............105
Whole-Wheat Pizza with Corn
and Pineapple................................106
Pastry-Wrapped Pears Stuffed with
Walnuts, Stilton, and Leeks.............107
Mushroom Coulibiac........................108
Broccoli and Pecorino Turnovers 109
Smoked Cheese Gougère with a
Lemon and Fennel Filling.................110
Steamed Leek and Celeriac
Pudding 111
Asparagus Strudel...........................112
Spinach and Nappa Cabbage Pie....113
Fennel, Endive, and Blue Cheese
Triangles..114
Bulgur-Stuffed Phyllo Packages 115

Fennel, Broccoli, and Okra Croustades

Mushrooms and Asparagus in Phyllo
Cases 116
Baguette and Brie Bake 117
Salsify and Asparagus Muffins.........118
Italian Peasant Salad.......................119
Bread, Cheese, and Onion Pudding ...120
Fennel, Broccoli, and Okra
Croustades......................................121
Making Croustades..........................121

4 Microwaving Vegetarian Dishes.....122

Cauliflower Cheese Mold.................123
Zucchini and Tomato Clafoutis........124
Mixed Vegetable Pipérade...............125
Jerusalem Artichoke Gratin.............126
Salad-Filled Potato Pie.....................127
Stuffed Grape Leaves with Bulgur
and Tomatoes 128
Warm Camembert and Fruit Salad 129
Potato, Carrot, and Cauliflower
Curry...130
Spiced Bean Medley 131
Oriental Parchment Parcels 132
Sweet-and-Sour Tumbled
Vegetables 133
Cabbage Timbale with
Tomato Sauce 134
Mushroom Quiche............................135

Nutritional Charts 136

Glossary..140
Picture Credits.................................141
Acknowledgments............................142
Index..142

The Vegetarian Alternative

In the prosperous West, where meat and fish have long been the cornerstones of a privileged diet, a significant change is under way. While entrenched carnivores continue to insist that a meal without animal flesh is not a true meal at all, a growing number of people are beginning to discover that meatless meals are not only possible but are positively enjoyable. They also are discovering the paradox of vegetarian cooking: Instead of less choice, there somehow seems to be more. Vegetables emerge from supporting roles as side dishes, challenging the imagination of a creative cook with their dazzling variety. Pasta and bread, no longer regarded as mere fillers, prove capable of the most sophisticated variations, while ordinary dried beans and grains—so long dismissed as humble food—become the respected, nutritious staples of the vegetarian alternative.

This book explores the wide world of cooking without meat, from simple suppertime casseroles of vegetables or dried beans to festive centerpieces for the dinner party. As with other volumes in the Healthy Home Cooking series, all of these dishes keep within low levels of sodium, cholesterol, and saturated fat. In adhering to these guidelines, Time-Life's cooks have been assisted by the ingredients themselves, for vegetables and grains are naturally low in these substances. The result is a revelatory anthology of original vegetarian dishes.

A wealth of nutrients

Enjoying a meatless meal requires no elaborate justification. The food is quite simply delicious. It is also very good for you. A mere glance at the nutritional charts on pages 136 to 139 offers reassurance to the novice in vegetarian cookery. Grains, dried beans, lentils, and peas, nuts, eggs, and cheese are all packed with proteins. Many of the green vegetables, including cabbage, broccoli, and asparagus, are also valuable sources of this body-building nutrient. A single sweet green pepper contains approximately three times the recommended daily minimum intake of vitamin C; two carrots a day provide more than enough vitamin A. Spinach is a storehouse of calcium and iron—along with a

whole alphabet of vitamins— while the lowly potato, so long a forbidden food for old-fashioned weight-watchers, is not only high in vitamins B_3 and B_6, but suprisingly low in calories, too.

Less familiar nutrients, all equally essential to good health, are also amply represented by vegetarian ingredients. Peanuts, vegetable oils, and egg yolk are among foods rich in vitamin E, necessary for healthy cells and the healing of wounds. Cabbage, lettuce, and cauliflower all contain vitamin K, which enables the blood to clot. Wheat bran, a major component of whole-wheat flour, is rich in magnesium, potassium, zinc, and copper.

Of all the essential nutrients, carbohydrates are the least appreciated. Our principal source of energy, they include sugars and starches. While sugars convert readily into energy but contain few nutrients, starches are a much misrepresented food group. Traditional slimming diets have frightened people away from starchy foods such as dried beans, potatoes, and bread, while persuading the impressionable dieter that even to look at a bowl of pasta is to gain weight. Yet these satisfying staples are not in themselves particularly fattening. A potato, for instance, contains fewer calories than an equal weight of lean steak. It is the topping—the butter, sour cream, or rich sauce with which starchy foods are traditionally served —that does the damage to a carbohydrate's reputation, and to our health. What is more, these foods are naturally full of proteins, vitamins, and minerals. When prepared with discretion, they can be eaten with a clear conscience.

Any vegetarian dish that is made with whole, unrefined ingredients has the added benefit of a high fiber content. Dietary fiber is itself indigestible, yet it assists the digestion of food and bulks up waste material, thus speeding the passage of waste through the intestines. Extravagant health claims have been made for this improbable nutritional hero; nevertheless, it is likely that fiber helps prevent diseases of the intestine—possibly including colon cancer—and reduces the body's absorption of cholesterol. Whole grains are a major source of dietary fiber, but so too are nuts and dried beans, as well as such fresh vegetables as celery, cabbage, spinach, broccoli, peas, and potatoes eaten in their skins.

A meatless way of life

There are many reasons for adopting a vegetarian diet. For some, it is simply a matter of a distaste for meat and fish; others may be attracted by the relatively low price of meatless meals; yet others find a persuasive moral justification for becoming vegetarians. Whatever the motivation, those reducing or abandoning meat in their diet must look closely at what they eat. In giving up meat they are abandoning a rich source of nutrients, especially of protein. In a diet that includes meat and fish, protein deficiency is very rare; just 4 ounces of beef, for instance, supplies half of the recommended daily intake of protein for an adult male. When meat is absent from the diet, eggs and cheese loom large as key sources of protein. Eggs are 12 percent protein and hard cheeses about 25 percent, compared with 20 to 30 percent in meat and about 20 percent in fish. Increasing one's intake of eggs and cheese to compensate for lost meat and fish protein, however, is not an ideal solution. Egg yolks are high in cholesterol, and many cheeses are full of saturated fat, which increases the level of cholesterol in the blood. Although some cholesterol is necessary to the proper functioning of the body, a diet high in cholesterol and saturated fat can lead to heart disease and the danger of strokes. Thus the wise vegetarian gains the bulk of his or her protein from grains, which are 6 to 13 percent protein, and dried beans, lentils, and peas—about 20 percent protein.

But percentages do not tell the whole story. Of the 20 amino acids that are the building blocks of proteins, 12 can be synthesized within the body; the other eight, known as essential amino acids, must be obtained from food. Only meat, fish, eggs, and dairy products have all eight of these essential amino acids in almost exactly the right proportion for the body's needs. Grains, dried beans, nuts, and seeds each contain only some of these eight amino acids. Thus to complete the protein jigsaw, vegetarians must be sure to eat a variety of foods. Dried beans and grains eaten together, or beans and nuts or seeds, complement each other to create a balanced amino acid intake.

Many traditional vegetarian diets strike just this balance. A poor Jamaican may cook no more than a dish of rice and peas for the main meal; a poor Indian eats lentils with a whole-wheat chapati. Lacking any precise nutritional knowledge, these two diverse cultures, like many others, have devised ways of providing a balanced supply of protein from vegetarian sources.

Variety is the key not just to consuming the right mix of amino acids, but also to gaining a good supply of all vitamins and minerals. Vegetarians must make a point of choosing widely from the vast range of vegetables, fruits, grains, dried beans, nuts, and seeds available. Provided they do so, and also eat modest quan-

tities of eggs and cheese, they have no need of vitamin supplements. Only vegans, who reject animal products entirely, must supplement their diets with vitamin B_{12}. Small amounts of this nutrient are essential to human life but are significantly present only in animal sources. It is readily available, however, in tablets or in fortified vegetarian foods such as yeast extracts.

Choosing and storing vegetarian ingredients

Few modern convenience foods are more truly convenient than grains, nuts, seeds, and dried beans. Supermarkets increasingly stock supplies of these ingredients, but many are still available only from health-food stores. Choose an outlet with a rapid turnover to ensure that the stock is fresh. It is not easy to guess the age of most dry ingredients. Beans with wrinkled skins, however, have almost certainly spent too long on the shelf.

Kept cool, dark, and dry in airtight containers, whole grains such as rice and millet will keep virtually forever. Under the same conditions, beans, peas, and lentils have a shelf life of up to six months. Kept much longer, they require more cooking, until finally they reach an age when they will not become tender no matter how long they are boiled.

Unshelled nuts also keep fresh-tasting for six months or more. Shelled whole nuts, which are more convenient for cooking, remain fresh for about three months when stored in airtight containers. Nut pieces or ground nuts go stale more quickly, and they should be used within six weeks.

Shopping for fresh ingredients is more of a challenge. Buy vegetables that are as fresh as possible, choosing those with crisp leaves and stalks, or firm skins. Avoid limp, pale-colored specimens; deep oranges, yellows, and greens promise a rich supply of vitamin A.

Vegetables are best not stored at all but eaten straight from the market or—better still—the garden. Green vegetables such as celery, lettuce, spinach, and broccoli are particularly affected by light and warmth, losing nutrients even while on display in the store. A shopworn cabbage may have lost half of its vitamin C by the time it reaches home.

If they must be stored, perishable vegetables keep best in the refrigerator at a temperature of between 35° and 40° F. Root vegetables are more durable. Stored in a dark, airy place at a temperature of about 50° F.—a basement or a cool pantry is ideal—carrots and onions will remain fresh for several weeks. Potatoes can last throughout the winter in these conditions, though they will inevitably lose some of their vitamin C in storage.

The best cooking methods

Much of the art of the preparation of nutritious vegetarian food lies in cooking vegetables so that they do not lose their inherent goodness. However carefully fresh ingredients have been select-

The Key to Better Eating

Healthy Home Cooking addresses the concerns of today's weight-conscious, health-minded cooks with recipes developed within strict nutritional guidelines.

The chart at right shows the National Research Council's Recommended Dietary Allowances of calories and protein for healthy men, women, and children, along with the council's recommendations for the "safe and adequate" intake of sodium. Although the council has not established recommendations for either cholesterol or fat, the chart includes what the National Institutes of Health and the American Heart Association consider the daily maximum amounts for healthy members of the population. The Heart Association, among other groups, has pointed out that Americans derive about 40 percent of their calories from fat; this, it believes, should be cut to less than 30 percent.

The volumes in the Healthy Home Cooking series do not purport to be diet books, nor do they focus on health foods. Rather, the books express a common-sense approach to cooking that uses salt, sugar, cream, butter, and oil in moderation while including other ingredients that also contribute flavor and satisfaction.

The recipes make few unusual demands. Naturally they call for fresh ingredients, offering substitutes should these be unavailable. (Only the first ingredient is calculated in

Recommended Dietary Guidelines

		Average Daily Intake		Maximum Daily Intake			
		CALORIES	PROTEIN grams	CHOLESTEROL milligrams	TOTAL FAT grams	SATURATED FAT grams	SODIUM milligrams
Children	7-10	2400	22	240	80	27	1800
Females	11-14	2200	37	220	73	24	2700
	15-18	2100	44	210	70	23	2700
	19-22	2100	44	300	70	23	3300
	23-50	2000	44	300	67	22	3300
	51-75	1800	44	300	60	20	3300
Males	11-14	2700	36	270	90	30	2700
	15-18	2800	56	280	93	31	2700
	19-22	2900	56	300	97	32	3300
	23-50	2700	56	300	90	30	3300
	51-75	2400	56	300	80	27	3300

the nutrient analysis, however.) Most of the ingredients can be found in any well-stocked supermarket; the exceptions can be bought in specialty shops or ethnic food stores.

About cooking times
To help the cook plan ahead effectively, Healthy Home Cooking takes time into account in all of its recipes. While recognizing that everyone cooks at a different speed, and that stoves and ovens may differ somewhat in their temperatures, the series provides ap-

proximate "working" and "total" times for every dish. Working time stands for the minutes actively spent on preparation; total time includes unattended cooking time, as well as time devoted to marinating, steeping, or soaking various ingredients. Because the recipes emphasize fresh foods, the dishes may take a bit longer to prepare than those that call for canned or packaged products, but the difference in flavor, and often in added nutritional value, should compensate for the little extra time involved.

ed and stored, careless cooking has the potential to undo their nutritional value in a matter of minutes. Boiling—which is traditionally the most popular way of preparing vegetables—can also be the most destructive to nutrients. Prolonged exposure to boiling water leaches out B vitamins and some minerals, while also destroying up to 80 percent of a vegetable's vitamin C supply. Ironically, the nutritious cooking liquid is then usually drained away, while the nutritionally decimated vegetable is respectfully consumed at the table.

For quickly cooked green vegetables, however, boiling is a very acceptable method. Plunged into a large open pan of rapidly boiling water, vegetables such as Brussels sprouts and green

beans cook swiftly and so retain a major part of their color, flavor, and nutrients.

Steaming, a gentler process than boiling, suits vegetables that require a longer cooking time. Cauliflower and roots—which take time to tenderize—lose less nutritive value in the steamer than by lengthy boiling in water. Various types of steamers are commercially available, including expanding steel baskets, which adjust to fit saucepans of various sizes, and multitiered steamers for cooking two or three vegetables at once. Lacking a steamer, use a colander or a frying basket; provided that the vegetables do not come in direct contact with the water, and that the saucepan can be tightly covered, an improvised steamer serves just as well. And remember that, whether steamed or boiled, vegetables cooked in their skins suffer less nutritional decimation than those that are first peeled and sliced.

Stir-frying, a technique that has been borrowed from Asian cuisine, is another successful way of preserving a vegetable's volatile nutrients. Rapidly heated and continually turned in a wok or skillet, finely cut vegetables have time to cook through, yet they retain their colors and suffer only an insignificant loss of vitamins and minerals.

About this book

Many of the recipes in this book include modest amounts of eggs and cheese, for these versatile, flavorful, and highly nutritious foods greatly extend the possibilities of vegetarian cuisine. However, the chefs and nutritionists at Time-Life Books have resisted the temptation to give them the major role that they occupy in many vegetarian cookbooks. This has enabled levels of saturated fat, cholesterol, and sodium to be kept within acceptable limits, while also ensuring that dried beans, grains, and vegetables assume a central importance.

This volume will appeal to many nonvegetarians who simply enjoy having some meals without meat. But the recipes have been devised to be acceptable to strict vegetarians. Thus gelatin, which is obtained from animal bones, makes no appearance. Similarly, vegetable stock *(recipe, right)* is used in place of meat stock. And although vegetarian cheeses are not called for in the ingredients lists, they may easily be purchased by those who prefer not to consume cheese set with animal rennet.

This volume divides the vast realm of vegetarian cuisine into four chapters. The first, quite properly, is devoted to vegetables themselves. Chapter two explores the grains and dried beans—crops as old as civilization—which have the potential both to nourish and to delight in a beguiling variety of combinations. Chapter three is a collection of recipes based upon pasta, pastry, or bread. In essence no more than flour and water, this international trio proves capable of the most toothsome and sophisticated of disguises. The concluding chapter is not about a type of food, but a method of cooking. The microwave oven, which is now an established part of the modern kitchen, is singularly suited to preparing vegetarian meals, preserving not just the freshness, flavor, and color of the ingredients but their wholesomeness as well.

Fresh Ways with Vegetarian Dishes serves as no more than an introduction to a healthful alternative way of eating. But whether you are a dedicated vegetarian, someone who likes to enjoy the occasional meatless meal, or perhaps someone who cooks for a vegetarian friend or member of the family, these recipes will furnish you with a multitude of fresh flavors and new ideas to enhance your diet.

Vegetable Stock

Makes about 1½ quarts
Working time: about 25 minutes
Total time: about 1 hour and 30 minutes

3 celery stalks with leaves, finely chopped
3 carrots, scrubbed, sliced into ⅛-inch rounds
3 large onions (about 1½ lb.), coarsely chopped
2 large broccoli stems, coarsely chopped (optional)
1 medium turnip, peeled and cut into ½-inch cubes
5 garlic cloves, coarsely chopped
2 tbsp. coarsely chopped parsley (with stems)
10 black peppercorns
2 sprigs fresh thyme, or 1 tsp. dried thyme leaves
2 bay leaves

Put the celery, carrots, onions, broccoli, if you are using it, turnip, garlic, parsley, and peppercorns in a heavy stockpot. Pour in enough water to cover them by 2 inches. Slowly bring the liquid to a boil over medium heat, skimming off any scum that rises to the surface. When the liquid reaches a boil, add the thyme and bay leaves. Stir the stock once and turn the heat to low; cover the pot, leaving the lid slightly ajar. Let the stock simmer undisturbed for one hour.

Strain the stock into a large bowl, pressing down lightly on the vegetables to extract all their liquid. Discard the vegetables. Allow the stock to stand until it is tepid, then refrigerate or freeze it.

Tightly covered and refrigerated, the stock may be safely kept for five to six days. Stored in small, tightly covered freezer containers and frozen, the stock may be kept for as long as six months.

1 Packed with vitamins, minerals, and flavor, fresh vegetables lie ready for the cook's attentions.

A Wealth of Vegetables

For their versatility and nutritional value, their wealth of flavors and sheer good looks, vegetables are in a class by themselves. Roots, stems, seeds, flowers, leaves—sometimes entire plants, sometimes only tiny parts of them—this vast family of food naturally provides the low-fat, low-sodium, high-fiber diet that nutritionists urge us to eat. When prepared with protein-rich dried beans and grain or with small quantities of eggs and cheese, vegetables need not be relegated to side dishes, the lowly accompaniment to meat; they increasingly take pride of place as a main course.

Nutritional awareness alone does not explain the vegetable's newfound prestige. Improved transport and storage, combined with a growing taste for international cuisine, have stocked markets with a rainbow of vegetable ingredients. In addition to familiar favorites such as cabbage, cauliflower, and carrots, such vegetables as eggplant, sweet peppers, tomatoes, and zucchini routinely bring year-round Mediterranean warmth to northern climes.

Some vegetables, admittedly, still require a little searching. Salsify, a thin, white-fleshed root with a flavor said to resemble oysters, is not in every market, for instance. But wild and exotic mushrooms such as porcini, morels, and shiitake—formerly to be found in dried form only in specialty stores—can now be purchased fresh from some large supermarkets.

With the move from side dish to center table, even the most ordinary vegetable assumes new aspects to suit its new station. Potatoes can be stewed with saffron (page 38); rutabagas curried and served as a soup (page 43). Layered with pine nuts and cheese (page 30), spinach proves to be one of the most socially mobile of vegetables, while the pumpkin becomes a delicate Cinderella of a dish in the soufflé on page 19.

For maximum flavor and goodness, vegetables should be as fresh as possible when cooked. Even the freshest homegrown ingredients, however, will lose nutrients if not prepared with care. As a general rule, the less chopping and paring the better. Whenever possible, cook and eat vegetables in their skins. When peeling is absolutely necessary, remove only a thin outer layer. Work with a light hand when trimming leaf vegetables; the outer leaves of a cabbage, for instance, contain many of its nutrients. Finally, prepare vegetables just before cooking and avoid soaking them, especially if they are peeled and chopped, since some vitamins and minerals leach out in water.

Zucchini Tian

THIS PROVENÇAL VEGETABLE GRATIN TAKES ITS
NAME FROM THE HEAVY EARTHENWARE POT IN WHICH
IT IS TRADITIONALLY COOKED.

Serves 4
Working time: about 45 minutes
Total time: about 1 hour and 15 minutes

Calories **190**
Protein **8g.**
Cholesterol **100mg.**
Total fat **9g.**
Saturated fat **3g.**
Sodium **195mg.**

1½ lb. zucchini, trimmed and finely sliced
3 tsp. virgin olive oil
¼ cup brown rice
1 garlic clove
¼ tsp. salt
3 shallots, finely chopped
2 small eggs, beaten
2 tbsp. freshly grated Parmesan cheese
1 tbsp. shredded fresh arugula or watercress leaves
1 tbsp. shredded fresh basil leaves
1 tbsp. finely chopped parsley
⅛ tsp. white pepper

Place the zucchini slices in a heavy-bottomed saucepan with 2 teaspoons of the oil and cook them gently over low heat, covered, until they are just tender—about 10 minutes. Stir the slices from time to time to prevent them from sticking.

Meanwhile, rinse the rice under running water and place it in a small, heavy-bottomed saucepan with 1¼ cups water. Bring the water to a boil, then lower the heat, cover the pan, and simmer for 15 minutes. Drain the rice well and set it aside, covered.

Preheat the oven to 350° F. Crush the garlic with the salt. Heat the remaining teaspoon of oil in a small, heavy-bottomed saucepan, add the shallots and garlic, and cook them over very low heat, covered, until soft—about five minutes.

Lightly grease a wide, shallow gratin dish. In a large mixing bowl, stir together the zucchini, rice, shallots, and garlic; add the eggs and 1 tablespoon of the Parmesan. Stir well, then mix in the arugula or watercress, basil, parsley, and pepper. Transfer the mixture to the prepared dish, level the zucchini slices so they sit flat, and sprinkle on the remaining tablespoon of Parmesan cheese.

Bake the tian in the oven, uncovered, for 20 minutes, then increase the oven temperature to 425° F. and bake it for 10 to 15 minutes more, until a crust has formed. Serve hot or warm.

SUGGESTED ACCOMPANIMENTS: *mixed salad of radicchio, curly endive, lamb's lettuce, and escarole; crusty French bread.*

Spanish Omelette

Serves 4
Working time: about 20 minutes
Total time: about 35 minutes

Calories **190**
Protein **7g.**
Cholesterol **110mg.**
Total fat **10g.**
Saturated fat **2g.**
Sodium **260mg.**

2 tbsp. virgin olive oil
1 onion, chopped
2 garlic cloves, chopped
2 small zucchini (about 4 oz.), trimmed and thinly sliced
2 eggs
2 egg whites
½ tsp. salt
freshly ground black pepper
1 large potato (about 10 oz.), peeled, cooked in boiling water for 25 to 30 minutes until tender, drained, and coarsely chopped
4 oz. green beans, trimmed, cooked in boiling water for 5 minutes, drained, refreshed under cold running water, and cut into 1-inch lengths
1 large tomato (about 6 oz.), peeled, seeded (technique, page 14), and chopped
½ tbsp. chopped fresh oregano, or ½ tsp. dried oregano

Heat 1½ tablespoons of the oil in a heavy frying pan over medium heat. Add the onion and cook it until it is soft—about three minutes. Add the garlic and zucchini, cover the pan, and cook the vegetables gently for 10 minutes, stirring them occasionally. Remove the pan from the heat.

In a large bowl, beat together the eggs and egg whites, salt, and some black pepper. Then add the cooked vegetables, potato, beans, tomato, and oregano. Stir gently to mix the ingredients.

Heat the remaining oil in a 10-inch nonstick flameproof skillet and pour in the egg mixture. Cook the omelette gently over medium heat for three to four minutes, until the underside is pale gold. Then place the pan under a preheated broiler and cook the omelette for two to three minutes more, or until it has set lightly. Cut it into quarters and serve.

SUGGESTED ACCOMPANIMENT: *mixed salad.*

Heat the oil in a heavy-bottomed saucepan and add the onion, sweet peppers, and zucchini trimmings. Cover the pan and cook the vegetables over low heat until soft—six to eight minutes. Add the eggplant, oregano or marjoram, coriander, and tomato paste, stir well, and cook for 10 minutes more. Then stir in the tomatoes and cornstarch, and simmer for a final two minutes. Season with the black pepper. Transfer the ratatouille to the lined pan and smooth the top. Let the terrine cool for 30 minutes, then cover it and chill it in the refrigerator for at least three hours.

Trim the zucchini slices level with the rim of the pan, if necessary, then turn the terrine out onto a serving plate. Remove the plastic wrap and slice the terrine with a serrated knife.

SUGGESTED ACCOMPANIMENTS: *hot herbed-garlic bread; crisp green salad.*

Ratatouille Terrine

Serves 4
Working time: about 1 hour
Total time: about 4 hours and 15 minutes (includes chilling)

Calories **120**	½ lb. eggplant, diced
Protein **3g.**	2 tsp. salt
Cholesterol **0mg.**	¾ lb. zucchini, trimmed
Total fat **8g.**	2 tbsp. virgin olive oil
Saturated fat **1g.**	1 small onion, coarsely chopped
Sodium **10mg.**	1 large sweet red pepper, seeded, deribbed, and coarsely chopped
	1 large sweet green pepper, seeded, deribbed, and coarsely chopped
	1 tsp. dried oregano or marjoram
	½ tsp. ground coriander
	1 tbsp. tomato paste
	½ lb. tomatoes, peeled, seeded (technique, right), and coarsely chopped
	1 tbsp. cornstarch
	freshly ground black pepper

In a bowl, toss the eggplant with the salt. Place the eggplant in a colander and weight it down with a plate small enough to rest on top of the dice. Let the eggplant drain for 30 minutes to eliminate its natural bitterness. Rinse the eggplant under cold running water to rid it of the salt, and drain it well.

Meanwhile, slice the zucchini very thinly lengthwise; chop and reserve any uneven pieces and trimmings. Blanch the strips in boiling salted water for 1 minute, then refresh them under cold water. Drain them well.

Line a 9-by-4-by-3-inch loaf pan with plastic wrap. Lay two strips of zucchini lengthwise down the center of the pan, then completely line the long sides of the pan with the remaining strips, placing one end of each strip on and perpendicular to the center seam of zucchini, and overlapping the strips slightly.

Peeling and Seeding a Tomato

1 *PEELING THE TOMATO. Core the tomato by cutting a conical plug from its stem end. Cut a shallow cross in the base. Immerse the tomato in boiling water for 10 to 30 seconds, then plunge it into cold water. When the tomato has cooled, peel the skin away from the cross in sections.*

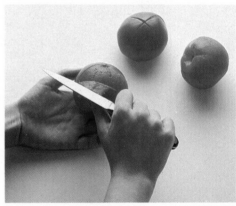

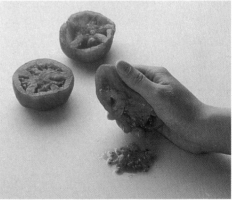

2 *REMOVING THE SEEDS. Halve the peeled tomato horizontally. Gently squeeze one of the halves, forcing out its seeds and juice. Rotate the tomato 90 degrees and squeeze once more. Dislodge any seeds from the inner chambers. Repeat the process with the other half.*

Eggplant and Mozzarella Ramekins

Serves 6
Working time: about 1 hour and 30 minutes
Total time: about 2 hours

Calories **275**
Protein **19g.**
Cholesterol **35mg.**
Total fat **13g.**
Saturated fat **6g.**
Sodium **385mg.**

3 medium eggplants (about 1 lb. each), sliced into ¼-inch rounds
1 tsp. salt
2 tbsp. virgin olive oil
¾ lb. low-fat mozzarella cheese, grated
2 tbsp. chopped fresh oregano
¼ cup sour cream
¾ cup plain low-fat yogurt
1 tbsp. chopped chives
Tomato coulis
1½ lb. ripe tomatoes (about 4 medium), peeled, seeded (technique, opposite), and chopped, or 14 oz. canned tomatoes, with their juice, chopped
1 carrot, finely chopped
1 small onion, finely chopped
1 celery stalk, trimmed and finely chopped
1 bay leaf
1 fresh red chili pepper, seeded and finely chopped (cautionary note, page 25)
¼ tsp. salt

First, prepare the tomato coulis. Place all the coulis ingredients in a heavy-bottomed, nonreactive saucepan with ⅓ cup of water. Bring the ingredients to a boil, then reduce the heat to low, cover the pan, and simmer for 45 minutes. At the end of this time, discard the bay leaf and process the coulis in a food processor or blender for two minutes. Strain the mixture, return it to the pan, and keep it warm.

While the coulis is cooking, prepare the eggplants. Arrange the slices on a wire rack set over a tray, and sprinkle them with ½ teaspoon of the salt. Allow them to drain for 15 minutes, then turn them over and repeat the process with the remaining ½ teaspoon of salt. At the end of the second draining period, rinse the slices well under cold running water to rid them of the salt. Pat them dry on paper towels.

Preheat the broiler. Lightly grease six ½-cup ramekins measuring 3 inches in diameter.

Lightly brush the eggplant slices on one side only with the oil. Broil the oiled side of the slices until they are lightly colored—three to four minutes.

Turn the oven setting to 375° F. Line the bottom of each ramekin with two or three slices of broiled eggplant, broiled side down, then sprinkle on a little grated mozzarella and chopped oregano. Continue adding layers of eggplant, mozzarella, and oregano until the ramekins are full, finishing with a layer of eggplant.

Put the ramekins on a baking sheet and bake them for 20 minutes. During this time, place the sour cream, yogurt, and chives in a food processor or blender and process them until smooth—about one minute.

Remove the ramekins from the oven and let them stand for two to three minutes. Carefully run a small metal spatula or knife around the inside of each one and invert the contents onto individual serving plates. Serve the eggplant ramekins with the tomato coulis and the yogurt sauce.

SUGGESTED ACCOMPANIMENTS: *crusty rolls; broccoli and fava beans.*

Eggplant Rolls with a Ricotta-Raisin Filling

Serves 4
Working time: about 45 minutes
Total time: about 1 hour and 15 minutes

Calories **270**
Protein **14g.**
Cholesterol **15mg.**
Total fat **13g.**
Saturated fat **5g.**
Sodium **275mg.**

4 long eggplants (about ½ lb. each)
2 tsp. virgin olive oil
¾ cup low-fat ricotta cheese
¾ cup raisins, chopped
1 oz. pine nuts (3 tbsp.), toasted
2 tbsp. freshly grated Parmesan cheese
¼ tsp. salt
freshly ground black pepper
2 oz. dry-pack (unoiled) sun-dried tomatoes, soaked in boiling water for 10 minutes
1 tbsp. balsamic vinegar or red wine vinegar
2 tbsp. fresh whole-wheat breadcrumbs
1 tsp. arrowroot
2 tbsp. tomato paste

Preheat the oven to 425° F. Lightly oil a 12-by-18-inch baking sheet.

Cut off and discard a little of the stem end and base of the eggplants. Remove a wide strip of skin from two opposite sides of each one, then cut the trimmed eggplants lengthwise into six equal slices, so that each slice has a border of skin at the sides. Lay the eggplant slices close together on the baking sheet. Using a wide pastry brush, quickly brush the exposed surfaces of the slices with the oil. Cover the baking sheet loosely with foil and roast the eggplant slices in the oven for about 10 minutes, until they are sufficiently soft to be rolled but are not browned. Remove the eggplant from the oven and lower the oven temperature to 350° F.

Meanwhile, put the ricotta in a bowl and beat in the raisins, pine nuts, 1 tablespoon of the Parmesan, the salt and some black pepper. Drain the tomatoes well, reserving the soaking liquid, then finely chop them and stir them into the ricotta mixture.

Lay the eggplant slices on a work surface and place a heaped teaspoonful of the filling near one end of each slice. Roll up the slices around the filling. Place all 24 rolls into a 9-by-13-inch shallow baking dish.

Blend the balsamic vinegar with 2 tablespoons of the reserved tomato-soaking liquid and pour this around the eggplant rolls. Grind black pepper generously over the top, and sprinkle them with the breadcrumbs and the remaining tablespoon of Parmesan. Cover the baking dish with foil and bake the rolls until they are tender—about 30 minutes. Remove the dish from the oven, and tilting it by carefully lifting one end, spoon out the juices from the other end into a 2-cup measuring container—there should be about 1 tablespoonful. Cover the dish again with the foil and set it aside in a warm place while you prepare the sauce.

Add the remaining tomato-soaking liquid to the cooking juices from the rolls, then add enough water to make 1¼ cups. Dissolve the arrowroot in 2 tablespoons of this mixture in a small bowl, then stir the arrowroot solution into the liquid in the measuring container. Transfer the mixture to a small saucepan and bring the liquid to a boil, stirring continuously. Lower the heat and simmer the sauce for a few seconds, until it is clear and thick. Remove the pan from the heat, stir in the tomato paste, and pour the sauce around the eggplant rolls.

Crisp the surface of the rolls by placing the dish under a hot broiler for five minutes.

SUGGESTED ACCOMPANIMENT: *saffron rice.*

EDITOR'S NOTE: *To toast pine nuts, place them in a small, heavy-bottomed skillet over medium-high heat and cook them for one to two minutes, stirring constantly, until they are golden brown and release their aroma.*

Eggplant Fans

Serves 4
Working time: about 45 minutes
Total time: about 3 hours

Calories **275**
Protein **20g.**
Cholesterol **60mg.**
Total fat **14g.**
Saturated fat **6g.**
Sodium **350mg.**

4 eggplants (about ½ lb. each), washed and dried
4 garlic cloves, peeled and quartered lengthwise
4 large, firm tomatoes, cut lengthwise into ½-inch slices
6 oz. low-fat mozzarella cheese, cut into thin slices
freshly ground black pepper
¾ cup fine fresh whole-wheat breadcrumbs
1 small egg, beaten
1 tbsp. freshly grated Parmesan cheese
Basil spread
¼ cup fresh basil leaves, very finely chopped
1 tbsp. extra virgin olive oil
2 tbsp. sour cream
1 tbsp. plain low-fat yogurt
1 tbsp. freshly grated Parmesan cheese
½ tsp. dry mustard

Preheat the oven to 350° F.

Cut the stems off the eggplants. Cutting from near the stem end of each eggplant, slice them lengthwise, making cuts about ½ inch apart; leave the slices joined by 1¼ to 1½ inches at the stem end. With the tip of a sharp knife, make four small cuts into the unsliced stem end of each eggplant. Press a slice of garlic into each of these cuts.

To make the basil spread, combine the chopped basil leaves with the oil in a small bowl. Add the sour cream, yogurt, Parmesan cheese, and mustard, and stir until evenly mixed. Divide the basil spread among the eggplants, spreading a little over each cut surface.

Sprinkle the slices of tomato and mozzarella with a generous grinding of black pepper. Place a slice or two of tomato and cheese between each segment of eggplant: the mozzarella will probably sit more easily near the stem end, the tomato near the thicker end. Cut any remaining tomato and mozzarella slices into smaller pieces and insert them between the eggplant slices where space allows.

Select a baking dish wide enough to take all four eggplants, packed close together. Brush the base of the dish lightly with olive oil and sprinkle it with 1 or 2 teaspoons of the breadcrumbs to absorb the juices produced during cooking. Use a pastry brush to paint a little beaten egg over the sides and top of each eggplant. Sprinkle on the remaining breadcrumbs, pressing them down lightly to keep them in place. Arrange the eggplants in the baking dish, pressing down on the upper surface of each to fan out the slices a little. Sprinkle the Parmesan cheese over the fans.

Cover the dish with foil, and bake the eggplants for two to two and a half hours, or until a thin skewer inserted at the stem end meets with little resistance. Remove the foil, increase the oven temperature to the maximum setting, and continue to cook the fans until the topping is crisp—10 to 15 minutes.

SUGGESTED ACCOMPANIMENT: *crusty bread.*

EDITOR'S NOTE: *For best results, select elongated eggplants for this recipe.*

Squash Soufflé

Serves 4
Working time: about 30 minutes
Total time: about 2 hours and 45 minutes

Calories **200**
Protein **11g.**
Cholesterol **85mg.**
Total fat **12g.**
Saturated fat **6g.**
Sodium **300mg.**

1½ lb. slice pumpkin, butternut or other winter squash, seeds removed
2 tbsp. dry breadcrumbs
2 tbsp. unsalted butter
2 tbsp. unbleached all-purpose flour
½ cup skim milk
1 egg yolk
¼ tsp. salt
1 tsp. ground cinnamon
3 tbsp. freshly grated Parmesan cheese
5 egg whites

Preheat the oven to 375° F. Wrap the slice of pumpkin or squash in a sheet of foil and place it on a baking sheet. Bake it in the oven for about one hour, until it is soft. Check the squash after this time; if it is still hard, return it to the oven for 20 minutes more to cook it through. When the squash is cooked, remove it from the oven and let it cool, uncovered. Meanwhile, grease a 1-quart soufflé dish and dust it with the dry breadcrumbs. Increase the oven temperature to 400° F.

Using a metal spoon, scoop all the squash pulp from the skin, and pass the pulp through a fine sieve; there should be about 1¼ cups of sieved squash. Put the squash in a saucepan, and stirring continuously, dry out the pulp over medium heat until it becomes fairly dense and no longer wet—about 10 minutes. Set the squash aside.

In a small, heavy-bottomed saucepan, melt the butter over gentle heat. Remove the pan from the heat, and using a wooden spoon, stir in the flour. Then stir in the milk a little at a time. Return the pan to the heat and cook the mixture for about 30 seconds, stirring constantly, until it thickens. Take the pan off the heat again, and stir in the egg yolk, followed by the squash, salt, cinnamon, and 2 tablespoons of the Parmesan. Set the mixture aside.

Whisk the egg whites until they hold their shape, then fold them gently into the squash mixture. Turn the mixture into the prepared soufflé dish and sprinkle it with the remaining Parmesan.

Bake the soufflé in the oven until it is well risen and set—about 40 minutes. Serve immediately.

SUGGESTED ACCOMPANIMENT: *salad of mixed greens, fennel, and avocado.*

Spring Vegetables in Watercress Crepes

Serves 4
Working (and total) time: about 1 hour

Calories **200**
Protein **13g.**
Cholesterol **55mg.**
Total fat **10g.**
Saturated fat **3g.**
Sodium **300mg.**

1 egg
¼ tsp. salt
½ cup unbleached all-purpose flour
½ cup skim milk
2 tsp. safflower oil
2 shallots
¾ cup loosely packed watercress leaves
1 lb. asparagus, trimmed and peeled
1 lb. baby corn, fresh or frozen, *trimmed if necessary*
1 lb. very small baby carrots, trimmed and peeled
⅓ cup plain low-fat yogurt
Sweet-pepper sauces
1 large sweet red pepper, broiled and peeled *(technique, opposite), coarsely chopped*
1 large sweet yellow pepper, broiled and peeled *(technique, opposite), coarsely chopped*
4 shallots, finely chopped
1 tsp. finely chopped fresh thyme
¾ cup unsalted vegetable stock (recipe, page 9)
4 tsp. fresh lemon juice

First make the crepe batter. Put the egg and ⅛ teaspoon of the salt into a food processor or blender, and blend them well. Add the flour, milk, 1 teaspoon of the oil, and the shallots, and blend again until the shallots are very finely chopped. Then add the watercress leaves and blend once more. Transfer the batter to a bowl, cover with plastic wrap, and place it in the refrigerator for 30 minutes while you prepare the vegetables and sauces.

Cut each asparagus spear into two or three pieces approximately 2 inches long. Bring a large saucepan of water to a boil. Add the carrots and corn, then, after 2 minutes, add the asparagus. Boil the vegetables until they are cooked but still crisp—two to three minutes. If you are using frozen corn, add it for the last minute of boiling only. Drain the vegetables and refresh them under cold running water. Drain the vegetables again and set them aside.

To make the two sweet-pepper sauces, put the red pepper in one small saucepan and the yellow pepper in another. Divide the shallots, thyme, and stock equally between the two pans, and bring them both to a boil. Reduce the heat under both pans and simmer the ingredients until the peppers are soft—about five minutes. Purée the two sauces separately in a food processor or blender; sieve them both and return them to separate pans. Season each sauce with 2 teaspoons of the lemon juice. Cover the pans and set them aside while you cook the crepes.

Heat a 6-inch crepe pan or nonstick skillet over low heat and brush a little of the remaining oil over the surface of the pan using a paper towel. Stir the batter well; if it has thickened, stir in 1 tablespoon of water to restore it to its former consistency. Pour one-eighth of the batter into the crepe pan. Swirl the pan to coat the bottom with an even layer of batter, and cook until the top side of the crepe becomes firm and starts to bubble—about one minute. Using a spatula, carefully turn the crepe over and cook it for 15 to 30 seconds more, until it is very lightly browned on the second side. Slide the crepe out of the pan onto a piece of wax paper and set it aside. Cook seven more crepes in the same way, brushing a little more oil over the pan as necessary and stacking the cooked crepes on top of one another, separated by wax paper.

Preheat the oven to 325°F. Stir the remaining ⅛ teaspoon of salt into the yogurt. Fold each crepe in half, then in half again, creating pockets between the layers. Place the folded crepes in pairs on top of one another on the work surface. Divide the cooked vegetables into four portions, and decoratively arrange one portion in the pockets of each pair of crepes; leave room in the top pocket of each pair for the yogurt.

Carefully arrange the eight crepes, still in their pairs, in a gratin dish. Spoon one-fourth of the yogurt into the top pocket of the four upper crepes and cover the dish loosely with foil. Bake the crepes in the oven until they are heated through—about 10 minutes. Meanwhile, gently reheat the sweet-pepper sauces.

Place a pair of crepes on each of four warmed serving plates and spoon a little of each sweet-pepper sauce around them.

SUGGESTED ACCOMPANIMENT: *breadsticks.*

Peeling Sweet Peppers

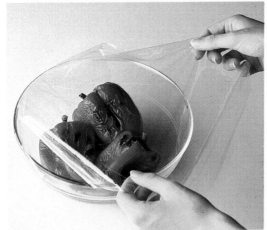 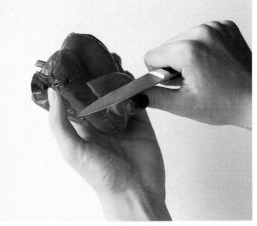

1 LOOSENING THE SKIN. Place the peppers about 2 inches below a preheated broiler. Turn the peppers as their sides become slightly scorched, until their skin has blistered on all sides. Transfer the peppers to a bowl and cover it with plastic wrap; the trapped steam will make the peppers limp and loosen their skins.

2 REMOVING THE SKIN. When the peppers are cool enough to handle, use a paring knife or other small, sharp knife to peel off a pepper's skin in sections, working from top to bottom. Repeat the process to peel the other peppers. The peppers may then be seeded and deribbed.

Asparagus Mousse with Goat Cheese Sauce

Serves 4
Working time: about 30 minutes
Total time: about 1 hour and 40 minutes

Calories **195**
Protein **17g.**
Cholesterol **90mg.**
Total fat **10g.**
Saturated fat **5g.**
Sodium **470mg.**

1½ lb. large asparagus, trimmed and peeled
1 tbsp. unsalted butter
1 onion, chopped
2 tsp. cornstarch
⅔ cup skim milk
¼ tsp. salt
freshly ground black pepper
¼ tsp. freshly grated nutmeg
1 tbsp. chopped parsley
1 egg yolk
3 egg whites
parsley sprigs for garnish
Goat cheese sauce
1 tsp. cornstarch
4 tbsp. white wine
1 garlic clove, crushed
freshly ground black pepper
¼ lb. soft goat cheese, rind removed, cubed

▶

Preheat the oven to 350°F. Lightly grease four 1-cup ring molds or ramekins.

To make the mousse, cut off the asparagus tips about ½ inch below the buds, and cut the remaining stalks in half. Cook the stalks in a little boiling water for one to two minutes. Add the tips and cook for one minute more, then drain the asparagus pieces and refresh them under cold running water. Cut the tips in half lengthwise and reserve them for the garnish.

Melt the butter in a small saucepan. Add the onion, cover the pan, and cook the onion over high heat, stirring occasionally, until it is soft—about three minutes. In a small bowl, blend the cornstarch with 2 tablespoons of the milk. Stir in the remaining milk, and add it to the pan along with the salt, some black pepper, and the nutmeg. Bring the mixture to a boil, and simmer it, stirring constantly, until it forms a smooth sauce—about two minutes.

In a food processor or blender, process the asparagus stalks, onion sauce, chopped parsley, and egg yolk and whites until completely smooth—about one minute. Turn the mixture into the prepared ring molds or ramekins. Cover each mold with lightly greased foil and place the molds in a baking dish containing boiling water ½ inch deep. Bake the molds until the mousse is just firm—about one hour.

Meanwhile, make the goat cheese sauce. In a small saucepan, blend the cornstarch with a little of the wine. Stir in the remaining wine, the garlic, and some freshly ground black pepper. Bring the mixture to a boil, stirring. Then remove the pan from the heat and add the cheese. Stir the sauce until the cheese has melted. Keep the sauce warm.

Remove the molds from the baking dish and let them stand for 10 minutes. Using a small metal spatula or table knife, loosen the edges and invert each mousse onto a warmed serving plate. Divide the asparagus tips among the mousses and garnish each one with a sprig of parsley. Spoon the sauce over and around the mousses, and serve them immediately.

SUGGESTED ACCOMPANIMENT: *new potatoes.*

Baked Fennel
in Roquefort Sauce

Serves 4
Working time: about 35 minutes
Total time: about 1 hour

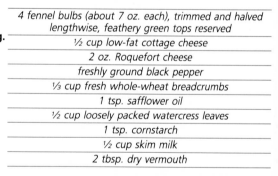

Calories **165**	4 fennel bulbs (about 7 oz. each), trimmed and halved lengthwise, feathery green tops reserved
Protein **13g.**	
Cholesterol **10mg.**	½ cup low-fat cottage cheese
Total fat **8g.**	2 oz. Roquefort cheese
Saturated fat **3g.**	freshly ground black pepper
Sodium **530mg.**	⅓ cup fresh whole-wheat breadcrumbs
	1 tsp. safflower oil
	½ cup loosely packed watercress leaves
	1 tsp. cornstarch
	½ cup skim milk
	2 tbsp. dry vermouth

Blanch the fennel bulbs in a large saucepan of boiling water until the layers have separated and softened slightly—about five minutes. Drain the fennel bulbs and set them aside.

Press the cottage cheese through a fine sieve into a bowl. Crumble the Roquefort into the bowl, add some black pepper, and beat well. In another bowl, blend the breadcrumbs with the oil.

Preheat the oven to 350°F. Open out the layers of the halved fennel bulbs. Reserve one-third of the Roquefort and cottage cheese mixture. Spread each layer of a half bulb with some of the remaining cheese mixture, and then with a few watercress leaves. Repeat with the other bulbs. Place two half bulbs, cut sides down, in each of four individual gratin dishes, or put all of the bulbs in a large, shallow ovenproof dish.

In a small saucepan, blend the cornstarch with 3 tablespoons of the milk. Add the remaining milk, then cook over medium heat, whisking continuously, until the sauce has thickened slightly. Remove the pan from the heat, and stir in the vermouth and remaining cheese mixture. Spoon the sauce over the fennel and sprinkle the bulbs with the oiled breadcrumbs.

Bake the fennel in the oven until the breadcrumbs are golden—approximately 20 minutes. Sprinkle the reserved feathery fennel tops over the baked fennel and serve the dish hot.

SUGGESTED ACCOMPANIMENT: *oven-baked French fries or potatoes and rutabaga mashed together and sprinkled with chopped parsley.*

Belgian Endive and Pistachio-Stuffed Tomatoes

Serves 4
Working time: about 30 minutes
Total time: about 45 minutes

Calories **200**
Protein **9g.**
Cholesterol **10g.**
Total fat **14g.**
Saturated fat **3g.**
Sodium **90mg.**

4 heads Belgian endive (about 4 oz. each)
8 firm cherry tomatoes
1 tbsp. virgin olive oil
2 oz. pistachio nuts (about ½ cup), peeled and coarsely chopped
3 garlic cloves, finely chopped
2 tbsp. dry whole-wheat breadcrumbs
¼ cup freshly grated Parmesan cheese
1 lemon, cut into wedges, for garnish

Preheat the oven to 425°F.

Trim the endive and slice each head lengthwise into fourths. Blanch the cut endive in a saucepan of boiling water for 30 seconds. Drain and refresh the endive under cold running water and set it aside. Slice off and discard the tops of the tomatoes. Using a teaspoon,

hollow out and discard the insides of the tomatoes, then turn them upside down on paper towels to drain.

Heat the olive oil in a skillet and sauté the pistachio nuts until they are crisp—about two minutes. Add the finely chopped garlic and sauté for another one to two minutes, until the garlic has softened. Remove the skillet from the heat.

Lay the endive slices in a rectangular baking dish, alternating them with rows of the hollowed-out tomatoes. Fill the tomatoes with the garlic and pistachio mixture, spooning any extra neatly around them. Brush the olive oil from the skillet over the endive. Mix the breadcrumbs with the Parmesan cheese and sprinkle this mixture over the endive. Bake until the vegetables are tender—about 15 minutes.

Serve hot, garnished with the lemon wedges.

SUGGESTED ACCOMPANIMENT: *crusty bread.*

EDITOR'S NOTE: *To peel pistachio nuts, drop them into boiling water and simmer them for one minute. Then drain them thoroughly, wrap them in a towel, and rub them briskly until they have shed their skins.*

Stuffed Leeks with Gruyère Sauce

Serves 4
Working time: about 1 hour
Total time: about 1 hour and 30 minutes

Calories **250**
Protein **10g.**
Cholesterol **25mg.**
Total fat **9g.**
Saturated fat **3g.**
Sodium **330mg.**

1 qt. unsalted vegetable stock (recipe, page 9)
¾ oz. dried porcini
5 medium leeks, tough outer leaves discarded, washed thoroughly to remove all grit, trimmed to 4-inch lengths
½ cup buckwheat groats (kasha), rinsed well
1 tbsp. unsalted butter
½ lb. mushrooms, 5 oz. finely diced, 3 oz. finely sliced and tossed in 1 tbsp. fresh lemon juice
1 large sweet yellow or red pepper, seeded, deribbed, and finely chopped
¼ tsp. salt
2 tbsp. fresh breadcrumbs
Gruyère sauce
¾ cup plain low-fat yogurt
2 oz. Gruyère cheese, grated (about ¼ cup)
⅛ tsp. grated nutmeg

Heat the stock in a saucepan over medium heat until hot but not boiling. Pour the stock over the porcini in a large bowl and let them soak for 10 to 15 minutes.

Meanwhile, separate 26 outer leaves from the leeks, blanch them in a saucepan of boiling water for one minute, then refresh them under cold running water. Drain the leaves and set them aside to dry flat on several layers of paper towels. Finely chop the remaining inner parts of the leeks and set them aside. There should be about ¾ cup of chopped leeks.

Remove the porcini from the stock. Squeeze them dry, chop them finely, and set them aside. Strain 2 cups of the stock through cheesecloth and reserve it.

Put the buckwheat in a saucepan, add the reserved stock, and bring it to a boil. Lower the heat, cover the pan, and simmer for 15 minutes. Remove the pan from the heat and let the buckwheat rest, covered, for another 10 minutes. At the end of this time all the liquid will have been absorbed.

Melt one-third of the butter in a nonstick skillet over low heat. Gently sauté the chopped leeks, diced mushrooms, and finely chopped porcini until they are lightly browned—about seven minutes. Remove the pan from the heat, stir in the chopped pepper and the buckwheat, and season with the salt.

Preheat the oven to 400° F. Divide the buckwheat mixture into 12 equal portions. Cut two of the blanched leek leaves lengthwise into six ribbons each. Lay two intact leaves next to one another on the work surface and overlap two adjacent long edges by about 1½ inches. Spoon a portion of the buckwheat mixture along one of the remaining outer long edges, then roll up the leaves around the filling and tie the roll with a leek ribbon. Repeat this process to make 12 rolls in all, and arrange them side by side in a single layer in a large rectangular gratin dish.

In a bowl, blend together the ingredients for the Gruyère sauce. Place the gratin dish in a large deep roasting pan and pour boiling water into the pan to reach two-thirds of the way up the side of the gratin dish. Pour the sauce over both ends of the leeks, leaving the middles uncovered. Melt half the remaining butter and brush it over the middle of the leeks. Cover the dish loosely with foil and bake the leeks in the oven for 25 minutes.

Preheat the broiler to medium hot. Remove the gratin dish from the oven and remove the foil. Sprinkle the breadcrumbs over the sauce, cover the middle of the leeks with a strip of foil, and place the gratin dish under the broiler for four to six minutes, until the crumbs are golden brown.

Meanwhile, melt the remaining butter in a nonstick skillet and gently sauté the sliced mushrooms for two to three minutes. Divide the stuffed leeks among four individual plates, allowing three rolls per portion, and serve garnished with the sautéed mushrooms.

Spicy Mold of Leeks, Zucchini, and Cabbage

Serves 6
Working time: about 30 minutes
Total time: about 14 hours and 30 minutes
(includes chilling)

Calories **295**
Protein **5g.**
Cholesterol **0mg.**
Total fat **10g.**
Saturated fat **2g.**
Sodium **220mg.**

1 lb. zucchini (about 3 medium), trimmed and coarsely grated
1 lb. Savoy cabbage, trimmed and very finely shredded
1 lb. leeks (about 4 medium), trimmed, washed thoroughly to remove all grit, sliced into very fine rings
¾ tsp. salt
4 tbsp. virgin olive oil
2-inch piece fresh ginger, peeled and grated
1 dried hot red chili pepper, crushed (cautionary note, below)
2 garlic cloves, crushed
1 tbsp. coriander seeds, crushed
2 tsp. curry powder
1 tbsp. low-sodium soy sauce
5 sheets nori seaweed, each about 8 inches square

Place the grated zucchini, shredded cabbage, and sliced leeks in separate bowls. Sprinkle ¼ teaspoon of salt over each vegetable and leave them to drain for one hour, to rid them of their bitter juices. At the end of this time, squeeze out each vegetable very thoroughly in a piece of cheesecloth. Once more place the vegetables in separate bowls.

Heat 2 tablespoons of the oil in a heavy skillet over medium heat. Add the ginger, chili, and garlic to the pan and sauté, stirring frequently, for about one minute. Pour the contents of the pan over the leeks and toss them in the flavored oil. Heat the remaining 2 tablespoons of oil in a clean pan and cook the coriander and curry powder for one minute. Pour the spiced oil over the shredded cabbage and toss it thoroughly. Let the cabbage and the leeks stand for one hour, to allow the flavors to develop.

Meanwhile, in a large, shallow square dish, mix the soy sauce with 2 tablespoons of water. Moisten the sheets of nori in the solution and leave them in the dish for five minutes. Then remove them, and using a sharp knife, cut each sheet diagonally into two triangles. Lay all the triangles out on the work surface facing the same way. Line a 1½-quart bowl or mold with the triangles, placing them in the mold one after another and overlapping them; one 45-degree corner should be placed in the bottom of the bowl and the other should overhang the rim at the top.

Place the cabbage mixture in the bottom of the mold, pressing it down firmly. Follow with the zucchini, and then the leeks. Fold over the overhanging sheets of nori to enclose the filling. Set a small plate on top of the mold and place a heavy weight on top of the plate. Refrigerate the mold for at least 12 hours.

To serve, turn the mold out onto a plate and slice it into wedges with a sharp knife.

SUGGESTED ACCOMPANIMENTS: *radicchio salad; potato gratin.*
EDITOR'S NOTE: *Nori, paperlike dark green or black sheets of dried seaweed, can be purchased from health food shops and Asian groceries. If nori is unavailable, spinach leaves, blanched in boiling water for 30 seconds, may be used to line the mold instead.*

Chilies—A Cautionary Note

Both dried and fresh hot chilies should be handled with care. Their flesh and seeds contain volatile oils that can make skin tingle and cause eyes to burn. Rubber gloves offer protection—but the cook should still be careful not to touch the face, lips, or eyes when working with chilies.

Soaking fresh chilies in cold, salted water for an hour will remove some of their fire. If canned chilies are substituted for fresh ones, they should be rinsed in cold water in order to eliminate as much of the brine used to preserve them as possible.

Chestnuts and Brussels Sprouts with Red Cabbage and Caraway Potatoes

Serves 8
Working time: about 45 minutes
Total time: about 1 hour

Calories **245**
Protein **7g.**
Cholesterol **10mg.**
Total fat **5g.**
Saturated fat **2g.**
Sodium **155mg.**

2 tbsp. caraway seeds
8 potatoes, scrubbed and halved
½ tsp. salt
1 tsp. virgin olive oil
1 onion, sliced
2 lb. red cabbage, shredded
¾ cup red wine
2 tbsp. red wine vinegar
1 bay leaf
1 cooking apple, peeled, cored, and chopped
½ orange, grated zest and juice
1 garlic clove, peeled
1 large sprig parsley
2 tbsp. unsalted butter
2 tsp. sugar
1 lb. fresh chestnuts, peeled (technique, page 37)
2 tbsp. unsalted vegetable stock (recipe, page 9) or water
1 lb. Brussels sprouts, trimmed, halved if large

Preheat the oven to 400° F. Place the caraway seeds on a small flat plate. Press each potato half, cut side down, into the seeds, ensuring that an even layer adheres to each cut surface. Place the potato halves, seeded side up, on a baking sheet and sprinkle them with ¼ tea-spoon of the salt. Bake the potatoes for 45 minutes, or until the flesh feels soft when pierced with a skewer.

Meanwhile, heat the olive oil in a very large, heavy-bottomed saucepan over medium heat. Add the onion and sauté it for about five minutes, until it is soft and lightly browned. Add the shredded red cabbage to the pan and stir-fry it for two minutes. Then mix in the wine, vinegar, bay leaf, apple, orange zest and juice, the whole garlic clove, the remaining ¼ teaspoon of salt, and the parsley sprig. Bring the contents of the pan to a boil, then lower the heat, cover the pan, and simmer until the cabbage is tender—35 to 40 minutes. At the end of this time, remove and discard the bay leaf, garlic clove, and parsley sprig.

While the red cabbage is simmering, prepare the chestnuts and Brussels sprouts. In a heavy skillet over medium heat, stir the butter and sugar together until both have melted—about two minutes. Add the peeled chestnuts and glaze them by stirring them in the butter and sugar mixture for about three minutes. Then add the stock or water, cover the pan with a tight-fitting lid, and reduce the heat to low. Simmer the chestnuts until they are soft—about 20 minutes. Toward the end of this time, place the Brussels sprouts in a steamer set over a pan of simmering water, and steam them until they, too, are tender—about five minutes. Add the sprouts to the pan with the chestnuts and mix both together thoroughly.

Transfer the baked potato halves, red cabbage, and chestnuts and Brussels sprouts to hot serving dishes.

Spiced Red Cabbage

Serves 6
Working time: about 20 minutes
Total time: about 1 hour and 50 minutes

Calories **330**
Protein **15g.**
Cholesterol **20mg.**
Total fat **13g.**
Saturated fat **4g.**
Sodium **390mg.**

1 tbsp. juniper berries
1 tbsp. coriander seeds
2 tbsp. virgin olive oil
5 garlic cloves, sliced
1 large red cabbage (about 4½ lb.), trimmed and sliced
1¼ cups sparkling apple cider
freshly ground black pepper
3 large green cooking apples (about 1½ lb.), cored, peeled, halved, and placed in acidulated water
3 oz. Edam cheese, thinly sliced

Preheat the oven to 350° F. Put the juniper berries and the coriander seeds into a mortar and then crush them with a pestle.

Heat the oil over medium heat in a very large flame-proof casserole. Add the garlic and crushed spices, and stir-fry them briefly, then add all of the red cabbage and continue to stir-fry for three to four minutes. Remove the casserole from the heat. Pour the cider over the cabbage and season it with some black pepper. Cover the casserole and cook the cabbage in the oven for one hour.

Stir the cabbage and transfer it to a 4-quart flame-proof casserole—the cabbage will have halved in volume by this stage. Drain the apple halves, pat them dry on paper towels, and lay them on top of the cabbage. Cover the casserole and return the cabbage to the oven for 30 minutes more.

Preheat the broiler to medium. Remove the casserole from the oven, take off the lid, and without stirring the contents, lay the slices of cheese over the apples. Put the casserole under the broiler for about five minutes, until the cheese melts and begins to brown. Serve the cabbage at once.

SUGGESTED ACCOMPANIMENT: *buckwheat, bulgur, couscous, or millet.*

Lacy Pancakes with Spinach Filling

Serves 4
Working time: about 45 minutes
Total time: about 1 hour

Calories **410**
Protein **18g.**
Cholesterol **25mg.**
Total fat **16g.**
Saturated fat **5g.**
Sodium **360mg.**

2 lb. spinach, washed and stemmed
1 tbsp. unsalted butter
1 onion, chopped
2 garlic cloves, crushed
1 sweet red pepper, seeded, deribbed, and cut into 1-inch-long strips
10 oz. potatoes, peeled and grated
freshly ground black pepper
1 cup less 2 tbsp. rice flour
⅛ tsp. salt
2 egg whites, with enough water added to make 1¼ cups
2 tbsp. safflower oil
¼ lb. low-fat mozzarella cheese, thinly sliced

Blanch the spinach in a saucepan of boiling water for one minute, then drain it and refresh it under cold running water. Drain the spinach again thoroughly, then squeeze it dry and chop it.

Melt the butter in a large nonstick skillet over low heat. Add the onion and garlic, and sauté for two minutes. Mix in the red pepper and grated potatoes, and cook, stirring frequently, until the potatoes are cooked through—about 20 minutes. Remove the skillet from the heat, and stir in the spinach and some freshly ground black pepper. Cover the skillet and set it aside while you make the pancakes.

Put the rice flour and salt into a bowl, and gradually beat in the egg whites and water to make a batter. Heat a 6-inch crepe pan or nonstick skillet over medium-high heat, then spread a little of the oil over the entire surface with a paper towel. Pour in 2 tablespoons of the batter and immediately swirl the pan to coat the bottom with a thin, even layer. Cook the pancake until it is firm—about one minute—then lift the edge with a spatula and turn the pancake over. Cook the second side until dry—about 30 seconds. Slide the pancake onto a plate. Make seven more pancakes in this way, spreading a little safflower oil over the pan as necessary. Stack the cooked pancakes on top of one another.

Preheat the oven to 375° F. Lay each pancake, in turn, out flat on the work surface and spoon an eighth of the spinach mixture down the center. Roll up the pancake to enclose the filling, then transfer it to a lightly oiled, shallow ovenproof dish. Lay the cheese slices evenly over the pancakes and cook them in the oven until the filling is heated through and the cheese melts and begins to brown—about 15 minutes. Serve the pancakes at once.

SUGGESTED ACCOMPANIMENT: *tomato salad.*

Spinach, Stilton, and Tomato Roulade

Serves 4
Working time: about 40 minutes
Total time: about 1 hour

Calories **200**
Protein **18g.**
Cholesterol **115mg.**
Total fat **10g.**
Saturated fat **5g.**
Sodium **410mg.**

1 lb. spinach, washed, stems removed
2 egg yolks
¼ tsp. grated nutmeg
¼ cup fresh whole-wheat breadcrumbs
¼ tsp. salt
freshly ground black pepper
4 egg whites
Stilton and tomato filling
½ cup low-fat ricotta cheese
1½ oz. Stilton cheese, mashed
2 tbsp. finely cut fresh chives
4 tomatoes, peeled, seeded (technique, page 14), and chopped
freshly ground black pepper

Preheat the oven to 400° F. Line the bottom and sides of a baking pan that measures 9 by 13 inches with nonstick parchment paper.

Cook the spinach in a saucepan of boiling water until it has wilted—approximately 30 seconds. Drain the spinach in a colander, refresh it under cold running water, then place it in a piece of cheesecloth and squeeze out all the liquid. Purée the spinach in a food processor or blender.

In a mixing bowl, stir together the puréed spinach, egg yolks, nutmeg, breadcrumbs, salt, and some black pepper. Whisk the egg whites until they are fairly stiff. Fold 1 tablespoon of the egg whites into the spinach mixture, then carefully fold in the remainder. Spread the roulade mixture evenly in the prepared baking pan and smooth the top. Bake the mixture until it is just firm to the touch—10 to 15 minutes. Do not overbake the roulade or it will be difficult to roll. Remove the roulade from the oven, cover it with a clean dishtowel, and allow it to cool.

To make the filling, blend the ricotta cheese in a bowl with the Stilton, and mix in the chives, tomatoes, and some black pepper. Turn the baked spinach rectangle out onto a sheet of wax paper and carefully peel off the lining paper. Spread the filling over the rectangle. Starting from one of the short sides, roll the base and filling into a cylinder: Lift one end of the underlying wax paper to start the roulade off, and nudge it along by gradually lifting the rest of the paper. Serve the roulade cut into slices.

SUGGESTED ACCOMPANIMENTS: *hot herbed bread; watercress and apple salad.*

Spinach and Pine Nut Layered Terrine

Serves 4
Working time: about 45 minutes
Total time: about 1 hour and 30 minutes

Calories **295**	2¼ lb. spinach, washed, stems removed
Protein **25g.**	⅔ cup low-fat ricotta cheese
Cholesterol **75mg.**	3 tablespoons low-fat cottage cheese
Total fat **13g.**	¼ cup freshly grated Parmesan cheese
Saturated fat **5g.**	¼ cup pine nuts, toasted
Sodium **530mg.**	freshly ground black pepper
	1 egg yolk
	2 egg whites
	Red-pepper sauce
	2 sweet red peppers, seeded, deribbed, and sliced
	1 onion, sliced
	2 garlic cloves, crushed
	1 cup unsalted vegetable stock (recipe, page 9)
	6 tbsp. fresh whole-wheat breadcrumbs
	⅛ tsp. salt
	freshly ground black pepper

Select 12 medium-size spinach leaves for lining the terrine. Blanch them in a saucepan of boiling water for 30 seconds, then drain them and refresh them under cold running water. Drain the leaves again and lay them out to dry on paper towels. Place the rest of the spinach, with water still clinging to the leaves, in a large, heavy-bottomed saucepan. Cover the pan, and cook the spinach over low heat until it has wilted and reduced in volume by a third—two to three minutes. Drain the spinach, squeeze out any excess moisture in a piece of cheesecloth, and chop the spinach coarsely. Place it in a bowl.

Preheat the oven to 400° F. Line a 1-quart rectangular terrine mold with the blanched spinach leaves, leaving enough overhanging the rim to fold over the top. Combine the cheeses in a bowl with the pine nuts, some black pepper, and the egg yolk. Whisk the egg whites until they are stiff but not dry, then fold them gently into the chopped spinach. Layer the prepared mold with a third of the spinach mixture, then half the cheese mixture, another third of the spinach, the rest of the cheese mixture, then a final layer of spinach; smooth each layer with a rubber spatula before adding the next. Fold over the leaves at the top of the terrine. Cover the mold with buttered wax paper or parchment paper. Place the mold in a deep baking dish and pour enough water into the dish to come two-thirds of the way up the sides of the mold. Bake the terrine until the top feels firm to the touch—about 45 minutes.

While the terrine is cooking, prepare the red-pepper sauce. Put the sweet red peppers, onion, garlic, and stock into a saucepan, and bring the liquid to a boil. Cover the pan, lower the heat, and simmer the mixture gently until the peppers and onion are soft—about 20 minutes. Stir in the breadcrumbs, salt, and some black pepper. Purée the mixture in a food processor or blender, and return it to the saucepan.

Remove the terrine from the oven and let it rest for five minutes. Meanwhile, gently reheat the pepper sauce. Turn the terrine out onto a warmed serving dish and serve it cut into slices. Spoon a little red-pepper sauce around each portion and serve the rest of it separately.

SUGGESTED ACCOMPANIMENT: *melba toast.*

EDITOR'S NOTE: *To toast pine nuts, place them in a small, heavy-bottomed skillet over medium-high heat, and cook them for one to two minutes, stirring constantly, until they are golden brown and release their aroma.*

Kohlrabi and Zucchini Gratin

Serves 4
Working time: about 35 minutes
Total time: about 1 hour and 10 minutes

Calories **145**
Protein **8g.**
Cholesterol **15mg.**
Total fat **7g.**
Saturated fat **4g.**
Sodium **415mg.**

1½ lb. kohlrabies, leaves and stems removed, unpeeled if young
½ lb. zucchini, trimmed
2 tbsp. unsalted butter
3 medium tomatoes, peeled, seeded (technique, page 14), and chopped
2 tbsp. finely chopped parsley
2 garlic cloves, crushed
⅛ tsp. cayenne pepper
½ tsp. salt
freshly ground black pepper
¼ cup fresh whole-wheat breadcrumbs

Using a sharp knife, cut the kohlrabies horizontally into very thin, even slices. Cut the zucchini lengthwise into equally thin slices. Steam the kohlrabi slices for 15 minutes, then add the zucchini slices to the steamer. Do not mix the two vegetables. Continue to cook the kohlrabi and zucchini slices until both vegetables are just tender—about five minutes more.

Meanwhile, melt the butter in a heavy-bottomed saucepan over low heat. Add the tomatoes, parsley, and garlic, and season the mixture with the cayenne pepper, salt, and some black pepper. Stir the ingredients well and cook them over medium heat, stirring occasionally, until the tomatoes have reduced to a fairly thick, dry purée—10 to 15 minutes.

Preheat the oven to 350° F. Lightly grease an oven-proof gratin dish.

Drain the kohlrabi and zucchini slices and pat them dry with paper towels. Arrange alternate layers of kohlrabi and zucchini slices in the prepared gratin dish. Spoon the tomato purée over the top and sprinkle with the whole-wheat breadcrumbs. Bake the vegetable gratin until the topping is crisp and lightly browned—20 to 30 minutes.

SUGGESTED ACCOMPANIMENT: *mashed potatoes with chives.*

Stuffed Mushrooms

Serves 6
Working time: about 35 minutes
Total time: about 1 hour and 10 minutes

Calories **185**
Protein **7g.**
Cholesterol **15mg.**
Total fat **6g.**
Saturated fat **3g.**
Sodium **260mg.**

6 large mushrooms, wiped clean, the stalks removed and finely chopped
½ tsp. salt
freshly ground black pepper
1 tbsp. virgin olive oil
1 onion, finely chopped
1 small sweet red pepper, seeded, deribbed, and finely chopped
½ cup short-grain rice
2 garlic cloves, crushed
¼ cup pine nuts
1½ cups unsalted vegetable stock (recipe, page 9)
2 tbsp. shredded fresh basil leaves
4 oz. low-fat mozzarella cheese, diced
¼ cup fresh whole-wheat breadcrumbs
1 tbsp. chopped parsley

Preheat the oven to 400° F. Place the mushroom caps in a shallow ovenproof dish. Add 2 tablespoons of cold water to the dish. Season the mushrooms with a little of the salt and some black pepper. Cover the dish with a lid or foil, and set it aside.

To prepare the stuffing, heat the oil in a large heavy-bottomed saucepan over medium heat. Add the onion and red pepper and cook gently until they are soft—six to eight minutes. Stir in the chopped mushroom stalks, rice, garlic, and pine nuts, and continue cooking, stirring occasionally, until the rice is very lightly browned—about five minutes. Add the vegetable stock, basil, remaining salt, and some freshly ground black pepper. Bring the mixture to a boil, then reduce the heat to low and cover the pan with a tight-fitting lid. Cook gently until the rice is cooked and the stock has been absorbed—20 to 25 minutes. Meanwhile, put the mushroom caps into the oven to cook until they are almost soft—about 20 minutes.

Remove the rice mixture from the heat and stir in the mozzarella, then divide the mixture evenly among the mushrooms, mounding it neatly on top of each one. Sprinkle on the breadcrumbs and return the mushrooms to the oven for another 10 minutes, or until the cheese begins to melt. Serve the mushrooms sprinkled with the chopped parsley.

SUGGESTED ACCOMPANIMENT: *green beans.*

Celeriac Rolls with Mustard Sauce

Serves 4
Working time: about 1 hour and 15 minutes
Total time: about 2 hours and 15 minutes

Calories **260**
Protein **15g.**
Cholesterol **15mg.**
Total fat **9g.**
Saturated fat **4g.**
Sodium **320mg.**

1 tbsp. virgin olive oil
1 garlic clove, crushed
1 small onion, finely chopped
½ lb. tomatoes, peeled, seeded (technique, page 14), and chopped
1 tbsp. tomato paste
½ tsp. dried mixed herbs
freshly ground black pepper
4 young leeks (about 4 oz. each), trimmed, washed thoroughly to remove all grit
2½ cups unsalted vegetable stock (recipe, page 9)
2 large celeriacs (about 2½ lb. each), scrubbed
1 tbsp. fresh lemon juice
2 tbsp. dry whole-wheat breadcrumbs

Mustard sauce
2 tbsp. cornstarch
¼ tsp. freshly grated nutmeg
2½ cups skim milk
½ bay leaf
3 tbsp. grainy mustard
2 oz. Cheddar cheese, grated (about ¼ cup)
⅛ tsp. salt
freshly ground black pepper

Heat the oil in a heavy-bottomed saucepan and sauté the garlic and onion over medium heat until the onion is transparent—three to four minutes. Stir in the tomatoes, tomato paste, and dried mixed herbs, and season the mixture generously with some black pepper. Simmer the sauce for 15 minutes, stirring frequently, until it is very thick. Let it cool.

While the tomato sauce cools, simmer the leeks, whole, in the vegetable stock until they are just tender—about seven minutes. Allow them to cool in the stock while you prepare the celeriac slices.

Peel the celeriacs. Using a very sharp knife, cut 12 horizontal slices about ⅛ inch thick from each one; take the slices from the widest part of each root. Drop the slices into acidulated water as you work, together with the unused top and bottom sections; these may be reserved for another use.

Bring a large saucepan of water to a boil and add the lemon juice. Cook the celeriac slices in the water until they are just tender and pliable—three to four minutes. Drain them in a colander and place them in a bowl of ice water to cool.

Drain the leeks thoroughly and squeeze out as much moisture as possible in paper towels. Cut each leek in half lengthwise, then cut each half crosswise into thirds, to give a total of 24 pieces. Drain the celeriac slices and dry them thoroughly on paper towels. Preheat the oven to 400° F. Lightly grease a large rectangular baking dish.

To assemble the celeriac rolls, put about 1 teaspoonful of the tomato sauce on one half of each slice of celeriac. Top the tomato sauce with a piece of leek and roll up each slice carefully and tightly. Arrange the celeriac rolls, seam side down, in a single layer in the prepared baking dish.

For the mustard sauce, place the cornstarch and nutmeg in a large bowl, and stir in ½ cup of the milk until smoothly blended. Bring the rest of the milk to a boil, with the bay leaf, in a heavy-bottomed saucepan. Pour the boiling milk into the bowl, stirring constantly, then return the mixture to the saucepan. Bring the sauce back to a boil, still stirring. Cook it over high heat for about two minutes, until it has thickened slightly. Take the saucepan off the heat, discard the bay leaf, and stir in the mustard, cheese, salt, and plenty of freshly ground black pepper.

Pour the mustard sauce over the celeriac rolls and sprinkle the breadcrumbs over the top. Bake the rolls until the surface appears bubbling and golden brown—about 30 minutes. Serve hot.

Salsify with Pepper and Onion Relish

Serves 6
Working (and total) time: about 45 minutes

Calories **190**
Protein **7g.**
Cholesterol **0mg.**
Total fat **5g.**
Saturated fat **1g.**
Sodium **140mg.**

2½ lb. salsify, scrubbed well
1 large sweet red pepper, seeded, deribbed, and coarsely chopped
9 pickled mild green chili peppers, finely chopped, or 1 large sweet green pepper, seeded, deribbed, and coarsely chopped
1 red onion, finely chopped
6 scallions, trimmed, white bottoms sliced, green tops coarsely chopped
4 tomatoes, peeled, seeded (technique, page 14), and finely chopped
½ cucumber, peeled and diced
1½ tbsp. capers
6 tbsp. coarsely chopped parsley
1 tbsp. virgin olive oil
1 lime, juice only
⅛ tsp. cayenne pepper
3 black olives, pitted and sliced
lamb's lettuce, or other salad leaves, for garnish

Peel the salsify with a vegetable peeler and trim both ends. Drop the peeled roots into acidulated water as you work, to prevent them from discoloring. Drain the salsify and put it in a large, heavy-bottomed saucepan. Add sufficient water to cover the roots and bring it to a boil. Cook the salsify over high heat until it is tender—8 to 12 minutes, depending on the thickness of the salsify. Test the roots for doneness with the point of a sharp knife.

While the salsify is cooking, prepare the relish. Place the sweet red pepper, chili peppers or sweet green pepper, onion, scallions, tomatoes, cucumber, capers, parsley, oil, lime juice, cayenne pepper, and olives in a large mixing bowl and combine them thoroughly.

Drain the salsify in a colander, arrange it on a hot serving dish, and garnish it with the lamb's lettuce. Spoon the relish over the roots and serve.

SUGGESTED ACCOMPANIMENT: *whole-wheat bread.*

Boiled Yams
with Hot-Pepper Sauce

Serves 4
Working (and total) time: about 50 minutes

Calories **350**
Protein **8g.**
Cholesterol **0mg.**
Total fat **4g.**
Saturated fat **0g.**
Sodium **245mg.**

1 tbsp. peanut oil
2 large onions, chopped
4 medium tomatoes, peeled, seeded (technique, page 14), and chopped
1 hot yellow chili pepper, or 1 to 2 hot red chili peppers, seeded and very finely chopped (cautionary note, page 25)
3 tbsp. tomato paste
½ tsp. salt
2¼ lb. firm yams or sweet potatoes, peeled
1 tbsp. finely chopped parsley, for garnish

In a heavy-bottomed saucepan, heat the oil over medium heat. Add the onions and cook them, stirring frequently, until they are golden—about five minutes. Add the tomatoes and hot pepper to the pan, and cook them, stirring briskly, for about eight minutes.

Stir in the tomato paste and 4 tablespoons of cold water, then add the salt. Mix the ingredients in the pan thoroughly. Lower the heat, cover the pan, and simmer the sauce for 10 minutes. Set the hot-pepper sauce aside and keep it warm.

Rinse the yams or sweet potatoes under cold running water, and cut them into ½-inch-thick slices. Place the slices in a large saucepan of water: The water should just cover them. Bring the water to a boil, lower the heat to medium, and cook the yam slices, partially covered, until they feel soft when pierced with a sharp knife—three to four minutes; be careful not to overcook them. Drain the slices in a colander.

Serve the yam slices with the hot-pepper sauce, garnished with the chopped parsley.

SUGGESTED ACCOMPANIMENT: *Belgian endive salad.*

EDITOR'S NOTE: *The yams in this recipe are available at stores that sell Latin American foods. Any root vegetable, such as sweet potatoes, rutabagas, or white potatoes, would go well with the pepper sauce. To avoid skin irritation, wear protective rubber gloves when peeling yams.*

Chestnut-Stuffed Sweet Potatoes with Chili Sauce

Serves 4
Working time: about 1 hour and 10 minutes
Total time: about 2 hours and 20 minutes

Calories **455**
Protein **6g.**
Cholesterol **0mg.**
Total fat **11g.**
Saturated fat **2g.**
Sodium **165mg.**

2 sweet potatoes (about 1 lb. each), scrubbed
14 oz. fresh chestnuts, peeled (technique, opposite)
1 tbsp. virgin olive oil
1 onion, finely chopped
1 garlic clove, crushed
¼ tsp. salt
½ lime, juice only
1 bunch watercress, stemmed, washed, and dried, for garnish
½ orange, the zest julienned, blanched for 1 minute in boiling water, and drained, the flesh segmented, for garnish

Chili sauce

1 tbsp. virgin olive oil
½ onion, finely chopped
1 garlic clove, crushed
½ red chili pepper, fresh or dried, finely chopped (cautionary note, page 25)
½ tsp. ground cumin
1 medium tomato, peeled, seeded (technique, page 14), and chopped
2 tsp. light brown sugar
1 tsp. red wine vinegar

Preheat the oven to 400° F. Prick the sweet potatoes with a fork and bake them on a rack in the oven for about one and a half hours, or until there is no resistance when the tip of a sharp knife is inserted. While the sweet potatoes are baking, prepare the chili sauce and chestnut stuffing.

For the chili sauce, heat the oil in a heavy-bottomed saucepan and sauté the onion, garlic, and chili pepper until they are soft—four to five minutes. Stir in the cumin, cover the pan, and cook over very low heat, covered, for four minutes more. Mix in the tomato, sugar, and vinegar, and simmer, covered, for 10 minutes. Let the sauce cool a little, then transfer it to a food processor or blender, and blend until smooth.

To prepare the chestnut stuffing, simmer the peeled chestnuts in a pan of boiling water until they are soft—about 10 minutes. Drain them thoroughly and chop them. Heat the oil in a nonreactive saucepan, add the onion and garlic, and cook them gently over medium heat until they are soft—about five minutes. Stir the chopped chestnuts into the pan, together with the salt and lime juice. Keep the stuffing warm until the sweet potatoes are ready.

Cut the cooked sweet potatoes in half lengthwise and carefully scoop out the flesh into a bowl, leaving a ¼-inch-thick shell. Mash the flesh, then spoon it back into the shells, making a well in the center. Pile the chestnut stuffing into the well. Meanwhile, gently reheat the chili sauce.

Arrange the stuffed sweet potatoes on a bed of watercress, and garnish them with the orange segments and zest. Pour the chili sauce into a bowl and serve it with the potatoes.

Peeling Chestnuts

1 *PREPARING THE CHESTNUTS. With a sharp knife, cut a cross in the rounded side of each chestnut. Drop the chestnuts into boiling water and parboil them for about 10 minutes, to loosen their shells. Remove the pan from the heat.*

2 *PEELING OFF THE SHELLS. With a slotted spoon, lift out the parboiled chestnuts a few at a time. Peel off the loosened shells and inner skins while the chestnuts are still hot.*

Sweet Potato Timbales with Two Paprika Sauces

Serves 6
Working time: about 1 hour
Total time: about 2 hours and 45 minutes
(includes chilling)

Calories **140**
Protein **5g.**
Cholesterol **10mg.**
Total fat **5g.**
Saturated fat **2g.**
Sodium **185mg.**

1 lb. sweet potatoes, peeled and cut into chunks
2 tbsp. whipping cream, chilled
4 egg whites, chilled
1 tsp. cut fresh chives, plus a few whole chives for garnish
1 tsp. virgin olive oil
3 sweet red peppers (about 1 lb.), seeded, deribbed, and thinly sliced
1 onion, thinly sliced
4 medium tomatoes, coarsely chopped
1 tsp. paprika
½ tsp. salt
freshly ground black pepper
2 tbsp. plain low-fat yogurt

Put the sweet potatoes into a saucepan of cold water and bring them to a boil. Cover the pan, lower the heat, and simmer the sweet potatoes until they are soft—20 to 25 minutes. Drain the potatoes well, allow them to cool for about 30 minutes, then chill them in the refrigerator for one hour.

Line six ½-cup ramekins with nonstick parchment paper: Cut a small disk to fit each base, and a strip long enough to fit around the inside and wide enough to stand above the rim by ½ inch. Preheat the oven to 350° F. ▶

Put the sweet potatoes and cream into a food processor or blender, purée the mixture until smooth, then transfer it to a large bowl. In another bowl, whisk the egg whites until they form soft peaks but are not stiff and dry. Using a rubber spatula, fold the egg whites into the potato mixture as lightly as possible, then fold in the cut chives. Divide the mixture among the prepared ramekins, smoothing the tops with a wet teaspoon. Arrange the ramekins in a large baking dish, pour in enough hot water to come two-thirds of the way up the sides of the ramekins, and cover them lightly with a sheet of nonstick parchment paper. Bake the timbales until they are risen and puffy and just firm to the touch—about 30 minutes.

While the timbales are cooking, prepare the paprika sauces. Heat the oil in a heavy skillet over low heat, and cook the peppers and onion in the oil for five minutes. Add the tomatoes and bring the mixture to a boil, then lower the heat, cover the skillet, and simmer the vegetables for 15 minutes. Add the paprika and simmer, covered, for five minutes more. Remove the skillet from the heat.

When the mixture has cooled slightly, season it with the salt and some black pepper, and purée it in a food processor or blender. Press the purée through a fine sieve into a bowl, then divide the purée between two small saucepans. Add the yogurt to one pan, stir well, and warm through gently, without boiling, to make a creamy, pale sauce. Gently heat the contents of the second pan as well.

Unmold the timbales onto individual plates, garnish them with the whole chives, and serve them at once with a spoonful of each sauce.

SUGGESTED ACCOMPANIMENTS: *steamed green beans and baby corn; crusty bread.*

Saffron and Potato Stew with Rouille

ROUILLE, A RED CHILI PEPPER AND GARLIC SAUCE FROM PROVENCE, IS USUALLY SERVED WITH FISH SOUPS. UNLIKE THE CLASSIC SAUCE, THIS VERSION CONTAINS NO OIL.

Serves 6
Working time: about 40 minutes
Total time: about 55 minutes

Calories **270**
Protein **7g.**
Cholesterol **0mg.**
Total fat **3g.**
Saturated fat **trace**
Sodium **350mg.**

1½ lb. potatoes, cut into ¾-inch chunks
1 tsp. virgin olive oil
2 large tomatoes, peeled, seeded (technique, page 14), and cut into ½-inch chunks
2 leeks, washed thoroughly to remove all grit, white and green parts separated and sliced
1 onion, sliced
2 tsp. chopped fresh thyme, or ½ tsp. dried thyme leaves
3 bay leaves
1 tsp. sugar
2 strips thinly pared orange zest
1 tsp. saffron threads, soaked in 1 tbsp. boiling water for 30 minutes
2½ cups unsalted vegetable stock (recipe, page 9)
1¼ cups dry white wine
¾ cup ditalini, macaroni, or other small pasta
½ lb. zucchini, sliced
3 tbsp. chopped parsley
1 sweet yellow pepper, seeded, deribbed, and sliced into fine strips
¾ tsp. salt
freshly ground black pepper
2 tbsp. plain low-fat yogurt

Rouille

2 slices white bread (crusts removed), broken into pieces
⅓ cup skim milk
2 hot red chili peppers, seeded and coarsely chopped (cautionary note, page 25)
3 garlic cloves, coarsely chopped
¼ tsp. salt
1 small sweet red pepper, seeded, deribbed, and coarsely chopped

First make the *rouille*. Place the bread in a bowl with the milk and set it aside to steep until the bread has softened—about five minutes. Meanwhile, purée the chilies, garlic, salt, and sweet red pepper with 2 tablespoons of water in a food processor or blender. Add the bread and milk, and blend again until smooth.

Transfer the *rouille* to a serving bowl and set it aside.

Put the potatoes in a saucepan with enough cold water to cover them. Bring the water to a boil, then lower the heat, cover the pan, and simmer until the potatoes are almost tender—about 10 minutes. Drain the potatoes well.

While the potatoes are cooking, heat the oil in a large flameproof casserole over medium heat. Add the tomatoes, white parts of the leeks, onion, thyme, and bay leaves, and cook, stirring, for five minutes. Stir in the sugar, orange zest, saffron and its soaking liquid, stock, and wine, and bring the mixture to a boil. Add

the pasta and cook, covered, until the pasta is almost *al dente*—five to seven minutes. Stir in the potatoes, green parts of the leeks, zucchini, parsley, sweet yellow pepper, salt, and some black pepper, and cook, stirring, for three to five minutes more, until the potatoes are heated through but the yellow pepper and zucchini still retain their crispness.

Ladle the stew into individual serving bowls, and top each serving with a swirl of the yogurt and a spoonful of *rouille*. Serve the remaining *rouille* separately.

SUGGESTED ACCOMPANIMENT: *crusty whole-grain bread.*

Potato, Carrot, and Celeriac Rösti

RÖSTI IS A SWISS DISH TRADITIONALLY MADE WITH POTATOES AS THE ONLY VEGETABLE. THIS VARIATION IS COOKED WITH SUBSTANTIALLY LESS BUTTER THAN THE CLASSIC VERSION.

Serves 4
Working time: about 40 minutes
Total time: about 1 hour and 10 minutes

Calories **200**
Protein **3g.**
Cholesterol **25mg.**
Total fat **9g.**
Saturated fat **5g.**
Sodium **165mg.**

1 lb. potatoes, scrubbed
½ lb. carrots (5 to 6 medium), peeled
10 oz. celeriac, peeled
¼ tsp. salt
freshly ground black pepper
3 tbsp. unsalted butter

Cook the potatoes in their skins in a saucepan of boiling water for six minutes, then drain them well. Carefully peel the potatoes while they are still hot. Allow them to cool for 10 minutes, then chill them for about 20 minutes.

Using a vegetable grater or the grating attachment of a food processor, coarsely shred the potatoes, carrots, and celeriac. Place the shredded vegetables in a large mixing bowl. Season them with the salt and some black pepper, and mix them well.

Heat half of the butter in a large nonstick skillet until it begins to bubble. Reduce the heat to low and add the *rösti* mixture, pressing it down gently with a spatula to form a flat cake. Cook until the *rösti* is golden brown underneath—about 10 minutes— shaking the skillet gently now and then to prevent sticking.

Place a large flat plate on top of the skillet, remove it from the heat, and carefully invert the *rösti* onto the plate. Return the skillet to the heat, add the remaining butter, and heat it until it is bubbling hot. Slide the *rösti* back into the skillet and cook the second side until it is golden brown—five to six minutes. Turn the *rösti* onto a hot plate and serve immediately.

SUGGESTED ACCOMPANIMENT: *salad of red and white cabbage tossed with chopped parsley and a vinaigrette dressing.*

Baked Potatoes with an Onion and Chive Filling

Serves 4
Working time: about 20 minutes
Total time: about 2 hours

Calories **270**
Protein **7g.**
Cholesterol **10mg.**
Total fat **3g.**
Saturated fat **1g.**
Sodium **245mg.**

2 large potatoes (about 1 lb. each), scrubbed and pricked
2 Spanish onions, unpeeled, halved lengthwise
½ cup plain low-fat yogurt
¼ cup sour cream
2 tbsp. finely chopped chives
½ tsp. salt
freshly ground black pepper

Preheat the oven to 400° F.

Place the potatoes and the onion halves on a rack in the middle of the oven and bake them until they are soft when pierced with a skewer; the onions will take about 45 minutes and the potatoes will need about one and a half hours. Do not turn off the oven at the end of this time.

When the onions are cooked, remove them from the oven. Allow them to cool a little, then peel them. Remove and reserve the centers of the onions and coarsely chop the remainder.

Cut the cooked potatoes in half lengthwise. Using a spoon, scoop the flesh into a bowl, leaving a ½-inch-thick potato shell. Mash the potato flesh, then mix in the yogurt, sour cream, chives, salt, and some freshly ground black pepper.

Half fill the shells with the mashed potato mixture. Add a layer of chopped roasted onion, and top the onion with the rest of the potato mixture. Garnish each potato half with a reserved onion center. Return the stuffed potatoes to the oven for about 15 minutes, to heat them through.

SUGGESTED ACCOMPANIMENT: *radish and watercress salad.*

Scandinavian Salad

THIS IS AN ADAPTATION OF A SALAD THAT IN SCANDINAVIAN COUNTRIES TRADITIONALLY ACCOMPANIES CURED HERRINGS. THE CLASSIC MIXTURE INCLUDES HARD-BOILED EGGS AND A RICH, CREAMY DRESSING; HERE THE PROPORTION OF EGGS IS REDUCED AND YOGURT REPLACES CREAM IN THE DRESSING.

Serves 6
Working time: about 45 minutes
Total time: about 2 hours and 15 minutes
(includes chilling)

Calories **195**
Protein **7g.**
Cholesterol **75mg.**
Total fat **4g.**
Saturated fat **1g.**
Sodium **190mg.**

1½ lb. small beets, washed and trimmed, 2-inch stem left on each
1½ lb. new potatoes, lightly scrubbed, halved if large
2 eggs, hard-boiled
1 tbsp. red wine vinegar
1 tsp. molasses
2 tbsp. plain low-fat yogurt
1 tsp. caraway seeds, lightly toasted
freshly ground black pepper
curly endive leaves for garnish
Mustard dressing
2 tsp. mild Dijon mustard
1 tsp. dry mustard
1 tsp. yellow mustard seeds, toasted
½ tsp. freshly grated horseradish or prepared horseradish
1 tsp. white wine vinegar
2 tsp. virgin olive oil
⅔ cup plain low-fat yogurt
2 tbsp. finely chopped fresh dill

Preheat the oven to 400° F. Wrap the beets, in a single package, in aluminum foil. Bake the beets until they are tender—about one hour. Remove them from the oven, and when they are cool enough to handle, peel them, removing the stems, and cut them into ½-inch cubes. Place the cubes in a large bowl.

While the beets are cooking, steam the new potatoes until they are just tender—15 to 20 minutes. Take care not to overcook them.

Cut one hard-boiled egg lengthwise into six wedges and set the wedges aside. Slice the second hard-boiled egg in half. Reserve the egg yolk for the mustard dressing; then finely dice the egg white and set it aside for garnishing the salad.

Put the red wine vinegar in a small bowl, add the molasses, and stir until smoothly combined. Pour this dressing over the beet cubes and toss them in it thoroughly. Add the yogurt, the caraway seeds, and some black pepper. Stir to combine all the ingredients, then set the bowl aside.

For the mustard dressing, sieve the reserved egg yolk into a small bowl and blend in the Dijon mustard. Add the dry mustard, mustard seeds, and horseradish, and stir thoroughly. Next, blend in the white wine vinegar, followed by the oil. Finally, mix in the yogurt and the chopped dill.

Cut the potatoes into slightly larger cubes than the beets and place them in a large bowl. Add the mustard dressing and toss the cubes in it thoroughly.

Line a serving dish with the curly endive leaves. Pile the beet cubes in the center of the dish, and arrange the new potatoes and hard-boiled egg wedges in a circle around them. Sprinkle the chopped egg white over the beets. Chill the salad for about 30 minutes before serving it.

SUGGESTED ACCOMPANIMENT: *a selection of breads.*

EDITOR'S NOTE: *To toast caraway or mustard seeds, place them in small, dry, heavy-bottomed skillet. Shake the skillet over medium heat for about three minutes, until the seeds are hot and aromatic.*

Jerusalem Artichoke and Walnut Soufflés

Serves 4
Working time: about 20 minutes
Total time: about 45 minutes

Calories **145**
Protein **8g.**
Cholesterol **60mg.**
Total fat **10g.**
Saturated fat **2g.**
Sodium **290mg.**

½ lb. Jerusalem artichokes, or ½ lb. potatoes, peeled and cut into small pieces
2 tsp. cornstarch
½ cup skim milk
¼ tsp. ground mace
½ tsp. salt
3 tbsp. chopped parsley
freshly ground black pepper
2 oz. shelled walnuts (about ½ cup), finely chopped
1 egg yolk
3 egg whites
1 tbsp. freshly grated Parmesan cheese

Preheat the oven to 350° F. Lightly grease the sides of four 1-cup soufflé dishes and place them on a baking sheet. Cook the artichokes in a saucepan of boiling water until they are tender—six to eight minutes. Drain and mash them, and set them aside.

In a large, heavy-bottomed saucepan, blend the cornstarch with a little of the milk. Stir in the remaining milk, followed by the mace, salt, parsley, and some freshly ground black pepper. Bring the contents of the pan to a boil, stirring continuously, then reduce the heat to medium and cook the sauce until it has thickened—about two minutes. Remove the pan from the heat and stir in the mashed Jerusalem artichokes. Set aside 1 tablespoon of the chopped walnuts; stir the remainder into the pan, together with the egg yolk, and mix the ingredients well.

Whisk the egg whites until they are stiff. Using a rubber spatula, carefully fold a quarter of the whites at a time into the artichoke mixture. Divide the mixture equally among the prepared dishes. Sprinkle the tops of the soufflés with the Parmesan and the reserved walnuts, and bake them in the oven until they are well risen and golden—20 to 25 minutes. Remove the soufflés from the oven and serve them immediately.

SUGGESTED ACCOMPANIMENTS: *crusty whole-wheat bread; green salad with a garlic dressing.*

Curried Rutabaga Soup

Serves 4
Working time: about 20 minutes
Total time: about 1 hour

Calories **185**
Protein **4g.**
Cholesterol **0mg.**
Total fat **7g.**
Saturated fat **2g.**
Sodium **425mg.**

1 tbsp. safflower oil
1 medium onion (about 4 oz.), chopped
¾ lb. rutabaga, peeled and cut into ¼-inch dice
6 oz. parsnip, peeled and cut into ¼-inch dice
1 small sweet red pepper, seeded, deribbed, and cut into ¼-inch dice
1 small cooking apple (about 3 oz.), cut into ¼-inch dice
3 tbsp. brown basmati rice or long-grain brown rice
½ tsp. medium-hot curry powder
½ tsp. ground coriander
¼ tsp. ground cumin
⅛ tsp. ground turmeric
⅛ tsp. ground ginger
1 garlic clove, crushed
½ tsp. salt
1¼ cups tomato juice
1 quart unsalted vegetable stock (recipe, page 9)
2 tbsp. golden raisins
2½ tbsp. unsweetened shredded coconut, toasted

Heat the oil in a large, heavy-bottomed saucepan or flameproof casserole, and cook the onion, rutabaga, and parsnip over medium heat for five minutes. Add the red pepper and cook for two to three minutes more, stirring occasionally. Then add the apple, rice, spices, and garlic, and cook, stirring constantly, for two minutes. Finally, mix in the salt, tomato juice, stock, and golden raisins, and bring the mixture to a boil. Lower the heat to a simmer, cover the pan, and cook the soup for 30 minutes. Just before serving, stir in the shredded coconut.

SUGGESTED ACCOMPANIMENT: *sourdough rye bread.*

EDITOR'S NOTE: *To toast coconut, spread it on a baking sheet and place the sheet in a 350° F. oven for 10 minutes, stirring the coconut once.*

Mixed Root Vegetables in Orange Sauce

Serves 4
Working time: about 30 minutes
Total time: about 1 hour

Calories **160**
Protein **4g.**
Cholesterol **15mg.**
Total fat **7g.**
Saturated fat **4g.**
Sodium **330mg.**

2 tbsp. unsalted butter
1 onion, chopped
1 garlic clove, crushed
2 tsp. freshly grated ginger
1 tsp. coriander seeds, crushed
6 oz. parsnips, peeled if necessary and cut into 1-inch chunks
6 oz. carrots, peeled if necessary and cut into 1-inch chunks
6 oz. rutabaga, peeled if necessary and cut into 1-inch chunks
6 oz. kohlrabies, peeled if necessary and cut into 1-inch chunks
6 oz. celeriac, peeled if necessary and cut into 1-inch chunks
6 oz. turnips, trimmed and cut into 1-inch chunks
1¼ cup fresh orange juice, mixed with ⅔ cup water
1 lemon, coarsely grated zest only
1 orange, coarsely grated zest only
½ tsp. salt
freshly ground black pepper

Melt the butter in a large, heavy-bottomed saucepan or flameproof casserole over medium heat. Add the chopped onion and crushed garlic, and sauté them until the onion is transparent—three to four minutes. Mix in the ginger and coriander, and cook the mixture for one minute more, stirring constantly. Add all the root vegetables, along with the orange juice and water mixture. Bring the contents of the pan to a boil. Turn the heat to low, cover the pan, and simmer the vegetables for 20 minutes.

Stir in the lemon zest and orange zest, the salt, and some black pepper. Cover the pan again and simmer the vegetables for another five minutes. Finally, to reduce and thicken the orange sauce, remove the lid from the pan and boil the vegetables rapidly for five minutes. At the end of this time, they should feel just tender when pierced with the tip of a sharp knife.

SUGGESTED ACCOMPANIMENT: *couscous or brown rice.*

EDITOR'S NOTE: *Since many valuable nutrients are contained in or just below the skin of root vegetables, select small, young specimens, which rarely need peeling, for this recipe.*

Stir-Fried Vegetables in a Sweet-and-Sour Sauce

Serves 4
Working and total time: about 30 minutes

Calories **240**
Protein **9g.**
Cholesterol **0mg.**
Total fat **13g.**
Saturated fat **2g.**
Sodium **30mg.**

1½ tbsp. safflower oil
¾ lb. baby corn, fresh or frozen, trimmed if necessary, halved lengthwise
1 large sweet red pepper, seeded, deribbed, and cut into strips
¾ lb. small carrots, trimmed and thinly sliced diagonally
¾ lb. bean sprouts
¾ lb. snow peas, strings removed
2 tsp. dark sesame oil
freshly ground black pepper
Sweet-and-sour sauce
3 tsp. arrowroot
1¼ cups unsweetened pineapple juice
2 tbsp. low-sodium soy sauce
1 tbsp. freshly grated ginger
1 garlic clove, crushed
⅔ cup unsalted vegetable stock (recipe, page 9)
1 tsp. honey
5 scallions, trimmed and finely sliced

First make the sweet-and-sour sauce. Place the arrow-root in a medium-size saucepan and gradually blend in the pineapple juice. Stir in the remaining sauce ingredients and bring the contents of the pan to a boil. Lower the heat and simmer the sauce for five minutes, stirring it frequently. Set the sauce aside.

Heat the safflower oil in a wok or large, heavy skillet over high heat. Add the corn, red pepper, and carrots, and stir-fry for four minutes. Add the bean sprouts and snow peas, and stir-fry until the vegetables are cooked but still slightly crunchy—one to two minutes more. If you are using frozen corn, add it with the bean sprouts and snow peas.

Add the sweet-and-sour sauce to the wok. Lower the heat and cook the mixture for one to two minutes more, still stirring, to warm the sauce through.

Season the stir-fry with the sesame oil and some black pepper. Serve immediately.

SUGGESTED ACCOMPANIMENT: *white or brown rice.*

Lohans' Feast

THIS IS ONE OF THE CLASSICS OF CHINESE BUDDHIST
VEGETARIAN CUISINE, SOMETIMES KNOWN AS "BUDDHA'S
DELIGHT" ON RESTAURANT MENUS. LOHANS ARE
THE GUARDIAN ANGELS OF THE BUDDHA. A GRAND VERSION OF
THIS DISH CONTAINS 18 DIFFERENT ITEMS—AMONG THEM
RARE AND EXOTIC FUNGI—REPRESENTING THE 18 LOHANS. THIS
COMPARATIVELY SIMPLE VERSION IS WHAT WOULD
BE FOUND ON THE DINING TABLE OF MOST CONTEMPORARY
CHINESE FAMILIES. COMMON TO ALL TRUE BUD-
DHIST VEGETARIAN DISHES, IT DOES NOT CONTAIN THE MORE
USUAL CHINESE FLAVORINGS OF GARLIC, GINGER, AND
SCALLIONS, BECAUSE THESE ARE CONSIDERED BY BUD-
DHISTS AS RANK FLAVORS AND ARE ALSO BELIEVED
TO AROUSE PASSION.

Serves 4
Working time: about 1 hour and 30 minutes
Total time: about 4 hours (includes soaking)

Calories **325**
Protein **11g.**
Cholesterol **0mg.**
Total fat **9g.**
Saturated fat **1g.**
Sodium **250mg.**

½ oz. dried hair algae (optional), soaked in cold water for 20 minutes or until pliable
2½ tbsp. safflower oil
12 dried shiitake mushrooms, soaked in warm water for 20 minutes
¾ oz. dried lily buds (golden needles), soaked in warm water for 20 minutes
⅓ oz. dried cloud-ear mushrooms, soaked in warm water for 20 minutes
4 oz. drained canned bamboo shoots, cut into ¼-inch-thick slices
2½ oz. dried bean curd sticks, soaked in cold water for 3 hours or until soft, drained, and cut into 2¼-inch lengths
3 oz. shelled ginkgo nuts (optional)
2 oz. dried cellophane noodles, soaked in cold water for at least 5 minutes, drained 5 to 10 minutes before cooking
1 tsp. dark sesame oil
½ carrot, sliced, slices cut into decorative shapes with aspic cutters, blanched in boiling water for 3 minutes, and drained

Bean curd sauce

2 cups unsalted vegetable stock (recipe, page 9)
1 cube red fermented bean curd, plus 1 tsp. pickling liquid from the can or jar
2 tbsp. low-sodium soy sauce
1½ tsp. sugar

Drain the hair algae, if you are using it, and rub into it 1 teaspoon of the safflower oil. Place the algae in a large bowl and cover it with fresh water. Stir the algae and rub it under the water to loosen any impurities lodged in the strands. Drain the algae carefully, press-ing it against the side of the bowl. Repeat the oiling and rinsing twice more, then rinse the algae in fresh cold water at least three times, or until all traces of oil are removed. Squeeze the algae dry, separate the strands into bunches, and knot the bunches into little balls. Set the balls aside.

Squeeze the shiitake mushrooms dry. Remove and discard the stalks, and set the caps aside. Strain and reserve the soaking liquid.

Drain the lily buds, squeeze them dry, and trim away and discard any hard bits at the stalk ends. Tie the buds into simple single knots—this is traditional and helps to preserve their crunchy texture. Set the knots aside.

Drain the cloud-ear mushrooms and rinse them in several changes of water to remove any grit. Remove any hard knobs with a sharp knife. Tear the cloud-ears into bite-size pieces, separating any large clusters. Let the pieces drain.

Next, prepare the bean curd sauce. Add enough of the vegetable stock to the mushroom-soaking liquid to make 2 cups. Blend the fermented bean curd with the teaspoon of its pickling liquid and a little of the veg-etable stock solution until smooth. Pass the mixture through a fine sieve, pressing the bean curd with the back of a spoon and adding a little more stock, if necessary, to get the bean curd through the sieve. Add the soy sauce, sugar, and any remaining vegetable stock to the purée, and mix it thoroughly. Set the bean curd sauce aside.

Heat a wok or large, heavy skillet over high heat, then add ½ teaspoon of the safflower oil and swirl it around in the wok to coat the sides. Add the lily buds and the cloud-ears, and let them sizzle in the oil for 30 seconds, stirring them with a spatula all the time. Remove them from the wok, using a slotted spoon, and set them aside. Add the remaining safflower oil to the wok, and stir-fry the bamboo shoots and shiitake mushrooms for about 30 seconds; remove them from the wok and set them aside.

Pour the bean curd sauce into a flameproof casse-role and bring it to a boil. Add the bean curd sticks and simmer them for 10 minutes. Add the previously browned lily buds, cloud-ears, bamboo shoots, and shiitake mushrooms to the casserole, together with the hair algae balls and ginkgo nuts, if used. Simmer the ingredients for 10 minutes, then add the cello-phane noodles and continue to simmer until most of the liquid has been absorbed—about 10 minutes more. (If you are using canned ginkgo nuts, add them with the cellophane noodles.)

Arrange the ingredients attractively on a heatproof serving platter. Sprinkle the sesame oil over the ingre-dients and garnish the dish with the carrot shapes. Before serving, set the platter over a large pan of boiling water to steam for 10 to 15 minutes.

SUGGESTED ACCOMPANIMENT: *boiled rice.*

EDITOR'S NOTE: *Lohans' Feast benefits from being cooked a day in advance, to allow the flavors to develop. Most of the unusual ingredients called for in this recipe can be obtained in stores that sell Asian foods, although hard-to-find ingre-dients may be replaced by any root vegetable. Since most of the ingredients are dried, any surplus can be stored almost indefinitely and used on another occasion. Fermented bean curd, which is available in cans or jars, will keep for several months in its pickling liquid. Once a can of fermented bean curd is opened, the contents should be transferred to a sterile, air-tight container for storage.*

Okra and Sweet Pepper Stew

Serves 4
Working time: about 30 minutes
Total time: about 45 minutes

Calories **200**
Protein **9g.**
Cholesterol **0mg.**
Total fat **12g.**
Saturated fat **3g.**
Sodium **230mg.**

2 tbsp. safflower oil
2 Spanish onions, cut lengthwise into eight wedges
1 tbsp. palm oil
2 large tomatoes, peeled, seeded (technique, page 14), and chopped
1 sweet red pepper, seeded, deribbed, and sliced into rings
1 sweet yellow pepper, seeded, deribbed, and sliced into rings
6½ tbsp. tomato paste
1¼ cups unsalted vegetable stock (recipe, page 9)
1½ lb. okra, trimmed and sliced
1 lb. mushrooms, wiped clean and quartered
2 tsp. ground coriander
½ tsp. salt

Heat the safflower oil in a large, heavy-bottomed saucepan over medium heat. Add the onions and sauté them gently for five minutes, stirring from time to time. Add the palm oil to the pan, and when it has melted, stir in the tomatoes and pepper rings. Reduce the heat to low, cover the pan, and cook the vegetables gently for five minutes.

Stir the tomato paste into the stock. When it has completely dissolved, pour this liquid into the saucepan. Add the okra, mushrooms, and coriander, and stir the mixture lightly.

Heat the stew slowly to the simmering point. Cover the pan and continue to simmer the stew, stirring from time to time, until the vegetables are tender—about 15 minutes. Stir in the salt and serve.

SUGGESTED ACCOMPANIMENT: *mashed sweet potatoes.*

EDITOR'S NOTE: *Palm oil—misleadingly named since at refrigerator temperature it has the consistency of butter—is bright orange in color and has a strong nutty flavor. It is available from African and Caribbean specialty food shops.*

Vegetable Curry with Coconut

Serves 4
Working time: about 45 minutes
Total time: about 1 hour

Calories **170**
Protein **5g.**
Cholesterol **10mg.**
Total fat **9g.**
Saturated fat **2g.**
Sodium **330mg.**

1 tbsp. clarified butter or unsalted butter
1 onion, finely chopped
1½ tsp. ground turmeric
2 tsp. ground coriander
1 tsp. ground fenugreek
2 tsp. black mustard seeds
¾ lb. carrots (3 to 4 medium), coarsely chopped and blanched in boiling water for 30 seconds
1 small cauliflower (about 1½ lb.), broken into florets and blanched in boiling water for 30 seconds
½ tsp. salt
6 oz. green beans, ends removed, cut in half, and blanched in boiling water for 30 seconds
6 tbsp. raisins
8 small hot green chili peppers, seeded and finely chopped (cautionary note, page 25)
3 small bananas, peeled and diced
2 oz. fresh coconut, grated, or ½ cup unsweetened shredded coconut
½ lemon, juice only
1 tbsp. chopped fresh mint
1 tbsp. chopped cilantro
freshly ground black pepper

Melt the butter in a large, heavy-bottomed saucepan over medium heat. Add the onion and sauté it, stirring frequently, until it is transparent—about three minutes. Stir in the turmeric, coriander, fenugreek, and mustard seeds, and sauté the spices with the onion for about two minutes. Then mix in the carrots, cauliflower, and salt. Reduce the heat to low, cover the pan, and cook the vegetables for five minutes. Add the green beans, re-cover the pan, and cook for three more minutes. Stir in 1¼ cups of water, then lightly stir in the raisins and half of the chopped chilies. Bring the mixture to a boil, cover the pan again, and reduce the heat to low. Simmer until the carrots are tender—approximately 10 minutes.

Gently mix in the bananas and coconut, and simmer the curry, uncovered, for three minutes. Finally, add the lemon juice, mint, cilantro, remaining chopped chilies, and some freshly ground black pepper. If the curry seems dry, add a little extra water. Simmer it for two minutes more and serve.

SUGGESTED ACCOMPANIMENTS: *rice; cilantro raita.*

EDITOR'S NOTE: *For a hotter curry, add a little cayenne pepper with the ground coriander. To make cilantro raita, whisk ½ teaspoon of cayenne pepper into 1 cup of chilled, plain low-fat yogurt. Stir in about 2 tablespoons of chopped cilantro, and sprinkle a little more over the top as a garnish.*

Mexican Sweet Potato Stew

Serves 4
Working time: about 40 minutes
Total time: about 1 hour and 10 minutes

Calories **270**
Protein **7g.**
Cholesterol **0mg.**
Total fat **9g.**
Saturated fat **1g.**
Sodium **150mg.**

1¼ lb. sweet potatoes, peeled and cut into large chunks
¾ lb. slice of pumpkin, peeled, seeded, and chopped
2 tbsp. safflower oil
1 onion, finely chopped
2 garlic cloves, crushed
½ tsp. chili powder
½ lb. okra, ends removed, chopped
1 sweet green pepper, seeded, deribbed, and chopped
4 fresh hot red chili peppers, seeded and finely chopped (cautionary note, page 25)
1½ cups fresh or frozen corn kernels
14 oz. canned tomatoes with their juice
5 cloves
1¼ cups unsalted vegetable stock (recipe, page 9)
2 tbsp. tomato paste
⅛ tsp. salt
freshly ground black pepper

Place the sweet potatoes in a saucepan, cover them with water, and bring it to a boil. Cover the pan, lower the heat, and simmer the sweet potatoes until they are tender—about 10 minutes. Remove them from the pan with a slotted spoon and set them aside. Put the pumpkin into the same cooking water and bring it to a boil. Cover the pan again, lower the heat, and simmer the pumpkin until it, too, is tender—five to seven minutes. Drain the pumpkin and set it aside.

Heat the oil in a large, heavy-bottomed saucepan and sauté the onion and garlic over very gentle heat until the onion is tender—about seven minutes. Add the chili powder, okra, sweet pepper, chili peppers, corn, tomatoes and their juice, cloves, and stock. Bring the mixture to a boil, then reduce the heat and simmer until the liquid has reduced and thickened—approximately 10 minutes.

Add the tomato paste, sweet potatoes, pumpkin, salt, and some black pepper to the pan and stir gently. Cover the pan and simmer the stew for 10 minutes more. Serve it hot.

SUGGESTED ACCOMPANIMENTS: *tacos or tortillas; green salad.*

Hot-and-Sour Potato and Turnip Casserole

Serves 4
Working time: about 45 minutes
Total time: about 1 hour and 20 minutes

Calories **270**
Protein **7g.**
Cholesterol **0mg.**
Total fat **12g.**
Saturated fat **3g.**
Sodium **265mg.**

1 tsp. coriander seeds
1 tsp. black peppercorns
5 cardamom pods
4 cloves
1½ tbsp. safflower oil
1 small onion, finely chopped
2 garlic cloves, crushed
1 tsp. grated fresh ginger
1 fresh or dried red chili pepper, halved lengthwise and seeded (cautionary note, page 25)
1 lb. potatoes, peeled and diced
½ lb. turnips, peeled and diced
½ lb. green beans or wax beans (about 2½ cups), cut into 1-inch lengths
5 or 6 fresh curry leaves (optional)
½ tsp. salt
3 medium tomatoes, peeled, seeded (technique, page 14), and chopped
1½ tbsp. fresh lemon juice
2 tsp. sugar
½ cup sour cream
2 tsp. ground turmeric
3 tbsp. chopped cilantro

Toast the coriander seeds, peppercorns, cardamom pods, and cloves in a dry, heavy-bottomed skillet over medium heat for one minute, to release their fragrance. Grind them finely in an electric coffee grinder, or by hand in a mortar with a pestle.

Heat the oil over medium heat in a large flameproof casserole or heavy-bottomed saucepan. Sauté the onion, garlic, ginger, chili pepper, and ground spices for five minutes, stirring frequently. Add the potatoes, turnips, beans, curry leaves, if you are using them, and salt. Stir the mixture well, cover the casserole or saucepan, and cook the vegetables for 10 minutes, stirring them occasionally.

Blend the tomatoes in a food processor or blender until smooth, and add them to the casserole. Continue simmering until the potatoes are almost done—about 15 minutes. Stir in ½ cup of water and cook for five minutes, then stir in another ½ cup of water and cook for five minutes more. Remove the casserole from the heat, and mix in the lemon juice and 1 teaspoon of the sugar. Discard the curry leaves and, if you wish, the chili pepper.

In a bowl, mix the sour cream with the remaining teaspoon of sugar and the turmeric. Stir half of the sour-cream mixture into the casserole. Pour the rest of the sour-cream mixture into the center of the casserole, sprinkle the chopped cilantro over the top, and serve immediately.

SUGGESTED ACCOMPANIMENT: *brown or white rice.*

EDITOR'S NOTE: *Curry leaves are available from Indian markets and some supermarkets.*

2 Red kidney beans, chickpeas, mung beans, and brown, white, and wild rice are but a sample of the many types of beans and grains used in this chapter.

Treasures from the Pantry

For 10,000 years or more, ever since Stone Age farmers first cultivated the banks of slow-flowing Asian rivers, grains and dried beans have been central to human nutrition. Today, these two vast families of food (there are 2,500 varieties of rice alone) still provide most of the calories and more than two-thirds of the protein consumed throughout the world. Their long association is no historical accident; eaten together, grains and dried beans complement each other to create a perfect protein balance.

In the wealthy Western countries of the world, where meat and fish are the principal sources of protein, health-conscious cooks are reawakening to this time-honored way of eating. Low in saturated fats and high in dietary fiber and carbohydrates, grains and dried beans are an ancient antidote to the modern ills of an affluent diet. And as the recipes in this chapter suggest, grains and beans adapt easily to the sophisticated tastes of the twentieth century.

Although most of the ingredients in these recipes are widely available, many of them are not yet common to every Western kitchen. Millet, a tiny, delicately flavored grain, is a staple of African and Asian diets, and it is rich in protein, iron, and B vitamins. Buckwheat is not strictly a wheat at all, being more closely related to rhubarb. The toasted seeds, or groats, which are known as kasha in Russian cookery, add a robust, earthy tang to any dish. Wild rice is a costly but delectable grass seed native to the Great Lakes region of the United States. Even when used in small quantities, it enhances any preparation with its distinctive though subtle flavor.

Several varieties of dried beans, peas, and lentils can be found on supermarket shelves. Tofu, once found only in health food stores and Asian markets, is now widely available. This high-protein soybean curd—which is nearly tasteless by itself—has a satisfying texture and a chameleon-like tendency to absorb flavors from other ingredients in which it is marinated or with which it is cooked.

Preparing beans often requires soaking time in addition to cooking time. Reward yourself for this little extra labor by cooking double the quantity of beans required by a recipe. Cooked beans freeze well, and they are delicious in salads and soups.

Salad of Avocado, Flageolets, Almonds, and Brown Rice

Serves 6
Working time: about 25 minutes
Total time: about 3 hours
(includes soaking)

Calories **300**
Protein **10g.**
Cholesterol **0mg.**
Total fat **11g.**
Saturated fat **2g.**
Sodium **80mg.**

½ cup flageolets or white beans, picked over	
1¼ cups brown rice	
¼ tsp. salt	
1 small ripe avocado	
1 lemon, juice only, strained	
2 oz. blanched almonds (about ½ cup), toasted	
6 tbsp. chopped parsley	
2 tbsp. chopped fennel	
¼ cup plain low-fat yogurt	
1 tbsp. virgin olive oil	
1 tsp. Dijon mustard	
1 garlic clove, crushed	
1 large head of lettuce, separated into leaves, for garnish	

Rinse the flageolets or white beans under cold running water, then put them into a large, heavy saucepan, and pour in enough cold water to cover them by about 3 inches. Discard any beans that float to the surface of the water. Cover the pan, leaving the lid ajar, and slowly bring the liquid to a boil. Boil the beans for two minutes, then turn off the heat and soak the beans, covered, for at least one hour. (Alternatively, soak the beans overnight in cold water.)

Drain the beans, then place them in a saucepan and pour in enough water to cover them by about 3 inches. Bring the liquid to a boil; then lower the heat to maintain a strong simmer and cook the beans, covered, until they are tender—about one hour. If the beans appear to be drying out at any point, add more hot water to the saucepan. Drain the beans in a colander, then rinse them and set them aside to cool for approximately 30 minutes.

Bring 2 quarts of water to a boil in a large saucepan. Stir in the brown rice and salt, lower the heat, and simmer, uncovered, until the rice is tender—approximately 40 minutes. Drain the rice in a sieve, rinse it under cold running water, and leave it in the sieve to drain and cool thoroughly.

Halve, pit, peel, and chop the avocado, and coat the pieces in half of the lemon juice to prevent them from discoloring. In a large bowl, mix the avocado, almonds, parsley, and fennel with the beans and the rice. In a small bowl, beat together the yogurt, oil, mustard, garlic, and remaining lemon juice. Fold this dressing into the rice salad.

To serve, line a large bowl with the lettuce leaves and spoon the rice salad into the middle.

SUGGESTED ACCOMPANIMENT: *tomato salad.*

EDITOR'S NOTE: *To toast almonds, place them on a baking sheet in a preheated 350° F. oven for 10 minutes.*

Caribbean Spiced Rice

CARIBBEAN COOKING IS INFLUENCED BY MANY CULINARY TRADITIONS: THE SIMPLE FOOD OF THE NATIVE INDIANS WAS ADAPTED AND DEVELOPED BY THE SPANISH, AFRICAN, AND INDIAN PEOPLES WHO LIVED AND WORKED IN THE ISLANDS.

Serves 4
Working (and total) time: about 50 minutes

Calories **540**
Protein **9g.**
Cholesterol **0mg.**
Total fat **6g.**
Saturated fat **2g.**
Sodium **250mg.**

1¾ cups basmati rice or other long-grain rice, rinsed under cold running water until the water runs clear
1 tsp. ground allspice
½ tsp. salt
2 garlic cloves, sliced
freshly ground black pepper
1 qt. unsalted vegetable stock (recipe, page 9)
2 green plantains
1 tbsp. vinegar
1 small carrot, finely chopped
¼ sweet red pepper, seeded, deribbed, and finely chopped
1 celery stalk, finely chopped
¼ lb. okra, finely sliced
2 small ripe mangoes
12 scallions, finely sliced
6 tbsp. chopped parsley
½ fresh lime, cut into slices, for garnish

Cilantro sauce

⅔ cup loosely packed cilantro leaves
4 scallions, coarsely chopped
1 garlic clove, coarsely chopped
½ onion, coarsely chopped
½-inch piece fresh ginger, peeled and coarsely chopped
½ green chili pepper, seeded and coarsely chopped (cautionary note, page 25)
freshly ground black pepper
4 tsp. wine vinegar
½ fresh lime, juice only
2 tbsp. virgin olive oil

First make the cilantro sauce. Put all the ingredients in a blender with 2 tablespoons of water and blend until smooth. Turn the sauce into a small serving bowl, cover it, and set it aside.

Put the rice in a saucepan with the allspice, salt, garlic, and some black pepper, and pour in the stock. Bring the stock to a simmer, cover the pan, and slowly simmer until the rice is cooked and the water is absorbed—about 20 minutes.

Meanwhile, cut the plantains in half lengthwise, without peeling them. With a sharp knife, score the skin through to the flesh in a few places. Put the plantains in a saucepan, cover them with cold water, and add the vinegar. Bring the liquid to a boil and simmer for 20 minutes. When the plantains are cooked, drain and peel them, and cut each half lengthwise into three or four thin slices. Set the plantains aside and keep them warm.

While the rice and plantains are cooking, steam the vegetables. Pour enough water into a saucepan to fill it 1 inch deep. Set a vegetable steamer in the pan and bring the water to a boil. Put the carrot in the steamer and steam it for three minutes, then add the sweet red pepper, celery, and okra. Steam the vegetables until they are cooked but still firm and crisp—five to six minutes more. Set them aside and keep them warm.

Peel the mangoes. Cut off the two cheeks from each mango, slice them thinly, and set them aside. Dice the remaining flesh and discard the pits.

When the rice is cooked, stir in the diced mangoes, scallions, steamed vegetables, and parsley, then turn the mixture into a serving dish. Serve the rice with the plantain slices, mango slices, and a slice of lime, accompanied by the cilantro sauce.

Basmati and Wild Rice Molds with Braised Artichokes

Serves 6
Working time: about 1 hour and 30 minutes
Total time: about 2 hours and 30 minutes
(includes soaking)

Calories **405**
Protein **14g.**
Cholesterol **25mg.**
Total fat **12g.**
Saturated fat **5g.**
Sodium **245mg.**

⅔ cup wild rice
⅔ cup basmati rice or other long-grain rice, rinsed under cold running water until the water runs clear, then soaked in 2½ cups water for 1 hour
½ tsp. salt
2 lemons, grated zest of one, juice of both
6 artichokes
1 tbsp. virgin olive oil
3 tbsp. chopped fresh mint
2 garlic cloves, finely chopped
4 oz. fresh chestnuts, peeled (technique, page 37), or 2 oz. dried chestnuts, soaked for at least 8 hours or overnight in hot water
4 tbsp. unsalted butter
white pepper

Bring 1½ quarts of water to a boil in a saucepan. Stir in the wild rice, lower the heat, and simmer the rice, uncovered, until it is tender but still chewy—about 45 minutes. Meanwhile, drain the basmati rice in a sieve and place it in a large saucepan with the salt. Add 1 quart of water, bring it to a boil, and boil it rapidly, uncovered, until the rice is cooked—about five minutes. Drain the basmati rice and set it aside.

While the wild rice is cooking, prepare the artichokes. Put 3 quarts of water in a large bowl and add a third of the lemon juice. Break or cut the stem off one of the artichokes. Snap off and discard the outer leaves, starting at the base, and continuing until the pale yellow leaves at the core are exposed. Cut the top two-thirds off the artichoke. Trim away any dark green leaf bases that remain on the artichoke bottom. Cut the artichoke bottom in half, and remove the hairy choke and all the pinkish central leaves. Then cut each half into six wedges. Drop the wedges into the acidulated water. Repeat these steps to prepare the remaining artichokes.

Heat the oil in a large skillet over medium-low heat. Add the mint and garlic, and cook for about one minute. Drain the artichokes, add them to the pan, and stir-fry them for one minute. Add the remaining lemon juice and 1 cup of water, cover, and simmer for about 10 minutes. Remove the lid and cook until the artichokes are tender—5 to 10 minutes more.

A few minutes before the artichokes are done, prepare the rice molds. Drain the wild rice in a sieve. Finely chop the chestnuts. Melt the butter in a pan, add the chestnuts, and cook them for two to three minutes. Add the basmati and wild rice to the chestnuts, mix

well, and heat through. Divide the rice mixture among six 1-cup molds, and carefully turn each one out onto a hot individual serving plate.

Arrange the artichokes alongside the rice. Stir the lemon zest and some white pepper into the juices remaining in the pan, and spoon the mixture over the artichokes. Serve immediately.

Gâteau of Crepes with Wild Rice and Mushrooms

Serves 6
Working time: about 1 hour
Total time: about 2 hours

Calories **215**
Protein **8g.**
Cholesterol **40mg.**
Total fat **7g.**
Saturated fat **2g.**
Sodium **185mg.**

1 cup unbleached all-purpose flour
1 tsp. freshly grated nutmeg
1 small egg
1 egg white
1¼ cup skim milk
⅓ cup wild rice
1 oz. dried porcini or other wild mushrooms
1½ tbsp. dry Madeira
1½ tbsp. safflower oil
½ lb. button mushrooms, wiped clean and thinly sliced
½ tsp. salt
freshly ground black pepper
3 tbsp. plain low-fat yogurt

First make the crepe batter. Sift the flour into a bowl and mix in the nutmeg. Make a well in the center, and add the egg, egg white, and a little of the milk. Beat the eggs and milk, gradually working in the dry ingredients; as the batter thickens, add the rest of the milk in several stages to make a smooth batter. Cover the bowl and let the batter stand for one hour.

Bring 1¼ cups of water to a boil in a saucepan. Stir in the wild rice, reduce the heat, and simmer, uncovered, until the rice is tender but still chewy—approximately 45 minutes.

Meanwhile, put the porcini in a small bowl, and add 1 tablespoon of the Madeira and 2½ cups of tepid water to cover them. Set the mushrooms aside to soak for 20 to 30 minutes.

When the batter has rested, heat an 8-inch crepe pan or nonstick skillet over medium heat. Add ¼ teaspoon of the oil and spread it over the entire surface with a paper towel. Continue heating the pan until it is very hot and the oil is almost smoking. Put about 3 tablespoons of the batter into the hot pan, and immediately swirl the pan to coat the bottom with a thin, even layer of batter. Pour any excess batter back into the bowl. Cook the crepe until the bottom is browned—about one minute. Lift the edge with a spatula and turn the crepe over. Cook the crepe on the second side until it, too, is browned—15 to 30 seconds. Slide the crepe onto a plate. Repeat the process with the remaining batter, brushing the pan lightly with more oil if the crepes begin to stick. Stack the cooked crepes on the plate. Cover the crepes with a towel and set them aside. There should be six crepes.

Preheat the oven to 350° F.

When the rice is cooked, drain it in a sieve, discard-

ing the cooking liquid. Drain and rinse the porcini, and strain their soaking liquid through cheesecloth or a coffee filter paper; reserve the liquid. Heat the remaining oil in a saucepan. Add the button mushrooms and sauté them until lightly cooked—three to five minutes. Add the porcini, the reserved soaking liquid, the salt, and the remaining ½ tablespoon of Madeira. Bring the liquid to a boil and boil it for 30 seconds. Lower the heat, stir in the wild rice, and cook over medium heat for about two minutes to heat the rice through. Drain the rice and mushroom mixture in a sieve, reserving the liquid. Return the mixture to the pan, season it with some black pepper, then cover it and keep it warm.

Pour the reserved liquid into a small saucepan and boil over high heat to reduce it to about 3 tablespoons in volume. Take the pan off the heat and stir in the yogurt. Reduce the heat to low, then gently warm the mixture; do not allow it to boil. Cover the yogurt sauce and keep it warm.

Place one of the crepes on a large ovenproof plate. Spoon one-fifth of the rice and mushroom mixture evenly over the crepe. Cover the mixture with another crepe, and continue alternating layers of rice and mushroom mixture with crepes to make a gâteau. Place the crepe gâteau in the oven for a few minutes to warm it through. Serve it at once, cut into wedges, accompanied by the yogurt sauce.

SUGGESTED ACCOMPANIMENTS: *carrot ribbons and peas.*

Wild and Brown Rice Pilaf with Mushroom Ragout

Serves 8
Working time: about 45 minutes
Total time: about 3 hours (includes soaking)

Calories **390**
Protein **14g.**
Cholesterol **5mg.**
Total fat **11g.**
Saturated fat **2g.**
Sodium **265mg.**

1¼ cups flageolets or white beans, picked over
2 bay leaves
⅔ cup wild rice
2 cinnamon sticks
1 tsp. salt
1½ cups brown basmati rice or other brown long-grain rice, rinsed under cold running water until the water runs clear, then soaked in 6 cups of water for 15 minutes
½ tsp. ground mace
2 tsp. light brown sugar
¾ lb. baby corn, fresh or frozen, thickly sliced
4 tbsp. hazelnut, walnut, or safflower oil
½ tsp. freshly grated nutmeg
freshly ground black pepper
Mushroom ragout
1 tbsp. unsalted butter
1 small onion, finely chopped
1 lb. mixed fresh wild mushrooms, such as chanterelles, porcini, or oyster or shiitake mushrooms, wiped clean
2 cups unsalted vegetable stock (recipe, page 9)
2 tbsp. cornstarch
2 tbsp. sour cream
¼ tsp. salt
freshly ground black pepper

Rinse the beans under cold running water, then put them into a large, heavy pan, and pour in enough cold water to cover them by about 3 inches. Discard any beans that float to the surface. Cover the pan, leaving the lid ajar, and slowly bring the liquid to a boil. Boil the beans for two minutes, then turn off the heat and soak the beans, covered, for at least one hour. (Alternatively, soak the beans overnight in cold water.)

Drain the beans, then place them in a saucepan and pour in enough water to cover them by about 3 inches. Add the bay leaves, bring the liquid to a boil, then lower the heat to maintain a strong simmer, and cook the beans, covered, until they are tender—about one hour. If the beans appear to be drying out at any point, add more hot water. Drain the beans, rinse them, and

drain them again. Set the beans aside and keep them warm. Preheat the oven to 325° F.

Place the wild rice with the cinnamon sticks and ½ teaspoon of the salt in a small ovenproof baking dish. Bring 2½ cups of water to a boil and pour it over the rice. Cover the dish with a lid and bake the rice in the oven for one hour. Drain off all but about 1 tablespoon of water. Leave the wild rice, covered, in a warm place for about 15 minutes, in order to allow it to absorb the remaining liquid.

Drain the brown rice, and place it in a large saucepan with the ground mace and the remaining ½ teaspoon of salt. Add 3 quarts of water and bring it to a boil. Reduce the heat to low, cover the pan, and simmer until the rice is tender—approximately 20 minutes. When the rice is cooked, drain it, cover it, set it aside, and keep it warm.

While the brown rice is cooking, prepare the mushroom ragout. Melt the butter in a large saucepan over medium heat, add the onion, and cook it gently until it is soft but not brown—five to six minutes. Add the mushrooms, and cook until they are slightly softened—two to three minutes more. Pour in the vegetable stock and bring it to a boil, then cover the pan and lower the heat. Simmer for 10 minutes, until the mushrooms are soft. Blend the cornstarch with the sour cream, and stir it into the mushrooms along with the salt and some freshly ground black pepper. Continue cooking for three to four minutes more, until the sauce thickens slightly. Transfer the mushroom ragout to a serving bowl and keep it warm.

Meanwhile, pour about 1½ inches of water into a large, nonreactive saucepan. Add the brown sugar and bring the mixture to a boil. Add the corn and bring the water back to a boil, turn down the heat, and simmer, covered, until the corn is just tender—about five minutes (one to two minutes for frozen corn). Drain the corn in a colander.

Place half the oil in a warmed serving bowl. Discard the bay leaves from the beans and the cinnamon sticks from the wild rice. Transfer the beans, rices, and corn to the oiled serving bowl. Pour the remaining oil over the vegetables, add the nutmeg and some black pepper, then toss all the ingredients together. Serve immediately, with the mushroom ragout.

EDITOR'S NOTE: *If wild mushrooms are unavailable, substitute button mushrooms. The pilaf is also delicious served cold as a salad, with a little cider vinegar added.*

Pumpkin and Pecorino Risotto

Serves 4
Working (and total) time: about 1 hour and 15 minutes

Calories **305**
Protein **6g.**
Cholesterol **5mg.**
Total fat **6g.**
Saturated fat **2g.**
Sodium **280mg.**

1 tbsp. virgin olive oil
2 shallots, finely chopped
1¼ cups Italian rice
1 lb. pumpkin, peeled, seeded, and finely grated
¼ tsp. powdered saffron
⅓ cup dry white wine
1 qt. unsalted vegetable stock (recipe, page 9)
1 tbsp. finely chopped fresh oregano, or 1 tsp. dried oregano
½ tsp. salt
freshly ground black pepper
¼ cup finely grated pecorino or romano cheese
2 tbsp. finely chopped parsley for garnish (optional)

Heat the oil in a large flameproof casserole. Add the shallots, and cook over medium heat, stirring from time to time, until they are soft but not brown—about five minutes. Reduce the heat to low, add the rice, and stir to ensure that each grain is coated with a little oil.

Add the pumpkin and stir well over medium heat until heated through—about three minutes. Stir the saffron into the white wine. Increase the heat and pour the wine into the casserole. Stir constantly until all the liquid has been absorbed—about three minutes. Meanwhile, heat the stock in a separate pan.

Reduce the heat under the rice to low, and pour a ladleful—about 1 cup—of hot stock into the casserole. Stir well, then cover the casserole, leaving the lid ajar. Simmer until the stock has been absorbed—about five minutes. Stir in another ladleful of stock and cover as before. This time, however, stir the contents of the casserole once or twice while the stock is being absorbed, replacing the lid after stirring. Mix in the oregano, then continue to add stock by the ladleful, stirring frequently, until the rice is soft but still a little resilient to the bite, and the pumpkin has all but melted into a sauce—approximately 30 minutes. Once this stage has been reached, stir in the remaining stock, and replace the lid on the casserole. Turn off the heat and let the risotto stand for five minutes, during which time the remaining stock will be absorbed. Meanwhile, warm the serving bowls.

Season the risotto with the salt, some freshly ground black pepper, and the pecorino or romano cheese, stirring well until the cheese melts. If you like, sprinkle ½ tablespoon of chopped parsley over each portion. Serve the risotto immediately.

Pea and Mushroom Risotto

Serves 6
Working time: about 45 minutes
Total time: about 1 hour and 15 minutes

Calories **410**
Protein **12g.**
Cholesterol **20mg.**
Total fat **10g.**
Saturated fat **5g.**
Sodium **430mg.**

¾ lb. peas, shelled, or ¼ lb. frozen peas, thawed
2 tbsp. unsalted butter
4 to 6 shallots, chopped
2½ cups brown rice
¾ cup dry white wine or dry vermouth
2 cups tomato juice
2 cups unsalted vegetable stock (recipe, page 9)
2 medium tomatoes, peeled, seeded (technique, page 14), and chopped
½ tsp. salt
½ lb. mushrooms, wiped clean and coarsely grated
½ cup freshly grated Parmesan cheese
freshly ground black pepper
chopped parsley for garnish

If you are using fresh peas, parboil them until they are barely tender—three to four minutes. Drain them, then refresh them under cold running water. Drain the peas again and set them aside. (Frozen peas do not need parboiling.)

In a large, heavy-bottomed saucepan, melt the butter and sauté the shallots over medium heat until transparent, stirring occasionally—three to five minutes. Stir the rice into the shallots and cook for two to three minutes, stirring constantly, to ensure that the grains are coated with the butter.

Pour the wine into the rice and simmer, stirring frequently, until the wine has been absorbed by the rice. Add the tomato juice and 1 cup of the stock, bring the liquid to a boil, then reduce the heat to a simmer. Cover the saucepan and cook the rice, stirring occasionally, for about 20 minutes. Stir the tomatoes and salt into the rice, cover the pan, and simmer for 10 minutes more, adding more stock, a ladleful at a time, if the rice dries out.

Add the mushrooms, peas, and any remaining stock, increase the heat to high, and cook rapidly, stirring constantly, until most of the liquid has been absorbed but the rice is still moist. Stir the Parmesan cheese into the risotto and season generously with some black pepper. Turn the risotto into a warmed serving dish and sprinkle it with chopped parsley.

SUGGESTED ACCOMPANIMENT: *salad of raw spinach leaves with a vinaigrette.*

EDITOR'S NOTE: *If preferred, 1 quart of vegetable stock may be used instead of the combination of tomato juice and stock.*

Eight Treasures in Lotus Leaves

IN CHINESE TRADITION, CERTAIN NUMBERS, SUCH AS THREE, FIVE, AND EIGHT, ARE CONSIDERED TO BRING LUCK; HENCE DISHES CONTAINING THREE MAIN INGREDIENTS ARE USUALLY KNOWN AS "THREE DELICACIES," WHILE THOSE WITH EIGHT OR MORE ARE KNOWN AS "EIGHT TREASURES."

Serves 4
Working time: about 1 hour and 30 minutes
Total time: about 12 hours (includes soaking)

Calories **553**
Protein **19g.**
Cholesterol **0mg.**
Total fat **14g.**
Saturated fat **3g.**
Sodium **250mg.**

4 dried lotus leaves, soaked in hot water for 30 minutes, rinsed in cold water, and dried carefully on a dishtowel
1 lb. fresh lotus roots, or 3 oz. dried lotus roots, dried roots soaked in tepid water for 8 to 10 hours
2 cups unsalted vegetable stock (recipe, page 9) or water
2 tbsp. rice wine or medium-dry sherry
½ tsp. sugar
⅛ tsp. salt
½-inch piece fresh ginger, sliced
1 garlic clove
3 scallions, each cut into 3 pieces
1½ oz. canned skinned whole lotus nuts, drained
1 tsp. low-sodium soy sauce
4 or 5 sprigs cilantro, leaves only, for garnish
Rice stuffing
24 fresh chestnuts, peeled (technique, page 37), or 24 dried chestnuts, soaked for at least 8 hours or overnight in hot water, drained
⅓ cup mung beans, soaked in water for 1 to 2 hours
⅓ cup adzuki beans, soaked in water for 1 to 2 hours

12 dried shiitake mushrooms, soaked in hot water for 20 minutes
1¼ cups long-grain rice
1 tsp. safflower oil
1 or 2 garlic cloves, finely chopped
½ tbsp. grated fresh ginger
6 oz. bamboo shoots, finely diced
2 carrots, diced
3 scallions, white and green parts separated and diced
¾ cup roasted unsalted peanuts
¼ tsp. sugar
¼ tsp. salt
1 tsp. low-sodium soy sauce

First prepare the rice stuffing. Simmer the chestnuts in water to cover until they are just tender—20 to 25 minutes. Bring the water to a boil and cook until nearly all the liquid has evaporated, stirring the chestnuts several times.

Drain the mung and adzuki beans, rinse them, and drain them again. Discard the soaking water, then simmer the two types of beans separately in fresh water to cover until tender—about 10 minutes for the mung beans, and up to 25 minutes for the adzuki beans—skimming several times during cooking. Drain and rinse the two types of beans, reserving the liquid from the adzuki beans.

Drain the mushrooms, and strain and reserve their soaking liquid. Dice the mushrooms, discarding the stalks, and set them aside.

Rinse the rice several times in cold water. Mix the adzuki-bean liquid with the mushroom-soaking liquid and add enough water to make 2 cups. Put this mixture in a large saucepan with the rice, and bring it to a boil; then cook the rice, uncovered, until most of the liquid has evaporated—10 to 15 minutes. Cover the pan tightly, reduce the heat to the lowest setting possible, and cook very gently for 10 minutes more. Turn off the heat and let the rice steam, covered, for about 10 minutes. Remove the lid, fluff up the rice with a pair of chopsticks, and let it cool. (The rice will be tinted pale pink from the adzuki-bean liquid.)

Heat a wok or a large, heavy skillet until very hot. Add the oil, and drop in the garlic and ginger to sizzle and become aromatic; then add the mushrooms, bamboo shoots, carrots, chestnuts, and white parts of the scallions at 10- to 12-second intervals, tossing and stirring all the time with a wok scoop or spatula. Turn the contents of the pan into a large bowl, add the rice, scallion greens, peanuts, sugar, salt, and soy sauce, and mix the ingredients well.

Make up four lotus leaf parcels, each filled with a quarter of the rice stuffing (steps 1 to 3, opposite). Steam the parcels in a bamboo or metal steamer over boiling water for 20 to 25 minutes.

Meanwhile, scrub the fresh lotus roots well and cut them diagonally into ¼-inch slices. (If you are using reconstituted dried lotus roots, rinse them well under running water before slicing them.)

Bring the stock or water to a boil, add the rice wine

or sherry, sugar, salt, ginger, garlic, and scallions, and return to a boil. Add the lotus nuts and roots, and simmer for 35 minutes. Remove the nuts, ginger, garlic, and scallions with a slotted spoon; reserve the nuts and keep them warm; discard the ginger, garlic, and scallions. (If you are using dried roots, simmer them for another 15 minutes.) Add the soy sauce to the cooking liquid, bring it to a boil, and reduce it until the sauce becomes syrupy—10 to 12 minutes. Return the nuts to the sauce to heat through.

Place a steamed lotus parcel on each of four individual plates and cut a square window in the parcel with scissors (step 4, below). Serve the rice-stuffed parcels with the braised lotus roots and nuts, garnished with cilantro leaves.

EDITOR'S NOTE: *All the unusual ingredients called for in this recipe can be obtained in Asian markets. Since most of the ingredients are dried, any surplus can be stored almost indefinitely and used on another occasion.*

Shaping a Lotus-Leaf Parcel

1 *PREPARING A LOTUS LEAF. Lay a lotus leaf flat on a clean work surface. Using a pair of kitchen scissors, snip off the center core where the stalk meets the leaf. Cut the lotus leaf in half to make two semicircles.*

2 *BEGINNING THE PARCEL. Lay the lotus-leaf halves on the work surface, vein side down, with their cut edges overlapping by about 2 inches. Place the stuffing in the center of the circle and shape the stuffing into a square mound with a knife blade. Fold over two opposite edges of the leaf circle by approximately 2 inches (below, left), then fold these edges firmly over the stuffing (below, right) to make a long package.*

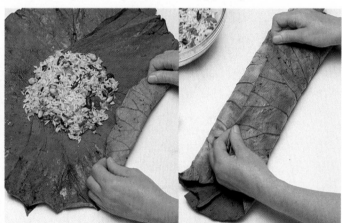

3 *COMPLETING THE PARCEL. Fold in the sides of one of the flaps that remain, so that the flap tapers. Make a fold ¾ inch from the end of the flap, then fold again so that the flap covers the stuffed part of the leaf. Repeat with the other flap, then secure the parcel with a wooden pick. Complete the remaining three lotus-leaf parcels in the same way.*

4 *OPENING THE COOKED PARCEL. When the parcels have been steamed (recipe, opposite), snip a square window in the top of each parcel, using kitchen scissors. The lids on the lotus-leaf parcels may be replaced for serving, if desired.*

Rice Cakes with Onion Relish

Serves 4
Working time: about 35 minutes
Total time: about 1 hour and 45 minutes
(includes soaking)

Calories **255**
Protein **8g.**
Cholesterol **15mg.**
Total fat **6g.**
Saturated fat **3g.**
Sodium **300mg.**

¾ cup basmati rice or other long-grain rice, rinsed under cold running water until the water runs clear, then soaked in 1 qt. water for 1 hour
½ tsp. safflower oil
1 onion, finely chopped
¼ lb. carrots (2 small), grated
2 hot green chili peppers, finely chopped (cautionary note, page 25)
2 garlic cloves, crushed
½ tsp. cardamom seeds, crushed
1 tbsp. chopped cilantro
½ tsp. ground cumin
¼ tsp. ground turmeric
¼ cup grated Cheddar cheese
¼ tsp. salt
Onion relish
1 onion, cut into paper-thin rings
½ sweet red pepper, seeded, deribbed, and chopped
1 lime, finely grated zest and juice
¼ tsp. salt
½ tsp. paprika
½ tsp. light brown sugar

First make the onion relish. Place the onion in a bowl with the sweet red pepper, and add the lime zest, lime juice, salt, paprika, and sugar. Toss the ingredients together until well combined, then transfer them to a serving bowl, and leave them for the flavors to develop while you prepare the rice cakes.

Drain the rice and put it in a large saucepan. Add 1½ quarts of water and bring it to a boil. Boil rapidly, uncovered, until the rice is thoroughly tender—about 10 minutes. The rice needs to be well cooked so that the rice cakes will hold together when they are grilled. Drain the rice and set it aside.

Heat the oil in a skillet over medium heat and sauté the onion until it is softened and begins to brown—three to four minutes. Stir in the carrots, chilies, garlic, cardamom, cilantro, cumin, and turmeric, and cook them, stirring continuously, until the carrots are soft—about two minutes. Remove the pan from the heat, stir in the rice, cheese, and salt, and mash with a potato masher until the rice is broken up and sticky.

Preheat the broiler to medium. With lightly floured hands, shape the mixture into 20 small balls. Thread five balls onto each of four skewers. Place the skewers on a foil-covered rack and broil the cakes, turning once, until they are a pale golden color—about 15 minutes. Serve hot, accompanied by the onion relish.

SUGGESTED ACCOMPANIMENTS: *Indian bread; tomato salad.*

EDITOR'S NOTE: *If you use wooden or bamboo skewers, soak them in water for about 10 minutes before threading them with the rice balls in order to prevent them from burning under the broiler.*

Buckwheat and Lentil Pilaf

Serves 8
Working time: about 1 hour
Total time: about 1 hour and 15 minutes

Calories **355**
Protein **19g.**
Cholesterol **0mg.**
Total fat **7g.**
Saturated fat **1g.**
Sodium **175mg.**

3 lb. peas, shelled, or 1 lb. frozen peas, thawed
1¾ cups lentils, picked over and rinsed
1¼ cups buckwheat groats (kasha)
1 tsp. salt
3 tbsp. virgin olive oil
2 small eggplants, cut into ½-inch cubes
2 sweet red peppers, seeded, deribbed, and sliced
2 sweet green peppers, seeded, deribbed, and sliced
8 garlic cloves, finely chopped
2 large onions, sliced
3 medium tomatoes, peeled, seeded (technique, page 14), and coarsely chopped
4 tbsp. finely cut fresh chives
2 tbsp. chopped fresh mint, or 1 tsp. dried mint
4 tbsp. chopped parsley
4 tbsp. capers (optional)
freshly ground black pepper

If you are using fresh peas, parboil them until they are barely tender—three to four minutes. Drain them, then refresh them under cold running water. Drain the peas again and set them aside. (Frozen peas do not need parboiling.)

Rinse the lentils and put them in a large, heavy-bottomed saucepan with 2½ quarts of water. Bring the water to a boil, then lower the heat and simmer the lentils until they are tender—approximately 40 minutes. When the lentils have finished cooking, drain them in a sieve.

While the lentils are cooking, add the buckwheat and ½ teaspoon of the salt to a saucepan containing 2½ cups of boiling water. Cook the buckwheat, stirring frequently, until the groats have tripled in size but still have a bite to them—about five minutes. Drain the groats in a sieve, rinse them well, and drain them again. Transfer them to a large bowl.

Heat the olive oil over medium heat in a large, heavy skillet. Add the eggplants, peppers, garlic, and onions, and sauté them, stirring constantly, until they become soft—10 to 15 minutes. Add the lentils, buckwheat, tomatoes, and peas to the eggplant mixture. Gently heat all the ingredients, stirring continuously.

Remove the pan from the heat. Add the chives, mint, and parsley, and if using them, the capers. Season with the remaining ½ teaspoon of salt and some black pepper. Serve immediately.

Semolina Gnocchi with Julienned Vegetables

Serves 6
Working time: about 1 hour
Total time: about 3 hours (includes chilling)

Calories **270**
Protein **13g.**
Cholesterol **5mg.**
Total fat **8g.**
Saturated fat **3g.**
Sodium **295mg.**

½ lb. celeriac, peeled and finely julienned, placed in acidulated water
¾ lb. carrots (4 medium), peeled and finely julienned
18 scallions, trimmed, quartered lengthwise, and cut into 2-inch pieces
3 garlic cloves, crushed
1¼ cups unsalted vegetable stock (recipe, page 9)
½ lemon, grated zest and juice
1½ tsp. cornstarch
1 oz. pine nuts (about ¼ cup)
½ tsp. sugar
½ tsp. salt
freshly ground black pepper
Semolina gnocchi
2½ cups skim milk
1¾ cup semolina
1 tbsp. unsalted butter
½ tsp. salt
½ tsp. freshly grated nutmeg
4 tbsp. freshly grated Parmesan cheese

First make the gnocchi. Pour the skim milk into a heavy-bottomed saucepan and bring it to a boil. Add the semolina gradually, stirring constantly, then cook over medium heat until the mixture is very thick—four to five minutes. Beat in half the butter, the salt, nutmeg, and 3 tablespoons of the cheese. Turn the mixture out onto a baking tray lined with plastic wrap, and spread it into a 7-by-7-by-1½-inch rectangle, using a dampened metal spreader or spatula. Allow the semolina mixture to cool for 20 minutes, then cover the pan loosely with plastic wrap and place the mixture in the refrigerator until it is well chilled—at least two hours, or overnight.

Preheat the oven to 350° F. Using a sharp, thin-bladed knife, cut the chilled mixture into thirty-six 1-inch squares. Transfer the gnocchi to a lightly greased baking sheet. Gently melt the remaining butter in a small saucepan and brush it over the gnocchi. Sprinkle them with the remaining Parmesan cheese. Bake the gnocchi until they are golden and crisp on top—20 to 25 minutes.

About 15 minutes before the gnocchi are cooked, put the celeriac, carrots, scallions, and garlic into a nonreactive saucepan, and pour in the vegetable stock. Bring the stock to a boil; lower the heat and simmer until the vegetables are soft—three to four minutes. Stir in the lemon zest and juice. Blend the cornstarch with 1 tablespoon of water and stir it into the stock. Add the pine nuts, sugar, salt, and some black pepper. Bring the mixture back to a boil, and cook over high heat, stirring, until the stock has formed a thick sauce—about two minutes. Spoon the vegetables onto warmed individual plates and top them with the gnocchi.

SUGGESTED ACCOMPANIMENT: *steamed broccoli.*

Chili Beans with Cornbread Topping

Serves 4
Working time: about 30 minutes
Total time: about 3 hours (includes soaking)

Calories **340**
Protein **15g.**
Cholesterol **60mg.**
Total fat **10g.**
Saturated fat **1g.**
Sodium **405mg.**

½ cup red kidney beans, picked over
1 tbsp. safflower oil
1 onion, chopped
½ tsp. chili powder
2 garlic cloves, chopped
4 ripe medium tomatoes, peeled, seeded (technique, page 14), and chopped, or 14 oz. canned tomatoes, chopped
1 sweet green pepper, seeded, deribbed, and coarsely chopped
1 sweet red pepper, seeded, deribbed, and coarsely chopped
2 celery stalks, trimmed and sliced
1 tbsp. tomato paste
6 tbsp. pitted green olives, rinsed, quartered or halved

Cornbread topping

1 cup cornmeal
¼ cup unbleached all-purpose flour
¼ tsp. salt
¼ tsp. freshly ground black pepper
2 tsp. baking powder
1 egg, beaten
½ cup skim milk
2 tbsp. chopped parsley
1 oz. Edam cheese, finely grated (about 2 tbsp.)

Rinse the kidney beans under cold running water, then put them into a large saucepan with enough cold water to cover them by about 3 inches. Discard any beans that float to the surface. Cover the saucepan, leaving the lid ajar, and slowly bring the liquid to a boil. Boil the beans for two minutes, then turn off the heat and soak the beans, covered, for at least one hour. (Alternatively, soak the beans overnight in cold water.)

If the beans have absorbed all of their cooking liquid, pour in enough water to cover them again by about 3 inches. Bring the liquid to a boil, then lower the heat to maintain a strong simmer, and cook the beans until they are tender—about 1 hour. Check the water level from time to time and add more hot water if necessary. Drain and rinse the beans when they are cooked.

Preheat the oven to 400° F.

Heat the oil in a heavy-bottomed saucepan and sauté the onion over medium heat until soft—about five minutes. Add the chili powder and garlic, and cook for one minute more. Stir in the tomatoes, peppers, celery, and tomato paste, cover the pan, and cook over medium-low heat for 10 minutes. Add the olives and cooked beans, and cook for five minutes more, stirring occasionally. Divide the bean mixture among four shallow, 1½-cup ovenproof dishes and set them aside.

To make the topping, mix the cornmeal, flour, salt, some black pepper, and baking powder in a large bowl, and make a well in the center. In a separate bowl, using a wooden spoon, beat together the egg, milk, and parsley. Beat this into the dry ingredients until a thick, smooth mixture is formed. Spoon the cornmeal mixture over the chili beans, using a fork to spread it to the edges of the dishes. Sprinkle with the grated cheese.

Place the dishes in the oven and bake until the topping is firm—15 to 20 minutes. Serve hot.

SUGGESTED ACCOMPANIMENT: *tossed salad.*

Polenta Pizza

Serves 4
Working time: about 40 minutes
Total time: about 1 hour

Calories **470**
Protein **19g.**
Cholesterol **25mg.**
Total fat **12g.**
Saturated fat **5g.**
Sodium **390mg.**

½ tsp. salt
3 cups cornmeal
1 tbsp. virgin olive oil
1 red onion, finely sliced
1 large garlic clove, chopped
2 carrots, chopped
4 celery stalks, finely sliced
3 medium tomatoes, peeled, seeded (technique, page 14), and chopped
6 tbsp. tomato paste, dissolved in ¾ cup hot water
1 tbsp. chopped fresh basil, or 1 tsp. dried basil
½ tbsp. chopped fresh oregano, or ½ tsp. dried oregano
cayenne pepper
freshly ground black pepper
¼ lb. low-fat mozzarella cheese, very thinly sliced
1 tbsp. freshly grated Parmesan cheese
½ tbsp. finely chopped parsley for garnish

Preheat the oven to 350° F. Thoroughly grease a 13-by-9-by-1-inch baking pan.

Put 9 cups of water into a large saucepan with the salt and bring it to a boil. Sprinkle in the cornmeal, stirring continuously with a wooden spoon. Lower the heat to medium, and cook the polenta, stirring constantly, until all the liquid has been absorbed and the polenta is quite stiff—10 to 15 minutes. Spoon the polenta into the prepared baking pan and spread it out to a uniform thickness. Cover the pan with foil and bake the polenta in the oven for 20 minutes.

Meanwhile, make the sauce. Heat the oil in a heavy-bottomed saucepan, add the onion, and sauté it over medium heat until it is soft and transparent—about 10 minutes. Add the garlic, carrots, celery, and tomatoes. Stir well for a few minutes, then mix the tomato paste solution into the sauce. Finally, add the basil, oregano, and some cayenne and black pepper. Simmer the sauce gently, covered, for 10 to 15 minutes.

When the polenta is ready, spread the sauce over it. Cover the sauce with the mozzarella slices, then sprinkle with the Parmesan cheese. Return the polenta to the oven until the cheese has melted—about 10 minutes. Serve the polenta pizza immediately, garnished with the chopped parsley.

SUGGESTED ACCOMPANIMENT: *steamed purple sprouting broccoli or green broccoli, tossed with lemon juice and freshly ground black pepper.*

Polenta Ring with Pine Nuts and Mozzarella

Serves 6
Working time: about 45 minutes
Total time: about 1 hour and 45 minutes
(includes cooling)

Calories **300**
Protein **13g.**
Cholesterol **20mg.**
Total fat **14g.**
Saturated fat **4g.**
Sodium **265mg.**

5 plum or small tomatoes, peeled (step 1, page 14)
2 tbsp. virgin olive oil
1 tsp. paprika
2 garlic cloves, one crushed, the other chopped
½ tsp. salt
1¼ cup cornmeal
¼ lb. low-fat mozzarella cheese, thinly sliced
1 onion, thinly sliced
1 sweet red pepper, seeded, deribbed, and cut into 1-inch strips
1 sweet green pepper, seeded, deribbed, and cut into 1-inch strips
1 tsp. ground cumin
½ cup pine nuts

Thinly slice three of the tomatoes crosswise and the remaining two tomatoes lengthwise; keep them separate. Grease an 8-inch ring mold with ½ tablespoon of the virgin olive oil.

Bring 3¾ cups of water to a boil in a large saucepan.

Add the paprika, crushed garlic, and salt, then stir in the cornmeal. Lower the heat to medium, and continue to cook, stirring, until the cornmeal has formed a thick porridge—10 to 15 minutes. Remove the pan from the heat and immediately pour half the polenta into the prepared ring mold. Press it down firmly using the back of a spoon. Quickly place the crosswise-sliced tomatoes and the mozzarella on top, and cover them with the remaining polenta. Let the polenta cool completely—at least one hour.

Preheat the oven to 350° F. When the polenta has cooled, carefully loosen all around the edges of the mold, using a small metal knife. Turn out the polenta ring onto a large, flat, heatproof plate, and bake it in the oven until the mozzarella has melted—approximately 15 minutes.

While the polenta is baking, heat the remaining oil in a skillet over low heat. Put the onion and chopped garlic in the pan, and cook gently to soften them—about three minutes. Add the peppers, cover the pan, and cook over very low heat for 10 minutes, then add the remaining tomato slices, the cumin, and half of the pine nuts. Cover the pan again and cook for two minutes more over very low heat.

Spoon some of the vegetables into the center of the polenta ring and the remainder around the edge. Sprinkle the remaining pine nuts over the vegetables and serve the polenta ring hot.

Provençal Casserole

Serves 6
Working time: about 30 minutes
Total time: about 3 hours (includes soaking)

Calories **180**
Protein **11g.**
Cholesterol **0mg.**
Total fat **3g.**
Saturated fat **1g.**
Sodium **90mg.**

1½ cups flageolets or white beans, picked over
1 medium eggplant, cut into large dice
½ tsp. salt
1 tbsp. virgin olive oil
1 large onion, sliced
1 garlic clove, crushed
1 sweet red pepper, seeded, deribbed, and sliced
1 lb. zucchini, thickly sliced
3 medium tomatoes, peeled, seeded (technique, page 14), and coarsely chopped, or 10 oz. canned tomatoes (about 1½ cups), drained and coarsely chopped
¼ lb. mushrooms, wiped clean, stems trimmed
⅔ cup unsalted vegetable stock (recipe, page 9)
2 tsp. chopped fresh oregano, or ½ tsp. dried oregano
freshly ground black pepper

Rinse the beans under cold running water, then put them into a large saucepan and pour in enough cold water to cover them by about 3 inches. Discard any beans that float to the surface. Bring the water to a boil

and cook the beans for two minutes. Turn off the heat, partially cover the pan, and then soak the beans for at least one hour. (Alternatively, soak the beans overnight in cold water.)

Drain the beans, place them in a saucepan, and pour in enough water to cover them by about 3 inches. Bring the liquid to a boil, then lower the heat to maintain a strong simmer, and cook the beans, covered, until they are tender—about one hour. If the beans appear to be drying out at any point, add more hot water. Drain and rinse the beans in a colander.

In a bowl, toss the eggplant with ¼ teaspoon of the salt. Place the eggplant in a colander. Weight it down with a plate and let it drain for 30 minutes. Rinse the eggplant under cold running water and drain it well.

Heat the oil in a large flameproof casserole or saucepan, and cook the onion and garlic over low heat for a few minutes, until softened but not browned. Add the pepper, zucchini, eggplant, and tomatoes, and cook over medium-low heat for one to two minutes, stirring frequently. Turn the heat to low, and add the mushrooms, beans, stock, oregano, pepper, and the remaining salt. Mix well, cover, and simmer over low heat, stirring occasionally, until the vegetables are tender—about 25 minutes. Serve hot.

SUGGESTED ACCOMPANIMENT: *garlic rolls.*

Tandoori Patties

Serves 4
Working time: about 45 minutes
Total time: about 2 hours and 45 minutes
(includes soaking)

Calories **305**
Protein **14g.**
Cholesterol **0mg.**
Total fat **6g.**
Saturated fat **1g.**
Sodium **290mg.**

1¼ cups pinto beans, picked over
1 tbsp. safflower oil
1 onion, chopped
2 garlic cloves, chopped
3 tsp. tandoori spice
1 tsp. ground cumin
¼ cup fresh whole-wheat breadcrumbs
2 tbsp. chopped cilantro
2 tbsp. tomato paste
¼ lb. parsnips or carrots, finely grated
½ tsp. salt
freshly ground black pepper
3 tbsp. whole-wheat flour
1 tsp. paprika
Cilantro-yogurt sauce
⅔ cup plain low-fat yogurt
½ tsp. ground coriander
1 tsp. tomato paste
1 garlic clove, crushed
2 tsp. chopped cilantro

Rinse the beans under cold running water, put them into a large, heavy pan, and pour in enough cold water to cover them by about 3 inches. Discard any beans that float to the surface. Cover the pan, leaving the lid ajar, and slowly bring the liquid to a boil. Boil the beans for two minutes, then turn off the heat and soak the beans, covered, for at least one hour. (Alternatively, soak the beans overnight in cold water.)

Drain the beans, place them in a saucepan, and pour in enough water to cover them by about 3 inches. Bring the liquid to a boil, then lower the heat to maintain a strong simmer, and cook the beans until they are tender—about one hour. Check the water level in the pan from time to time, and add more hot water if necessary. Drain the cooked beans in a colander, rinse them under cold running water, and set them aside.

Heat ½ tablespoon of the oil in a heavy skillet and sauté the onion over medium heat until soft—about three minutes. Add the garlic, 2 teaspoons of the tandoori spice, and the ground cumin, and cook for one minute more.

Put the onion mixture and the beans into a food processor with the breadcrumbs, cilantro, tomato paste, parsnips or carrots, salt, and some black pepper. Blend these until smooth, scraping down the sides of the processor bowl as necessary.

Preheat the broiler. With dampened hands, shape the blended mixture into eight balls, then flatten the balls into patties. Mix the flour with the remaining tandoori spice and the paprika. Roll the patties in the spiced flour to coat them. Brush the tandoori patties with the remaining safflower oil and broil them until

they are crisp—three to four minutes on each side.

Meanwhile, mix all the sauce ingredients together. Serve the patties hot, with the cilantro-yogurt sauce.

SUGGESTED ACCOMPANIMENTS: *green salad; hot potato salad.*

EDITOR'S NOTE: *Tandoori spice, a curry powder containing coriander, chili, ginger, turmeric, fenugreek, garlic, and other spices, is used in Indian cuisine to flavor food baked in a tandoor, a clay oven.*

Gingered Black Beans with Saffron Rice

Serves 6
Working time: about 35 minutes
Total time: about 2 hours and 45 minutes
(includes soaking)

Calories **390**
Protein **12g.**
Cholesterol **0mg.**
Total fat **14g.**
Saturated fat **2g.**
Sodium **150mg.**

¾ cup black kidney beans or turtle beans, picked over
2 tbsp. virgin olive oil
3-inch piece fresh ginger, peeled, 2 inches thinly sliced, the remainder grated
1 tbsp. chopped fresh oregano, or 1 tsp. dried oregano
1 tsp. chopped fresh sage, or ¼ tsp. dried sage
1 tsp. saffron threads
½ tsp. salt
1¼ cups long-grain white rice
3 oz. shelled walnuts (about ¾ cup), coarsely chopped
3 garlic cloves, crushed
2 oz. dried cloud-ear mushrooms, soaked in hot water for 20 minutes and drained
¼ lb. button mushrooms, wiped and sliced
2 limes, grated zest and juice
freshly ground black pepper
¼ tsp. paprika for garnish

Rinse the beans under cold running water, then put them into a large, heavy pan and pour in enough cold water to cover them by about 3 inches. Discard any beans that float to the surface. Cover the pan, leaving the lid ajar, and slowly bring the liquid to a boil. Boil the beans for two minutes, then turn off the heat and soak the beans, covered, for at least one hour. (Alternatively, soak the beans overnight in cold water.)

In a large clean saucepan, heat 1 tablespoon of the oil over medium heat; add the sliced ginger, oregano, and sage, and sauté them for one minute. Drain the beans, then add them to the pan. Pour in enough cold water to cover the beans by about 3 inches. Bring the water to a boil, then lower the heat to maintain a strong simmer, and cook the beans until they are tender—at least one hour. Drain the beans, return them to the pan, with all the flavorings, and keep them warm while you prepare the rice.

Bring 2½ cups of water to a boil in a saucepan. Add the saffron, salt, and rice, and stir once. Turn the heat to low, cover the pan, and simmer until the rice is just cooked and the water is absorbed—about 15 minutes. Remove the pan from the heat and stir in the chopped walnuts. Cover the pan again and let it stand for a few minutes while the walnuts warm through.

While the rice is cooking, heat the remaining tablespoon of oil in a wok or large skillet over medium heat, then add the garlic, cloud-ear mushrooms, button mushrooms, and the grated ginger. Increase the heat to high and stir-fry the ingredients until they are soft—five to six minutes. Add them to the beans, together with the lime zest and juice, and some black pepper.

Pile the bean mixture in the center of a large platter and arrange the rice around it. Sprinkle the rice with the paprika and serve at once.

SUGGESTED ACCOMPANIMENT: *watercress, curly endive, and orange salad.*

Tuscan-Style Beans

THIS ADAPTATION OF A TRADITIONAL TUSCAN RECIPE REPLACES
THE USUAL SAUSAGES WITH CEPS
AND USES LESS OIL AND MORE TOMATOES.

Serves 4
Working time: about 45 minutes
Total time: about 3 hours (includes soaking)

Calories **330**
Protein **22g.**
Cholesterol **0mg.**
Total fat **6g.**
Saturated fat **trace**
Sodium **245mg.**

1¾ cups borlotti beans or white beans, picked over
2 bay leaves
1 tbsp. virgin olive oil
2 garlic cloves, crushed
3 sprigs fresh rosemary
6 leaves fresh sage, finely shredded
½ lb. fresh ceps, or ¾ oz. dried ceps, soaked in hot water for 20 minutes, drained, and well rinsed
2½ lb. fresh tomatoes, peeled, seeded (technique, page 14), and chopped
1 tbsp. red wine vinegar
1 tbsp. molasses
½ tsp. salt
freshly ground black pepper
12 basil leaves, torn in pieces

Rinse the beans under cold running water, then put them into a large, heavy pan and pour in enough cold water to cover them by about 3 inches. Discard any beans that float to the surface. Cover the pan, leaving the lid ajar, and slowly bring the liquid to a boil. Boil the beans for two minutes, then turn off the heat and soak the beans, covered, for at least one hour. (Alternatively, soak the beans overnight in cold water.)

Drain the beans, place them in a saucepan, and pour in enough water to cover them by about 3 inches. Add the bay leaves, bring the liquid to a boil, then lower the heat to maintain a strong simmer, and cook the beans until they are tender—about one hour. Check the water level in the pan from time to time, and add more hot water if necessary. Drain the beans in a colander and discard the bay leaves. Rinse the beans, drain again, and set them aside.

Heat the oil in a flameproof casserole; sauté the garlic in the oil over medium-low heat for one to two minutes. Add the rosemary, lower the heat to the lowest possible setting, cover the casserole with a lid, and leave it for 10 minutes to allow the rosemary to infuse the oil. Discard the rosemary, and add the cooked beans to the casserole along with the sage, stirring well to coat the beans evenly with oil. Increase the heat to medium-low, add the mushrooms, and cook, stirring constantly, until the contents of the casserole are heated through—about two minutes. Cover the casserole closely, and remove it from the heat while you prepare the tomato sauce.

In a large, shallow saucepan, combine the tomatoes with the vinegar, molasses, salt and, some black pepper. Cook briefly over high heat to allow excess moisture to evaporate as the tomatoes break down into a sauce. Pour the sauce over the beans and mushrooms, add the torn basil leaves, and return the casserole to medium-high heat. Simmer briefly until the beans are just heated through; do not overcook.

SUGGESTED ACCOMPANIMENT: *crusty Italian bread.*

EDITOR'S NOTE: *If you use dried ceps, the soaking liquid can be added to the water in which the beans are cooked to enhance their flavor. Strain the mushroom-soaking liquid through a double layer of cheesecloth or a coffee-filter paper before adding it to the beans. Borlotti beans, an Italian variety of bean, are a speckled, pale tan color. White beans can be substituted for them.*

Lima Beans Baked with an Herbed Crust

Serves 6
Working time: about 30 minutes
Total time: about 3 hours (includes soaking)

Calories **310**	
Protein **19g.**	2½ cups dried lima beans, picked over
Cholesterol **0mg.**	2 onions, one finely chopped
Total fat **5g.**	1 large carrot, trimmed
Saturated fat **1g.**	1 small leek, trimmed, washed thoroughly to remove all grit
Sodium **280mg.**	2 sprigs fresh thyme, one chopped
	2 sprigs fresh rosemary, one chopped

2 bay leaves
1½ tbsp. virgin olive oil
8 medium tomatoes, peeled, seeded (technique, page 14), and coarsely chopped
2 garlic cloves, one crushed, the other chopped
1 tsp. salt
freshly ground black pepper
¾ cup fresh whole-wheat breadcrumbs
1 cup loosely packed parsley leaves, chopped
1 lemon, grated zest only

Rinse the beans under cold running water, then put them into a large saucepan with enough cold water to cover them by about 3 inches. Discard any beans that float to the surface. Cover the saucepan, leaving the lid ajar, and slowly bring the liquid to a boil. Boil the beans for two minutes, then turn off the heat and soak the beans, covered, for at least one hour. (Alternatively, soak the beans overnight in cold water.)

Drain the beans and put them in a saucepan with the whole onion, the carrot, the leek, the whole sprigs of thyme and rosemary, and one of the bay leaves. Pour in enough cold water to cover the ingredients by about 3 inches. Bring the liquid to a boil; then lower the heat, cover the pan, and simmer until the beans are tender—about one hour. Check the water level in the pan from time to time, and add more hot water if necessary. Drain the beans in a colander. Discard the vegetables and herbs, and set the beans aside.

Heat 1 teaspoon of the oil in a saucepan over medium heat, and add the finely chopped onion, half the chopped thyme and rosemary, and the remaining bay leaf, and sauté for three minutes. Add the tomatoes and the crushed garlic, bring to a boil, then lower the heat to a simmer. Season with the salt and some black pepper, and cook, uncovered, until the mixture has reduced to a sauce—30 to 40 minutes.

Meanwhile, preheat the oven to 350° F. In a bowl, combine the remaining garlic, rosemary, and thyme with the whole-wheat breadcrumbs and chopped parsley, until they form a green-flecked, crumbly mixture. Add the grated lemon zest and the remaining oil, and mix well.

When the tomato mixture is ready, add the beans to the saucepan, stir gently, and transfer the mixture to a large gratin dish. Spread the herbed crumbs on top of the beans and bake them in the oven, uncovered, until the crust is crisp—about 40 minutes.

SUGGESTED ACCOMPANIMENTS: *asparagus or broccoli; crisp green salad.*

Butter Bean Succotash

Serves 4
Working time: about 30 minutes
Total time: about 2 hours and 45 minutes
(includes soaking)

Calories **325**
Protein **15g.**
Cholesterol **10mg.**
Total fat **6g.**
Saturated fat **2g.**
Sodium **300mg.**

1 cup dried butter or lima beans, picked over
½ tbsp. safflower oil
1 onion, sliced
2 garlic cloves, crushed
3 celery stalks, trimmed and sliced
1 large potato, chopped
1 sweet green pepper, seeded, deribbed, and chopped
1 sprig summer savory, or ½ tsp. dried savory
2 cups fresh or frozen corn kernels
½ tsp. salt
1 tsp. sugar
freshly ground black pepper
3 tbsp. sour cream
1 tsp. fresh lemon juice
2 tbsp. chopped parsley

Rinse the beans under cold running water, then put them into a large, heavy saucepan and pour in enough cold water to cover them by about 3 inches. Discard any beans that float to the surface. Cover the pan, leaving the lid ajar, and slowly bring the liquid to a boil. Boil the beans for two minutes, then turn off the heat and soak the beans, covered, for at least one hour. (Alternatively, soak the beans overnight in cold water.)

Drain the beans, place them in a saucepan, and pour in enough cold water to cover them by about 3 inches. Bring the liquid to a boil, lower the heat to maintain a strong simmer, and cook the beans until they are tender—about one hour. Check the liquid in the pan from time to time, and add more hot water if necessary. Drain the cooked beans in a sieve over a bowl and reserve the cooking liquid. Rinse the beans under cold running water. Drain the butter or lima beans again and then set them aside.

Heat the oil in a heavy-bottomed saucepan and sauté the onion until soft—about three minutes. Add the garlic, celery, potato, green pepper, savory, and the reserved bean-cooking liquid, mixed, if necessary, with enough water to make 2½ cups. Cover the saucepan, bring the liquid to a boil, and simmer the ingredients for 10 minutes.

Add the cooked beans to the saucepan, together with the corn, salt, sugar, and some black pepper. Cook the mixture for 10 minutes more. Remove the saucepan from the heat, and stir in the sour cream and the lemon juice. Ladle the succotash into individual bowls and sprinkle with the chopped parsley.

SUGGESTED ACCOMPANIMENT: *crusty bread.*

Cabbage Stuffed with Black-Eyed Peas and Mushrooms

Serves 4
Working time: about 1 hour
Total time: about 3 hours and 15 minutes

Calories **155**
Protein **8g.**
Cholesterol **20mg.**
Total fat **7g.**
Saturated fat **2g.**
Sodium **220mg.**

⅓ cup dried black-eyed peas, picked over
1 tbsp. virgin olive oil
1 tbsp. unsalted butter
1 firm green cabbage (about 2½ lb.), hollowed out (technique, right), ½ lb. of the leaves reserved and chopped (about 2 cups)
3 garlic cloves, chopped
1 onion, chopped
¼ lb. mushrooms, wiped clean and chopped
1 tbsp. rolled oats
½ cup unsalted vegetable stock (recipe, page 9)
½ tsp. salt
freshly ground black pepper
1 tbsp. finely chopped cilantro
1 tbsp. finely chopped summer savory, or 1 tsp. dried savory

Rinse the black-eyed peas under cold running water, then put them into a large saucepan and pour in enough cold water to cover them by about 3 inches. Discard any peas that float to the surface. Bring the water to a boil and cook the peas for two minutes. Turn off the heat, cover the pan, and soak the peas for at least one hour. (Alternatively, soak the peas overnight in cold water.)

Discard the soaking water and rinse the peas. Place them in a clean saucepan and pour in enough water to cover them by about 3 inches. Bring the liquid to a boil; then lower the heat to medium-low, tightly cover the pan, and simmer the peas, occasionally skimming any foam from the surface of the liquid, until they are tender—about one hour. Check the water level in the pan from time to time, and add more hot water if

necessary. Transfer the peas to a colander to drain, rinse them and drain them again, then set them aside.

Preheat the oven to 400° F.

In a large skillet, heat the oil and butter together until the butter has melted. Add the reserved chopped cabbage, the garlic, onion, and mushrooms, and cook, stirring frequently, over medium heat until the vegetables are softened but not browned—five to seven minutes. Remove the pan from the heat.

Stir the cooked black-eyed peas into the vegetables. Add the rolled oats and the stock. Stir lightly, return the pan to the heat, and bring the mixture to a simmer. Simmer for five minutes. Remove the pan from the heat, season the stuffing with the salt and some black pepper, then mix in the cilantro and savory.

Fill the hollowed-out cabbage to the top with the stuffing. Put the cabbage lid over the stuffing, and place the cabbage in the middle of a 20-inch square of nonstick parchment paper. Fold the paper up to enclose the cabbage completely.

Place the wrapped cabbage on a baking sheet and bake it until the cabbage is tender—30 to 40 minutes. Let it rest for a few minutes before unwrapping it. Remove the lid and serve the cabbage cut into wedges.

SUGGESTED ACCOMPANIMENT: *tomato coulis.*

Hollowing a Whole Cabbage

SCOOPING OUT THE CENTER. Trim the protruding stem of the cabbage just enough to allow the cabbage to be stood on end. Cut a lid about 4 inches in diameter and ½ inch thick off the top of the cabbage and set it aside. With a sturdy tablespoon, dig into the exposed center and scoop out leaves until the cabbage walls are about ½ inch thick. Reserve the loosened cabbage leaves for the stuffing.

Chickpea and Okra Casserole with Couscous

Serves 4
Working time: about 30 minutes
Total time: about 3 hours and 30 minutes
(includes soaking)

Calories **450**
Protein **15g.**
Cholesterol **0mg.**
Total fat **10g.**
Saturated fat **1g.**
Sodium **320mg.**

⅔ cup dried chickpeas, picked over
2 tbsp. virgin olive oil
1 large onion, chopped
1 tbsp. paprika
1 tsp. ground turmeric
3 fresh thyme sprigs
2 fresh bay leaves
1 qt. unsalted vegetable stock (recipe, page 9) or water
½ tsp. salt
½ lb. carrots (3 medium), thickly sliced
¼ cup dried apricots
¼ lb. baby corn, fresh or frozen
⅔ cup dried pears
3 tbsp. currants
½ lb. small okra, trimmed
1⅓ cups whole-wheat couscous or couscous

Rinse the chickpeas under cold running water, then put them in a large, heavy pan and pour in enough cold water to cover them by about 3 inches. Discard any chickpeas that float to the surface. Cover the pan, leaving the lid ajar, and slowly bring the liquid to a boil.

Boil the chickpeas for two minutes, then turn off the heat and soak them for at least one hour. (Alternatively, soak the peas overnight in cold water.)

Drain and rinse the chickpeas, return them to the pan, and pour in enough water to cover them again by about 3 inches. Bring the liquid to a boil, lower the heat to maintain a strong simmer, and cook the peas until they are just tender—about one hour. If the chickpeas appear to be drying out at any point, add more hot water. Drain the peas in a colander and rinse them under cold running water.

In a large saucepan, heat half the oil and sauté the onion over medium heat until transparent—about three minutes. Add the paprika and turmeric, and cook, stirring, for one to two minutes. Add the thyme, bay leaves, chickpeas, and stock, and bring to a boil. Lower the heat, cover, and simmer for 45 minutes. Add the salt, carrots, apricots, corn, pears, and currants. Cover the saucepan and simmer the ingredients for 15 minutes more.

Heat the remaining tablespoon of oil in a heavy skillet and sauté the okra for five minutes. Using a slotted spoon, transfer the okra to the vegetable mixture and simmer for 15 minutes more.

Meanwhile, place the couscous in a bowl and pour 2 cups of boiling water over it. Stir it with a fork and let it stand until all of the water is absorbed—approximately 10 minutes.

Arrange the couscous on a large serving dish, and pile the fruit and vegetable stew in the center, having first removed the bay leaves and thyme sprigs.

Chickpea and Bulgur Kofta

KOFTA IS AN INDIAN DISH, USUALLY MADE OF MINCED, HERBED MEAT SHAPED INTO SMALL BALLS OR OVALS. IN THIS RECIPE, THE MEAT IS REPLACED WITH CHICKPEAS.

Serves 4
Working time: about 45 minutes
Total time: about 4 hours (includes soaking and chilling)

Calories **430**
Protein **21g.**
Cholesterol **0mg.**
Total fat **12g.**
Saturated fat **2g.**
Sodium **60mg.**

1¼ cup dried chickpeas, picked over
⅔ cup bulgur, soaked in warm water for 30 minutes, drained, and squeezed dry in paper towels
2 tbsp. tahini (sesame paste)
⅓ cup plain low-fat yogurt
1 small onion, grated
1 garlic clove, crushed
¼ cup chopped parsley
¼ cup chopped fresh mint
2 lemons, juice of one, the other cut into wedges for garnish
lettuce leaves for garnish
Chili-tomato relish
1 tbsp. virgin olive oil
1 lb. tomatoes (3 medium), chopped
1 small onion, very finely chopped
1 cucumber, very finely chopped
2 or 3 fresh hot red or green chili peppers, seeded and finely chopped (cautionary note, page 25)

Rinse the chickpeas under cold running water, then transfer them to a large pan and pour in enough water to cover them by about 3 inches. Discard any chickpeas that float to the surface. Cover the pan, leaving the lid ajar, and bring the liquid to a boil. Boil the peas for two minutes, then turn off the heat, cover the pan, and soak the peas for at least one hour. (Alternatively, soak the peas overnight in cold water.)

Drain and rinse the peas, return them to the pan,

and pour in enough water to cover them by 3 inches. Bring the liquid to a boil, then lower the heat to maintain a strong simmer and cook the peas, covered, until they are soft—about one and a half hours. If the peas appear to be drying out, add more hot water.

Drain the chickpeas, then purée them in a food processor. Stir in the bulgur, tahini, yogurt, onion, garlic, parsley, mint, and lemon juice. Form the mixture by hand into 16 ovals. Chill them for one hour.

To make the relish, heat the oil in a heavy-bottomed pan over low heat and add the tomatoes. Cover the pan, and cook for 15 minutes, then press the tomatoes through a sieve. Chill the purée for one hour.

Preheat the broiler. Cover a baking sheet with foil. Place the kofta on the foil, and broil them until they are golden brown—three to four minutes per side. Stir the onion, cucumber, and chilies into the tomato purée. Serve the kofta hot, garnished with the lettuce and lemon wedges, and pass the relish.

Chickpea Salad in Artichoke Cups

Serves 4
Working time: about 1 hour
Total time: about 3 hours (includes soaking)

Calories **230**
Protein **13g.**
Cholesterol **5mg.**
Total fat **10g.**
Saturated fat **2g.**
Sodium **135mg.**

¾ cup dried chickpeas, picked over
1 small onion, peeled
1 garlic clove, peeled
1 chili pepper, seeded and halved (cautionary note, page 25)
2 bay leaves
6 fresh sage leaves
4 large artichokes
1 large lemon, halved
mixed salad leaves for garnish
Herb dressing
1½ tbsp. virgin olive oil
1 garlic clove, peeled
¼ cup sour cream
2 tbsp. plain low-fat yogurt
½ oz. dry-pack (unoiled) sun-dried tomatoes (about 4), soaked in boiling water for 10 minutes, drained, and finely diced
1 tbsp. finely chopped parsley
2 fresh sage leaves, finely sliced
¼ tsp. cayenne pepper
¼ tsp. salt

Rinse the chickpeas under cold running water, then put them in a large, heavy pan and pour in enough cold water to cover them by about 3 inches. Discard any chickpeas that float to the surface. Cover the pan, leaving the lid ajar, and slowly bring the liquid to a boil over medium-low heat. Boil the chickpeas for two minutes, then turn off the heat and soak them, cov-

ered, for at least one hour. (Alternatively, soak the chickpeas overnight in cold water.)

Drain and rinse the chickpeas, return them to the pan, and pour in enough water to cover them by about 3 inches. Bring the liquid to a boil, then lower the heat to medium-low and add the onion, garlic, chili, bay leaves, and sage leaves. Cover the pan and simmer gently until the chickpeas are tender—about one hour. If the chickpeas appear to be drying out at any point, add more hot water. Let the chickpeas cool in their cooking liquid.

Following the instructions in step 1, below, trim the artichokes, using one of the lemon halves to rub the cut surfaces. Place the artichokes in a large nonreactive saucepan wide enough to hold all four in a single layer.

Grate the zest and squeeze the juice from the un-used lemon half. Set the grated zest and one table-spoon of juice aside for the dressing. Add the remaining lemon juice to the pan containing the artichokes. Pour in sufficient cold water to come level with the tops of the artichokes. Bring the water to a boil, cover, and boil until the center and base of each artichoke can be pierced easily with a thin skewer or the tip of a sharp knife—30 to 40 minutes.

While the artichokes are cooking, make the herb dressing. Place the oil and garlic clove in a small, heavy-bottomed saucepan, and heat them gently until the garlic sizzles. Remove the pan from the heat and allow the oil to infuse for 5 to 10 minutes. Discard the garlic, and blend the oil with the sour cream and yogurt. Add the sun-dried tomatoes to the dressing, along with the parsley, sage, cayenne pepper, and salt. Stir in the reserved lemon zest and as much of the tablespoon of juice as needed to sharpen the dressing.

Drain the chickpeas and discard the flavoring ingre-

dients added to their cooking liquid. Stir the chickpeas into the dressing.

Use a slotted spoon to lift the artichokes from the pan; set them upside down to drain. When the artichokes are cool enough to handle, remove the choke from each one (step 2, below). Remove a few more leaves from the center of each artichoke to form a cup large enough to hold a quarter of the chickpeas.

Place the artichoke cups on individual plates and pile the dressed chickpeas into them. Serve garnished with the salad leaves.

EDITOR'S NOTE: If you prepare the artichokes in advance, return them to their cooking liquid until required; this will prevent them from discoloring and drying out. Drain them upside down before filling them with the chickpeas.

Preparing Artichokes for Stuffing

1 TRIMMING THE LEAVES. Cut off the stem and small outer leaves from the base of each artichoke with a stainless steel knife. Rub the cut surfaces with freshly cut lemon to keep them from turning brown. Cut off the top third of each artichoke. Then snip off the sharp tips of the outer leaves with kitchen scissors. Cook the artichokes following the instructions given in the recipe.

2 REMOVING THE CHOKE. Lift the artichokes from the pan, and set them upside down to drain and cool. With a teaspoon, scoop out the tiny inner leaves and the hairy choke from the center of each artichoke to reveal the smooth, edible green heart.

Indonesian Vegetable Stew

Serves 6
Working time: about 45 minutes
Total time: about 1 hour and 20 minutes

Calories **290**
Protein **10g.**
Cholesterol **0mg.**
Total fat **10g.**
Saturated fat **1g.**
Sodium **30mg.**

7 oz. eggplant (½ medium), cut into ½-inch cubes
1 tsp. salt
3 tbsp. safflower oil
1 tbsp. black mustard seeds
1 tbsp. ground fenugreek
2 dried hot red chili peppers, seeded and broken into small pieces (cautionary note, page 25)
2 fresh hot green chili peppers, seeded and thinly sliced (cautionary note, page 25)
6 garlic cloves, chopped
1 tsp. freshly ground green cardamom pods
1 tsp. concentrated tamarind paste
⅔ cup dried mung beans, picked over and rinsed
5 cups unsalted vegetable stock (recipe, page 9)
1 lb. potatoes, thickly sliced
¼ lb. dried porcini, soaked in hot water for 20 minutes, drained, and coarsely chopped
½ lb. okra, trimmed and sliced
1 lb. green beans, trimmed and halved
2 spears fresh lemon grass, finely chopped (optional)
1 lemon, grated zest and juice
2 tbsp. unsweetened shredded coconut

In a bowl, toss the cubed eggplant with the salt. Place the eggplant cubes in a colander, weight them down with a plate, and let them drain for about 30 minutes. Rinse the eggplant cubes under cold running water and drain them well.

Meanwhile, in a large, heavy-bottomed saucepan, heat the oil over medium-high heat. Add the mustard seeds, fenugreek, red and green chilies, garlic, cardamom, and tamarind paste. Sauté these ingredients for about two minutes, stirring them occasionally, then add the mung beans and stock. Bring the contents of the pan to a boil, lower the heat, and simmer, uncovered, for 15 minutes.

Add the potatoes, eggplant, porcini, and okra to the pan, and simmer, covered, for 10 minutes more. Stir in the green beans, and add the lemon grass if you are using it. Simmer the stew for 10 minutes more. Finally, mix in the grated lemon zest, lemon juice, and coconut, and simmer the stew for one minute more. Let the vegetable stew rest, uncovered, for about five minutes before serving, to allow the coconut and lemon flavors to develop.

SUGGESTED ACCOMPANIMENTS: *a mixture of wild and brown rice; onion and chili chutney; fruit pickle.*

EDITOR'S NOTE: *Lemon grass, green cardamom, and tamarind paste are available at stores where Asian foods are sold.*

Lentils with Spinach and Carrots

Serves 4
Working time: about 20 minutes
Total time: about 50 minutes

Calories **330**
Protein **18g.**
Cholesterol **0mg.**
Total fat **10g.**
Saturated fat **1g.**
Sodium **80mg.**

1 cup lentils, picked over and rinsed
1 bay leaf
2 tbsp. safflower oil
1 garlic clove, crushed
1 tbsp. freshly grated ginger
½ lb. carrots (2 to 3 medium), peeled and cut into bâtonnets
12 scallions, cut into 1-inch lengths
¾ lb. spinach, stems discarded, washed, dried, and coarsely chopped
2 tbsp. low-sodium soy sauce
⅓ cup dry sherry
1 tbsp. sesame seeds, toasted

Put the lentils in a large, heavy-bottomed saucepan with 3 cups of water. Bring the water to a boil, then lower the heat to medium, add the bay leaf, cover the pan tightly, and simmer the lentils until they are tender—about 40 minutes. Drain the lentils and remove the bay leaf. Rinse the lentils under cold running water and drain them again.

Heat the oil in a wok or large, heavy skillet over high heat. Add the garlic and ginger, and stir them until the garlic sizzles. Add the carrots and scallions, and stir-fry them for one minute, then transfer them to a plate using a slotted spoon. Place the spinach in the pan and stir it over high heat until it begins to wilt—one to two minutes. Then return the carrots and scallions to the pan, add the cooked lentils, and stir them for two minutes to heat them through. Add the soy sauce and the sherry, and bring the liquid to a boil. Stir the ingredients once more, then transfer them to a heated serving dish. Scatter the sesame seeds over the dish and serve it immediately.

SUGGESTED ACCOMPANIMENT: *long-grain brown rice.*

EDITOR'S NOTE: *To toast sesame seeds, put them in a small, heavy-bottomed skillet over medium-low heat until they are golden—one to two minutes.*

Lentil and Potato Cakes with Mustard Pickle

Serves 4
Working time: about 40 minutes
Total time: about 1 hour and 40 minutes

Calories **295**
Protein **15g.**
Cholesterol **10mg.**
Total fat **4g.**
Saturated fat **1g.**
Sodium **245mg.**

½ lb. starchy potatoes, peeled and cut into 1-inch cubes
½ tsp. safflower oil
12 scallions, trimmed, white parts chopped, green parts sliced into thin rings
1-inch piece fresh ginger, peeled and finely chopped
¼ tsp. ground cinnamon
¼ tsp. freshly grated nutmeg, or ¼ tsp. ground nutmeg
½ tsp. salt
freshly ground black pepper
¾ cup split red lentils, picked over, rinsed
2 cups unsalted vegetable stock (recipe, page 9)
½ tsp. garam masala
⅓ cup sour cream
⅓ cup plain low-fat yogurt
Mustard pickle
¼ tsp. safflower oil
1 small onion, finely chopped
1 tbsp. mustard seeds, lightly crushed
2 tbsp. white wine vinegar
¼ cup dry white wine
1 tbsp. light brown sugar
1 tbsp. grainy mustard
1 red-skinned mango, peeled and pitted, flesh coarsely diced

First make the mustard pickle. Heat the oil in a small, heavy-bottomed saucepan, add the onion and mus-

tard seeds, and cook over medium heat, stirring, until the onion has softened—about three minutes. Stir in the vinegar, wine, sugar, mustard, and mango. Bring to a boil, then lower the heat, cover, and cook gently until the mango is tender and the mixture thick and pulpy—about 15 minutes. Transfer the contents of the pan to a bowl and set it aside.

Cook the potatoes in boiling water until tender—about 20 minutes. Drain well, then mash them with a potato masher. Heat the oil in a large skillet and add the white parts of the scallions, the ginger, cinnamon, nutmeg, salt, and some black pepper. Cook over medium heat, stirring continuously, for three minutes. Add the lentils and stock, and bring to a boil; then cover the pan, lower the heat, and simmer gently, stirring frequently, until the lentils are completely tender—about 25 minutes. Remove the lid, and increase the heat, stirring continuously, until the mixture is dry—about two minutes. Beat in the mashed potatoes and garam masala, then set the mixture aside to cool. Stir together the sour cream and yogurt.

Preheat the broiler and lightly grease a baking sheet. Shape the lentil mixture into 12 flat cakes about 3 inches in diameter, and place them on the baking sheet. Broil the cakes until they are golden—about five minutes on each side—then transfer them to individual serving plates. Top the cakes with the sour-cream mixture and mustard pickle, and garnish them with the green scallion rings.

SUGGESTED ACCOMPANIMENT: *stir-fried cucumber wedges.*

EDITOR'S NOTE: *Garam masala is a mixture of ground spices used in Indian cookery. It usually contains coriander, cumin, cloves, ginger, and cinnamon. In this recipe, a pinch each of some or all of these spices can be substituted if garam masala is not available.*

Lentils with Cumin
and Onion

Serves 4
Working time: about 15 minutes
Total time: about 1 hour

Calories **215**
Protein **9g.**
Cholesterol **0mg.**
Total fat **7g.**
Saturated fat **1g.**
Sodium **225mg.**

1½ cups lentils, picked over and rinsed
1 tsp. ground cumin
½ tsp. salt
⅓ cup brown rice
1 tbsp. virgin olive oil
1 lb. onions, thinly sliced
6 to 8 radishes, thinly sliced
2 tbsp. chopped parsley

In a heavy-bottomed saucepan, bring 1 quart of water to a boil; then add the lentils, cumin, and salt, and boil, uncovered, for 20 minutes. Add the rice, lower the heat, and simmer, covered, until the liquid has been absorbed but the rice is still moist—30 to 40 minutes.

Meanwhile, heat the oil in a skillet and sauté the onions over low heat, partially covered, stirring frequently, until they are soft and golden brown—approximately 15 minutes.

Remove half of the onions and stir them into the lentil mixture. Transfer the mixture to the center of a shallow serving dish. Distribute the remaining sautéed onions around the lentil mixture, then arrange the radishes around the onions on the edge of the dish. Sprinkle the parsley over the lentil mixture. Serve hot.

SUGGESTED ACCOMPANIMENT: *salad of lettuce and cucumber.*

Lentil Soufflés Baked in Sweet Pepper Cases

Serves: 6
Working time: about 40 minutes
Total time: about 2 hours

Calories **165**
Protein **10g.**
Cholesterol **75mg.**
Total fat **5g.**
Saturated fat **1g.**
Sodium **130mg.**

1 tbsp. virgin olive oil
1 large onion, finely chopped
1 large carrot, finely chopped
1 garlic clove, crushed
¾ cup split red lentils, picked over and rinsed
2 cups unsalted vegetable stock (recipe, page 9)
¼ tsp. salt
2 tbsp. tomato paste
3 large sweet green peppers
freshly ground black pepper
2 eggs, separated

Heat the oil in a large, heavy-bottomed saucepan over medium heat. Add the onion and carrot, and cook for five minutes, then stir in the garlic, lentils, stock, salt, and tomato paste. Bring the mixture to a boil, then lower the heat. Cover the pan with a tight-fitting lid, and simmer until the lentils are soft and the stock has been absorbed—about 45 minutes.

Meanwhile, carefully remove the stalk from each pepper. (The lentil filling is too stiff to seep through the small hole left by the stalk.) Cut the peppers in half horizontally, and remove their seeds and any thick white ribs. Cook the pepper cups in gently simmering water to cover until they are softened—four to five minutes—then drain them well on paper towels. Place the cups in a lightly oiled, shallow ovenproof dish. Preheat the oven to 375° F.

When the lentils are cooked, remove them from the heat and allow them to cool for 10 minutes. Season them with some black pepper, then beat in the egg yolks. Whisk the egg whites until stiff but not dry, and fold 1 tablespoon into the lentil mixture to lighten it. Then fold in the remaining egg whites. Spoon the soufflé mixture into the pepper cups, and cook them until the soufflés are well risen and lightly browned—30 to 35 minutes. Serve immediately.

SUGGESTED ACCOMPANIMENTS: *tomato and basil salad; crusty bread.*

Sichuan Tofu with Sweet Pepper and Peanuts

SICHUAN CUISINE, ONE OF THE FIVE STYLES OF CHINESE COOKING, IS CHARACTERIZED BY ITS USE OF PEPPERS AND IMAGINATIVE SEASONINGS.

Serves 6
Working (and total) time: about 35 minutes

Calories **220**
Protein **15g.**
Cholesterol **0mg.**
Total fat **15g.**
Saturated fat **1g.**
Sodium **50mg.**

2 tbsp. safflower oil
2 lb. firm tofu, well drained (box, opposite), cut into ¾-inch cubes
2 garlic cloves, thinly sliced
1½-inch piece fresh ginger, peeled and finely shredded
3 fresh or dried red chili peppers, seeded and thinly sliced (cautionary note, page 25)
8 scallions, thinly sliced, green and white parts separated
2 small sweet green peppers, seeded, deribbed, and cut into ¾-inch squares
⅛ tsp. salt

1 tbsp. rice wine or sherry
1½ oz. peanuts (about ¼ cup), toasted
Seasoning sauce
2 tbsp. low-sodium soy sauce
2 tsp. rice vinegar or wine vinegar
1½ tsp. sugar
½ cup unsalted vegetable stock (recipe, page 9) or water
1½ tsp. cornstarch
½ tsp. hot red-pepper sauce

In a heavy, nonstick skillet, heat 2 teaspoons of the oil and cook half of the tofu cubes over medium-high heat until they are golden brown all over—three to five minutes. Turn the cubes continuously with a spatula to prevent the tofu from sticking to the pan. Transfer the cubes to paper towels to drain. Pour another 2 teaspoons of oil into the skillet, cook the remaining tofu cubes in the same way, and again transfer them to paper towels.

In a small bowl, mix together all of the ingredients

for the seasoning sauce, then set the sauce aside.

Heat the remaining oil in a wok or large, heavy skillet, swirling it around to coat the sides. Drop in the garlic and allow it to sizzle for a few seconds. Add the ginger and sauté it, stirring continuously, until it is golden brown—about two minutes. Add the chilies and the white parts of the scallions, and stir-fry for 10 seconds, turning and tossing the ingredients with a spatula. Add the sweet peppers, and stir-fry for another 10 seconds; then add the tofu cubes, and continue to stir-fry for about 20 seconds. Add the salt and the wine or sherry.

Stir the seasoning sauce well and pour it into the wok. Continue to stir until the sauce thickens. Add the peanuts and mix them in. Remove the wok from the heat and mix in most of the green parts of the scallions. Transfer the tofu stir-fry to a serving dish, and sprinkle with the remaining scallions.

SUGGESTED ACCOMPANIMENT: *rice or Chinese egg noodles.*

EDITOR'S NOTE: *To toast peanuts, place them on a baking sheet and put them under a hot broiler for two to three minutes, stirring the nuts from time to time.*

Storing and Draining Tofu

Tofu—the Japanese name for soybean curd—is usually sold in a pressed form, either fresh or vacuum packed. Fresh tofu may be stored in the refrigerator, submerged in a bowl of cold water, for up to a week; the water should be changed daily. Unopened, vacuum-packed tofu will keep for many months. Once opened, however, it should be treated in the same way as fresh tofu.

Because it is stored underwater, tofu is moist, and for many recipes it needs to be thoroughly drained before use. To drain tofu, wrap it in a double layer of cheesecloth or a clean dishtowel, and place it between two flat, heavy boards; raise one end of the boards a few inches, and position the lower end over a sink or tray to catch the fluid that drains away. Let the tofu drain for 30 minutes to an hour.

Tofu and Vegetable Dumplings

Serves 4
Working time: about 45 minutes
Total time: about 1 hour

Calories **220**
Protein **16g.**
Cholesterol **0mg.**
Total fat **8g.**
Saturated fat **trace**
Sodium **235mg.**

1 lb. firm tofu, well drained (box, page 85)
4½ tbsp. cornstarch
1 egg white
½ tsp. salt
¼ cup shelled peas, blanched for 1 minute, drained, and refreshed under cold running water, or ¼ cup frozen peas, thawed
½ medium carrot, peeled and very finely diced, blanched for 1 minute, drained, and refreshed under cold running water
6 fresh water chestnuts, peeled and finely diced, or 6 canned water chestnuts, drained and finely diced
2½ tsp. sesame seeds, toasted
2 cups unsalted vegetable stock (recipe, page 9)
½ lb. baby corn, fresh or frozen
½ lb. center leaves of small bok choy
¼ lb. snow peas, strings removed

Put the tofu in a food processor with the cornstarch and blend for about one minute. In a bowl, whisk the egg white with the salt until it is stiff but not dry. Add the egg white to the tofu and process the ingredients briefly to form a smooth paste. Transfer the paste to a bowl, cover it with plastic wrap, and chill it in the refrigerator for 30 minutes.

Mix the peas, carrots, water chestnuts, and 2 teaspoons of the sesame seeds into the tofu paste, then divide the mixture into 16 equal portions, and mold each portion into a ball. Bring a large saucepan of water to a boil. Set a cheesecloth-lined steamer over the pan, and carefully place the tofu dumplings in the steamer in a single layer, then steam them over high heat for 12 minutes. Set the tofu dumplings aside and keep them warm.

Meanwhile, put the vegetable stock in a saucepan and bring it to a boil. Add the corn to the stock and cook for three minutes (one minute if you are using frozen corn); add the bok choy leaves and continue to cook for one minute; then add the snow peas and cook for two minutes more.

Reduce the heat to low and gently lower the dumplings into the stock. Heat them through for about one minute. Transfer the dumplings and vegetables to individual plates. Sprinkle the remaining sesame seeds over the tofu dumplings and serve immediately.

EDITOR'S NOTE: *To toast sesame seeds, heat them in a small, heavy-bottomed skillet over medium-low heat until they are golden—one to two minutes.*

Tofu and Vegetable Stir-Fry with Noodles

Serves 4
Working (and total) time: about 30 minutes

Calories **480**
Protein **18g.**
Cholesterol **0mg.**
Total fat **15g.**
Saturated fat **2g.**
Sodium **340mg.**

2 tbsp. low-sodium soy sauce
2 tbsp. honey
½ tsp. Chinese five-spice powder
7½ oz. firm tofu, cut into thin slices
4 tsp. light sesame oil
1 garlic clove, crushed
8 scallions, sliced
¼ lb. snow peas, strings removed
1 large sweet yellow pepper, seeded, deribbed, and sliced
1 large sweet red pepper, seeded, deribbed, and sliced
¼ lb. baby corn, fresh or frozen
¾ lb. fresh Chinese egg noodles, or ½ lb. dried vermicelli or thin spaghetti

Mix together the soy sauce, honey, and five-spice powder in a medium-size bowl. Add the tofu to the bowl, spoon the marinade over it, and set it aside to absorb the flavors while you cook the vegetables.

Heat 3 teaspoons of the sesame oil in a wok or a large, heavy skillet, and stir in the garlic and scallions.

Add the snow peas, peppers, and corn, and sauté over medium heat, stirring frequently, until the vegetables are cooked but still crisp—four to five minutes. Using a slotted spoon, lift the cooked vegetables out of the wok onto a heated dish. Cover the vegetables with foil and keep them warm.

Meanwhile, bring 4 quarts of lightly salted water to a boil. When the water boils, add the noodles. Cook the noodles until they are *al dente:* Start testing them after three minutes. When the noodles are done, drain them, rinse them with cold water, and set them aside in a colander.

Drain the tofu, reserving the marinade. Add the remaining teaspoon of oil to the wok and cook the tofu for about 20 seconds on each side.

Pour boiling water over the noodles in the colander to reheat them. Place the noodles on a heated serving dish, cover them with the vegetables, and arrange the tofu on top of the vegetables.

Pour the reserved marinade with 2 tablespoons of water into the wok. Heat the liquid through and pour it over the tofu. Serve immediately.

Tofu, Zucchini, and Mushroom Kabobs

Serves 4
Working (and total) time: about 45 minutes

Calories **240**
Protein **15g.**
Cholesterol **0mg.**
Total fat **15g.**
Saturated fat **2g.**
Sodium **100mg.**

4 zucchini (about 6 oz. each), ends removed
24 small shallots (about 8 oz.)
1 sweet red pepper, seeded, deribbed, and cut into 1-inch squares
1 lb. firm tofu, well drained (box, page 85), cut into 24 cubes
24 small mushrooms (about 1 lb.), wiped clean
2 tbsp. virgin olive oil
white pepper

Olive and caper sauce

4 black olives, pitted and finely chopped
1 tbsp. finely chopped capers
2 tsp. grainy mustard
1 tbsp. finely chopped parsley
5 tbsp. plain low-fat yogurt
2 tbsp. fresh lemon or lime juice

In a small bowl, mix together all the ingredients for the olive and caper sauce, then set the sauce aside to allow the flavors to mingle and develop.

Using a vegetable peeler or the point of a small, sharp knife, remove thin strips of peel lengthwise from each zucchini to create a striped effect. Slice the zucchini into 1-inch-thick rounds. Blanch the zucchini, shallots, and pepper squares in boiling water for two minutes, refresh them under cold running water, and drain them well. Preheat the broiler.

Thread each skewer with two each of the zucchini rounds, shallots, tofu cubes, mushrooms, and sweet red pepper squares. There should be 12 kabobs in all. Brush the kabobs with the olive oil and season them with some white pepper.

Place the kabobs under the broiler until they are lightly browned—four to six minutes on each side. Arrange the kabobs on a serving platter, and serve the sauce separately.

SUGGESTED ACCOMPANIMENT: *long-grain rice flavored with 1 to 2 tablespoons of tomato paste.*

Barley and Mushroom Broth with Smoked Tofu

Serves 4
Working time: about 30 minutes
Total time: about 1 hour

Calories **140**
Protein **6g.**
Cholesterol **0mg.**
Total fat **5g.**
Saturated fat **trace**
Sodium **85mg.**

⅓ cup pearl barley, rinsed under cold running water and drained
1 qt. unsalted vegetable stock (recipe, page 9)
1 tbsp. safflower oil
1 small onion, finely chopped
2 small carrots, diced
2 celery stalks, diced
¼ lb. mushrooms, wiped clean and sliced
1 tsp. cider vinegar
2 tbsp. tomato paste
¼ lb. smoked tofu, cut into ½-inch cubes
freshly ground black pepper
2 tbsp. chopped parsley
2 tbsp. cut chives

Place the barley and the vegetable stock in a large saucepan, and bring the liquid to a boil. Lower the heat to maintain a simmer, cover the saucepan, and cook the barley for 30 minutes.

Meanwhile, heat the oil in a heavy skillet, add the onion, carrot, and celery, and cook them over medium heat for about 10 minutes. Add the mushrooms, and cook for two minutes more.

Add the vegetables, vinegar, and tomato paste to the barley and stock, and simmer, covered, for 20 minutes. Then add the tofu, and simmer, covered, for 10 minutes more. Season the broth with some freshly ground black pepper, and stir in the parsley and chives. Serve the broth hot.

SUGGESTED ACCOMPANIMENT: *a selection of rye breads.*

3 *Bread, pasta, and the ingredients of numerous pastry dishes await metamorphosis into satisfying vegetarian meals.*

A Sustaining Trio

Pasta, pastry, and bread are the nutritious corner-stones of many vegetarian dishes. They derive nearly all of their goodness from wheat flour, which is rich in carbohydrates and includes six of the eight essential amino acids. White flour is also a good source of B vitamins, calcium, and iron, while its whole-wheat counterpart contains even higher concentrations of these valuable nutrients. Combined with vegetables and dried beans, and small quantities of dairy products or eggs, the time-honored staples made with flour create perfectly balanced meatless meals.

Pasta is not only one of the simplest of foods; provided that one bears in mind a few basic techniques, it is also simplicity to cook. Boil it in plenty of water—at least 5 quarts for 1 pound of fresh or dried pasta. Cooking times given in any recipe are no more than guidelines; you really know when pasta is done only by testing it. When it is tender but still slightly resistant to the bite—*al dente,* that is—drain it immediately, or it will continue to cook.

Shortcrust pastry is indispensable to any cook's repertoire. For a light, crumbly piecrust, keep the ingredients cool. Make sure that the fat is chilled; if your fingertips are warm, use a pastry blender to combine the fat and flour. Mix the dry and liquid ingredients just enough to form a compact ball; do not overwork the dough, or the pastry will be tough.

Yeast pastry prefers a heavy-handed approach, requiring a period of vigorous kneading after the ingredients have been combined. Dry or fresh yeast works equally well to create this breadlike crust. Take care, however, that the liquid is at the correct temperature when activating the yeast: Too cold a temperature will retard the yeast's development; too hot will kill it. Ideally, the liquid should be 110° F., a temperature that feels hot to the touch.

Phyllo pastry, paper-thin and crisp, is an ideal wrapping for low-fat vegetarian dishes. It can be made at home—and still is in some Greek and Turkish households—but is now available from most supermarkets. After peeling a sheet of phyllo from its stack, work swiftly so the pastry does not dry out and tear; keep the remaining sheets covered by a damp cloth.

Bread, one of the most ancient and revered of foods, is a traditional accompaniment to most meals. At the conclusion of this chapter, the staff of life also lends its able support to a variety of ingredients—from Brie to okra—in a number of inventive main-course dishes.

Ricotta and Zucchini Tortellini with Mint Yogurt Sauce

Serves 6
Working (and total) time: about 1 hour and 40 minutes

Calories **215**
Protein **11g.**
Cholesterol **45mg.**
Total fat **7g.**
Saturated fat **4g.**
Sodium **145mg.**

6 oz. zucchini (1 medium)
¼ tsp. salt
1½ cups unbleached all-purpose flour
1 egg
1 egg white
1 tbsp. safflower oil
½ cup part-skim ricotta cheese
freshly ground black pepper
chopped mint leaves for garnish
Mint yogurt sauce
⅔ cup plain low-fat yogurt
⅓ cup sour cream
½ cup part-skim ricotta cheese
4 sprigs fresh mint (about 40 leaves), chopped
white pepper

Grate the zucchini into a bowl, sprinkle it with the salt, and set it aside for 30 minutes.

Meanwhile, make the pasta dough. Put the flour into a bowl and make a well in the center. Add the egg, egg white, and oil, and stir them with a fork or wooden spoon, gradually mixing in the flour. Transfer the dough to a lightly floured surface and knead it for a few minutes. The dough should come cleanly away from the surface; if it is too wet, add flour by the tablespoon until the dough is no longer sticky. If the dough is too dry and crumbly to work with, add water by the teaspoon until it is pliable. Continue kneading the dough until it is smooth and elastic—approximately 10 minutes. (Alternatively, place the dough ingredients in a food processor and process for about 30 seconds.) Wrap the dough in wax paper or plastic wrap, and let it rest for 15 minutes before rolling it out.

To prepare the filling, break up the ricotta with a fork in a large bowl and season it with some black pepper. Squeeze the grated zucchini dry, a quarter at a time, in a double layer of cheesecloth or a clean dishtowel, and add it to the ricotta. Stir well and set the mixture aside.

Divide the dough into three equal portions. Cover two portions with plastic wrap or an inverted bowl to keep them moist. Using a rolling pin, roll out the third portion on a floured surface into a sheet about ¹⁄₁₆ inch thick. With a 2½-inch-round pastry cutter, cut out 24 circles from the pasta and form them into tortellini (technique, below), using 1 teaspoon of filling for each circle. Repeat the procedure with the remaining pieces of dough and filling to make about 72 tortellini. Set the tortellini aside.

To make the sauce, place all the ingredients in a food processor or blender, and blend until smooth. Transfer the sauce to a small saucepan, and warm it over very gentle heat while you cook the pasta. Do not allow the sauce to boil.

Add the tortellini to 3 quarts of boiling water with 1½ teaspoons of salt. Start testing the tortellini one minute after the water returns to a boil, and cook them until they are al dente. Drain the pasta and serve it immediately with the mint yogurt sauce, garnished with a little chopped mint.

SUGGESTED ACCOMPANIMENT: red and yellow pepper salad.
EDITOR'S NOTE: Instead of kneading and rolling out the pasta by hand, you can use a pasta machine.

Shaping Tortellini

1 FILLING THE TORTELLINI. With a 2½-inch pastry cutter, cut circles from the dough. Stack them or store them under a bowl to keep them from drying out. Place some filling on a circle, then moisten half the edge with water.

2 ENCLOSING THE FILLING. Fold the circle in half so that the moist and dry edges meet. Press the edges firmly shut to seal them.

3 JOINING THE ENDS. Curl the ends around the filling and pinch them together, moistening the inner surfaces, if necessary, to make them stick. Repeat the steps with the remaining circles.

Savory Pumpkin Pie

Serves 6
Working time: about 30 minutes
Total time: about 1 hour and 15 minutes

Calories **175**
Protein **13g.**
Cholesterol **75mg.**
Total fat **3g.**
Saturated fat **1g.**
Sodium **80mg.**

1 lb. pumpkin or butternut squash, peeled and cut into ½-inch chunks
¾ cup plain low-fat yogurt
2 eggs, beaten
1 onion, sliced into rings
1 tsp. safflower oil, plus a little extra for glazing
1 garlic clove, crushed
½ tsp. ground ginger
½ tsp. chili powder
⅛ tsp. salt
white pepper
Yeast dough
1½ cups whole-wheat flour
1 tsp. fast-acting dry yeast
½ cup skim milk

To make the dough, mix together the flour and yeast in a large bowl. Heat the milk in a saucepan until it is hot to the touch—about 110° F.—then pour it into the dry ingredients. Knead the mixture well for 10 minutes, adding a little water if necessary, to make a smooth, soft dough. Allow the dough to rest for 10 minutes, then roll it out. Line a lightly greased 8-inch quiche pan or pie pan with the dough.

Preheat the oven to 400° F.

Steam the pumpkin chunks over a saucepan of boiling water until they are soft—10 to 15 minutes. Transfer them to a bowl and mash them. When the pumpkin has cooled slightly, beat in the yogurt and the eggs.

Meanwhile, set a quarter of the onion rings aside and chop the remainder. Heat the oil in a small, heavy-bottomed saucepan over medium heat. Add the chopped onion and the garlic, and sauté them until they are soft but not brown—about three minutes. Stir in the ginger and chili powder.

Transfer the pumpkin mixture to a food processor or blender, and add the contents of the saucepan, the salt, and some white pepper. Blend the mixture until it is smooth. Pour the filling into the pastry shell and level the surface. Press the reserved onion rings lightly into the filling and then brush them with a little extra safflower oil.

Bake the pie in the oven until it is golden brown and firm in the center.

SUGGESTED ACCOMPANIMENT: *steamed fresh vegetables.*

Mustard-Cauliflower Quiche

Serves 4
Working time: about 40 minutes
Total time: about 1 hour and 30 minutes

Calories **330**
Protein **11g.**
Cholesterol **55mg.**
Total fat **15g.**
Saturated fat **4g.**
Sodium **285mg.**

1 small cauliflower (about ¾ lb.), trimmed and divided into small florets
1 tsp. virgin olive oil
1 onion, finely chopped
1 large cooking apple, peeled, cored, and coarsely chopped
1½ tbsp. Dijon mustard
2 tbsp. unbleached all-purpose flour
1 egg, lightly beaten
1¼ cups skim milk
¼ tsp. salt
white pepper
paprika
Herb pastry
1 cup whole-wheat flour
4 tbsp. polyunsaturated margarine, chilled
2 tbsp. finely chopped cilantro
2 tbsp. finely chopped parsley

First make the pastry. Place the flour in a mixing bowl and rub in the margarine with your fingertips until the mixture resembles fine breadcrumbs. Stir in the cilantro and parsley. Using a wooden spoon, blend 3 to 4 tablespoons of water into the dry ingredients to form a dough. Gather the dough into a ball and knead it briefly on a lightly floured surface, until it is smooth. Roll out the dough and use it to line an 8-inch quiche pan or pie pan approximately 1½ inches deep. Prick the insides of the pastry shell with a fork, then chill it in the refrigerator for 30 minutes. Meanwhile, preheat the oven to 400° F.

Bake the pastry shell until the pastry is crisp—10 to 15 minutes. Remove it from the oven and lower the temperature to 350° F.

While the pastry shell is baking, parboil the cauliflower florets in a saucepan of boiling water until they are just tender—about three minutes. Drain them, rinse them under cold running water, and drain them again thoroughly. Set the florets aside until required. Heat the oil in a heavy skillet over medium heat. Add the onion and sauté it until it is soft and transparent—about three minutes—then add the apple and cook for another four minutes, until the apple is just tender.

Spread the onion and apple mixture over the bottom of the pastry shell, and arrange the cauliflower florets on top. In a mixing bowl, blend the mustard and flour together to form a smooth paste. Using a whisk, beat in the egg, then beat in the milk a little at a time. Add the salt and some white pepper, and pour the mixture into the pastry shell. Bake the quiche until the filling is set—30 to 45 minutes. Serve the quiche hot or cold, sprinkled with a little paprika.

SUGGESTED ACCOMPANIMENTS: *salad of mixed lettuce leaves; sliced tomatoes sprinkled with chives.*

Whole-Wheat Pizza with Corn and Pineapple

Serves 4
Working time: about 40 minutes
Total time: about 1 hour and 45 minutes

Calories **395**
Protein **17g.**
Cholesterol **15mg.**
Total fat **8g.**
Saturated fat **4g.**
Sodium **390mg.**

2 tbsp. grainy mustard
¾ lb. corn kernels, cut from 2 large ears, or ¾ lb. frozen corn kernels (about 2 cups), thawed
½ tsp. safflower oil
1 large onion, sliced into rings
2 tsp. chopped fresh basil, plus shredded basil leaves for garnish
⅛ tsp. paprika
½ small ripe pineapple, skin and core removed, chopped into small dice
1 red sweet pepper, seeded, deribbed, and cut into ½-inch dice
4 black olives, pitted and quartered
3 oz. Gouda cheese, grated (about 1 cup)
Pizza dough
1 cup whole-wheat flour
1 cup unbleached all-purpose flour
½ tsp. salt
1 tsp. dry yeast

First make the dough for the pizza crust. Place both types of flour in a bowl with the salt. In a small bowl, sprinkle the yeast over ⅔ cup of warm water. Leave the mixture in a warm place for about 10 minutes, until its surface becomes frothy. Make a well in the center of the dry ingredients and pour in the yeast liquid. Using a wooden spoon, mix the ingredients to form a soft dough. Turn the dough out onto a floured surface and knead it for five minutes. Return the dough to the bowl, cover the bowl with plastic wrap, and leave it in a warm place for about 40 minutes, until the pizza dough has doubled in size.

Punch down the dough to its original size, then roll it out on a floured surface into a circle approximately 12 inches in diameter. Place the circle on a lightly greased baking sheet or pizza tray. Brush the dough with the mustard, leaving a ½-inch border of dough around the edge. Cover the dough once more and leave it in a warm place to rise again. Meanwhile, preheat the oven to 400° F.

While the pizza dough is rising, prepare the filling. Cook the corn kernels in a pan of simmering water for three minutes, then drain them. (Frozen corn does not need cooking.) Heat the safflower oil over medium heat in a heavy-bottomed skillet. Add the onion rings and cook them until they are soft—five to six minutes. Stir in the chopped basil.

Arrange the cooked onions over the pizza crust and sprinkle them with the paprika. Mix the corn with the pineapple and scatter the mixture over the onions. Add the sweet pepper and olives, then sprinkle the cheese over the pizza.

Bake the pizza until the dough is crusty around the edges and the cheese has melted—20 to 25 minutes. Serve the whole-wheat pizza hot, garnished with the shredded basil leaves.

Pastry-Wrapped Pears Stuffed with Walnuts, Stilton, and Leeks

Serves 4
Working time: about 1 hour
Total time: about 1 hour and 30 minutes

Calories **605**
Protein **14g.**
Cholesterol **65mg.**
Total fat **17g.**
Saturated fat **7g.**
Sodium **430mg.**

5 oz. leeks, trimmed, leaves separated and washed thoroughly to remove all grit
4 firm sweet pears (about 6 oz. each)
2 tbsp. fresh lemon juice
1 oz. Stilton cheese, rind removed
1 oz. shelled walnuts (about ¼ cup), chopped
¼ cup finely chopped parsley
1 egg yolk
1 tbsp. skim milk
⅔ cup dry breadcrumbs
oakleaf lettuce leaves for garnish
8 walnut halves for garnish
Shortcrust pastry
2 cups unbleached all-purpose flour
6 tbsp. polyunsaturated margarine, chilled
1 egg white, lightly beaten

First make the pastry. Sift the flour into a mixing bowl and rub in the margarine with your fingertips until the mixture resembles fine breadcrumbs. Using a wooden spoon, mix in the egg white and 2 to 3 teaspoons of ice water to form a dough. Knead the dough briefly on a lightly floured surface until it is smooth, then wrap it in plastic wrap and chill it in the refrigerator for at least 15 minutes.

Meanwhile, blanch the leeks in a saucepan of boiling water for 20 seconds. Refresh them under cold running water and allow them to drain. Chop the leeks finely and squeeze out any remaining water in a piece of cheesecloth or a dishtowel.

Peel the pears and brush them with some of the lemon juice to prevent discoloration. Cut the pears in half, and trim away the stems and the center rib. Using a teaspoon, remove the cores and discard them. Then scoop out and reserve more flesh from each pear half until only ½-inch-thick shells remain. Chop the reserved pear flesh, sprinkle it with a little lemon juice, and let it drain. Brush the insides of the pear shells with the remaining lemon juice and let them drain also.

Crumble the cheese into a bowl, and mix in the walnuts, leeks, pear flesh, and parsley. Chill the stuffing mixture in the refrigerator until required.

Make a paper template slightly larger all around than the flat side of a pear half, then make a second template large enough to cover the convex side of a pear half, with ½ inch to tuck under all around. Roll out the dough into a large rectangle measuring about 26 by 16 inches. With the point of a sharp knife, cut out eight shapes with each template. Reroll the pastry

trimmings and cut out eight stems and eight leaves with a small knife. Arrange all the shapes on a flat tray and chill them for 10 to 15 minutes. Meanwhile, preheat the oven to 425° F.

Remove the eight small pear shapes from the refrigerator and prick them well with a fork. Place them on a baking sheet and bake them until they are crisp and lightly colored—about 10 minutes. Let them cool.

Mix the egg yolk and the milk together to make a glaze. Fill the pear shells with the stuffing mixture, dip the flat sides into the breadcrumbs, and shake off any excess. Brush the underneath edges of each small pastry pear shape with some of the glaze, then place a stuffed pear half on top, flat side down. Cover each pear with a large pastry pear shape, and tuck the edges well under. Place the pastry-wrapped pears on a baking sheet.

Brush the pastry with the glaze, and attach the stalks and leaves. Make a few diagonal slashes on each shape, just cutting through the pastry. Cover the pears with plastic wrap and chill them in the refrigerator for about 15 minutes.

Bake the pastry-wrapped pears in the oven until they are golden brown—about 25 minutes. Watch the pastry carefully during this time and cover with foil any parts likely to burn.

To serve, place two pastry-wrapped pear halves on each plate, and garnish them with the oakleaf lettuce leaves and walnut halves.

Mushroom Coulibiac

COULIBIAC IS A TRADITIONAL RUSSIAN PIE OF FLAKED
SALMON, CABBAGE, AND KASHA, BAKED IN AN EGG AND
BUTTER-RICH YEAST DOUGH. THIS VEGETARIAN VERSION USES A
LIGHTER PASTRY AND REPLACES THE CUSTOMARY HARD-BOILED
EGGS AND SOUR CREAM IN THE FILLING WITH AN ABUNDANCE
OF FRESH MUSHROOMS AND HERBS.

Serves 8
Working time: about 1 hour and 30 minutes
Total time: about 4 hours and 30 minutes (includes rising)

Calories **355**
Protein **13g.**
Cholesterol **70mg.**
Total fat **12g.**
Saturated fat **6g.**
Sodium **240mg.**

1½ lb. Savoy cabbage, shredded
1 tbsp. unsalted butter
2 small onions, finely chopped
¾ lb. mushrooms, wiped clean and sliced
6 tbsp. buckwheat groats (kasha)
1 cup unsalted vegetable stock (recipe, page 9)
1 tbsp. finely chopped parsley
1 tbsp. finely chopped fresh dill
freshly ground black pepper
¼ tsp. salt
2 oz. Brie, rind removed, finely diced
½ beaten egg, for glazing

Yeast dough

2½ cups unbleached all-purpose flour
¾ cup plus 2 tbsp. barley flour or whole-wheat flour
½ tsp. dry yeast
⅔ cup skim milk, tepid
1 egg, beaten
4 tbsp. unsalted butter, melted

First make the yeast dough. Sift the flours into a large bowl and make a well in the center. Sprinkle the yeast over the milk and set it aside until the surface becomes frothy—5 to 10 minutes. Pour the yeast liquid into the well in the flour, add the egg and butter, and mix well. Turn the dough out onto a floured surface and knead it for about 10 minutes, or until it is no longer sticky but pliable and elastic. Return the dough to the bowl, cover it with plastic wrap, and leave it in a warm place to rise until it has doubled in volume—approximately one and a half hours.

While the dough is rising, prepare the filling. Cook the cabbage in a saucepan of boiling water for five minutes. Drain it well, and squeeze out as much liquid as possible. Set the cabbage aside.

Melt the butter in a large, heavy-bottomed sauce-pan over medium heat. Add the onions, and cook them until they are soft and transparent—about three minutes. Add the mushrooms, cover the pan, and cook the vegetables gently until the mushrooms are soft —about three minutes. Remove the lid and continue cooking until all the moisture has evaporated. Then add the cabbage and stir it well to coat it in butter. Cover the pan, and cook the cabbage over very low heat until it is soft—10 to 15 minutes.

To prepare the kasha, warm the grains of buck-wheat gently in a heavy-bottomed saucepan while bringing the stock to a boil in another pan. Pour the stock over the buckwheat, stir it, then cover the pan and simmer gently for 10 minutes. Remove the pan from the heat and leave it, covered, until all the stock has been absorbed and the buckwheat grains are soft—5 to 10 minutes more. Set the buckwheat aside to cool a little.

When the dough has doubled in size, punch it down and knead it again briefly. Cut off and reserve about ½ cup of dough, then divide the remaining dough into two equal portions. Roll out one portion into a rec-tangle about 14 by 10 inches and transfer it to a lightly greased baking sheet. Using your fingertips, build up the edges a little, to make a wall to contain the filling. Spread the buckwheat evenly over the dough, leaving ½ to ¾ inch clear at the edges. Spoon the cooked vegetable mixture evenly on top of the buckwheat, then sprinkle with the parsley, dill, plenty of freshly ground black pepper, and the salt. Finally, distribute the diced cheese evenly over the filling.

Roll out the second piece of dough into a rectangle about 16 by 12 inches and place it over the filling. Trim the edges, adding the scraps to the reserved dough. Press the edges of the upper and lower rectangles of dough firmly together, twisting them a little between your fingertips to form a crimped edge. Knead the reserved dough until smooth, then divide it into six portions and roll out six long, thin strands. Plait these together to form two braids long enough to join two diagonally opposite corners. Lay the braids across the pastry, then cut a 1-inch slit in the center of each of the four triangles formed by the crossed braids. Brush the pastry with the beaten egg, and leave the coulibiac in a warm place to rise a little longer. Meanwhile, preheat the oven to 400° F.

Bake the coulibiac in the center of the oven until the pastry is golden brown—40 to 45 minutes. Protect the edges with strips of foil if they appear to be browning too rapidly. Remove the coulibiac from the oven and wrap it in a clean, dry dishtowel for 15 minutes, to soften the pastry. Transfer it to a serving platter and slice it into squares at the table.

SUGGESTED ACCOMPANIMENTS: *grated raw carrot; salad of mixed lettuce leaves.*

Broccoli and Pecorino Turnovers

Serves 8
Working time: about 1 hour
Total time: about 2 hours and 15 minutes

Calories **320**
Protein **12g.**
Cholesterol **60mg.**
Total fat **13g.**
Saturated fat **5g.**
Sodium **150mg.**

1 tsp. virgin olive oil
1 red onion, finely chopped
10 oz. purple sprouting broccoli or green broccoli, divided into florets, the stalks and leaves finely chopped
3½ oz. kale, washed, stemmed, and chopped
2 small tomatoes, peeled, seeded (technique, page 14), and finely chopped
¼ fresh hot chili pepper, seeded and finely chopped (cautionary note, page 25), or ¼ tsp. cayenne pepper
1 tbsp. pine nuts, toasted
⅓ cup part-skim ricotta cheese
6 tbsp. finely grated pecorino or Parmesan cheese
¼ tsp. salt
Lemon shortcrust pastry
3½ cups unbleached all-purpose flour
2 tbsp. virgin olive oil
2 tbsp. unsalted butter
2 eggs, beaten
½ lemon, juice only, added to enough warm water to make ½ cup

First make the pastry. Sift the flour into a mixing bowl and rub in the oil and butter with your fingertips until the mixture resembles fine breadcrumbs. Make a well in the center, and pour in three quarters of the beaten egg, together with the lemon juice and water mixture. Stir the ingredients together with a wooden spoon, then gather the dough into a ball and knead it on a lightly floured surface until it is smooth. Cover the dough with a dishtowel and let it rest in a cool place for at least an hour.

Meanwhile, prepare the filling. Heat the oil over low heat in a heavy-bottomed saucepan. Add the onion, cover the pan, and cook until the onion is soft and transparent—about five minutes. Steam the broccoli and kale together over a saucepan of rapidly boiling water until they are no longer tough but still very crisp—about five minutes. Drain well, then toss them with the onion and allow the mixture to cool a little. Stir in the tomatoes, chili or cayenne pepper, pine nuts, cheeses, and salt.

Divide the dough into two equal portions. On a floured work surface, roll out each piece of dough into a rectangle measuring approximately 36 by 9 inches. Using a round plate or a cake pan as a guide, cut out four 7- to 8-inch circles from each piece of dough.

Preheat the oven to 400° F. Place one-eighth of the filling slightly off-center on each round of dough, then fold the rounds in half over the filling. Pinch the edges of the dough together, sealing the filling inside and creating a decorative border; a little water may be used to help seal the edges. Brush each turnover lightly with a little of the remaining beaten egg and place them on a baking sheet.

Bake the turnovers until they are a light golden color—about 25 minutes. Serve them hot.

EDITOR'S NOTE: *To toast pine nuts, place them in a small, heavy-bottomed skillet over medium-high heat, and cook them, stirring constantly, until they are golden brown—one to two minutes.*

Smoked Cheese Gougère with a Lemon and Fennel Filling

Serves 6
Working time: about 40 minutes
Total time: about 1 hour and 15 minutes

Calories **240**
Protein **7g.**
Cholesterol **80mg.**
Total fat **15g.**
Saturated fat **5g.**
Sodium **260mg.**

3 fennel bulbs (about 1¼ lb.), and quartered lengthwise
2 sprigs of lemon balm (optional)
1 celery stalk, trimmed and coarsely chopped
⅛ tsp. salt
freshly ground black pepper
1 lemon, grated zest and juice
1½ tbsp. cornstarch
1 oz. walnuts (about ¼ cup), coarsely chopped
finely chopped fennel leaves, for garnish
Chou-puff dough
1 cup unbleached all-purpose flour
⅛ tsp. salt
⅛ tsp. cayenne pepper
3 tbsp. polyunsaturated margarine
2 eggs
1 egg white
1 oz. smoked cheese, grated (about ⅓ cup)

Preheat the oven to 425° F.

First make the chou-puff dough for the gougère. Sift the flour, salt, and cayenne pepper onto a sheet of wax paper. Put the margarine and 1 cup of water into a heavy-bottomed saucepan, and heat them gently until the margarine melts. Increase the heat to medium high, and bring the water and margarine to a boil. Remove the pan from the heat and slide all the dry ingredients off the paper into the liquid, beating vigorously with a wooden spoon. Return the pan to the heat and continue to beat the mixture until it forms a ball in the center of the pan. Remove the pan from the heat and allow the mixture to cool for a few minutes.

Lightly beat the eggs and egg white together. Using an electric hand-held mixer, or beating vigorously with a wooden spoon, gradually incorporate the eggs a little at a time into the cooled flour mixture, beating well after each addition. Then beat in the grated smoked cheese and continue until the mixture forms a smooth shiny paste. Pipe or spoon the chou-puff dough around the edge of a greased 11-inch quiche pan or pie pan, making small mounds of dough that just touch one another.

Bake the gougère in the oven for 10 minutes. Then lower the oven temperature to 375° F. and continue baking until the gougère is golden brown and well risen—35 to 40 minutes more.

Meanwhile, prepare the filling. Bring 2½ cups of water to a boil in a heavy-bottomed saucepan. Add the fennel, lemon balm (if using), celery, salt, and some

black pepper to the pan. Lower the heat and simmer the fennel until it is tender but still crisp—about five minutes. Drain the contents of the pan, reserving the liquid; keep the fennel and celery warm until required. Discard the lemon balm. Return the liquid to the pan, and add the lemon zest and juice. Bring the liquid to a boil and boil it rapidly until it has reduced to half its original quantity.

In a small bowl, blend the cornstarch with 3 tablespoons of water, to form a smooth paste. Add the paste to the lemon-flavored stock, and cook it, stirring frequently, until the sauce thickens—approximately two minutes more.

Place the fennel and celery in the center of the gougère, and pour the lemon sauce over the top. Scatter on the walnuts and garnish with a few finely chopped fennel leaves.

Steamed Leek and Celeriac Pudding

Serves 6
Working time: about 1 hour
Total time: about 4 hours and 45 minutes

Calories **300**
Protein **7g.**
Cholesterol **0mg.**
Total fat **15g.**
Saturated fat **5g.**
Sodium **330mg.**

1 tbsp. virgin olive oil
2 lb. leeks (about 4 medium), trimmed, washed thoroughly to remove all grit, and thinly sliced
2 garlic cloves, crushed
1 eggplant (about ½ lb.), cut into small dice
¾ lb. celeriac or potatoes, peeled and grated
2 tbsp. cornstarch
14 oz. canned tomatoes, sieved
½ tsp. salt
freshly ground black pepper

Pastry

2 cups unbleached all-purpose flour
1 tsp. baking powder
⅛ tsp. salt
2 tsp. mixed dried herbs
1 tbsp. chopped parsley
½ cup vegetable shortening

Thoroughly grease a 2-quart pudding mold or deep, heatproof bowl. Line the bottom with a small circle of nonstick parchment paper.

For the filling, heat the oil in a large, heavy skillet over medium heat. Add the leeks and cook them gently until they are soft—10 to 15 minutes. Add the garlic, eggplant, and celeriac, and continue cooking for five minutes more. Remove the pan from the heat. Blend the cornstarch with a little of the sieved tomatoes until smooth, then stir in the rest of the tomatoes. Add the tomato mixture to the cooked vegetables, together with the salt and some black pepper. Stir the mixture well, then set it aside.

To make the pastry, sift the flour, baking powder, and salt into a mixing bowl. Add the dried herbs, parsley, and shortening, mix them thoroughly, then make a well in the center of the ingredients. Add ⅔ cup of cold water and stir to form a soft dough. Knead the dough lightly on a floured surface until it is smooth.

Cut off and reserve one-third of the dough. Roll out the rest of the dough on a floured surface into a large circle about 16 inches in diameter. Carefully lift the circle of dough into the prepared pudding mold, pressing it gently into the bottom and against the sides; allow a little to overhang the rim. Fill the lined mold with the vegetable mixture. Roll out the reserved piece of dough into a circle large enough to cover the pudding. Brush the edges of the pastry in the mold with cold water, then place the lid in position. Press the edges together well to seal them.

Cover the pudding with a circle of nonstick parch-ment paper, then cover the top completely with a large piece of foil pleated in the center to allow for expansion. Pleat and press the foil tightly under the rim of the mold, to seal it.

Place the pudding in a large saucepan, then pour boiling water into the saucepan to come halfway up the side of the mold. Cover the pan with a tight-fitting lid and cook the pudding over low heat for three and a half hours, ensuring that the water in the pan maintains a steady boil. Add boiling water as required.

Remove the foil and parchment paper from the pudding, and carefully turn it out onto a large hot plate. Serve the pudding hot, cut into wedges.

SUGGESTED ACCOMPANIMENTS: *tomato sauce; new potatoes; spring cabbage.*

Asparagus Strudel

Serves 4
Working time: about 40 minutes
Total time: about 1 hour and 10 minutes

Calories **225**
Protein **10g.**
Cholesterol **60mg.**
Total fat **13g.**
Saturated fat **5g.**
Sodium **380mg.**

¾ lb. asparagus, trimmed, peeled, and sliced diagonally into ¼-inch thick pieces
½ cup part-skim ricotta cheese
2 tbsp. finely cut fresh chives
2 tbsp. chopped fresh marjoram
1 tbsp. chopped parsley
1 egg, separated
¼ tsp. salt
freshly ground black pepper
5 sheets phyllo pastry, each about 18 by 12 inches
2 tbsp. polyunsaturated margarine, melted
¼ cup fresh whole-wheat breadcrumbs

Preheat the oven to 400° F. Lightly grease a baking sheet. Place the asparagus pieces in a steamer set over a saucepan of boiling water and steam them until they are tender—four to five minutes. Refresh them under cold running water and drain them well. Pat the asparagus pieces dry on paper towels.

Put the ricotta into a mixing bowl with the chives, marjoram, parsley, egg yolk, salt, and some black pepper. Beat the ingredients together well and stir in the drained asparagus. In a clean bowl, whisk the egg white until it is stiff, then fold it carefully into the asparagus mixture.

Lay one of the sheets of phyllo pastry out flat on the work surface, with a long side toward you. Keep the other sheets covered with a clean, damp cloth to prevent them from drying out. Brush a little of the melted margarine over the sheet on the work surface and sprinkle it with one-fifth of the breadcrumbs. Lay another sheet of phyllo on top of the first; brush it with margarine and sprinkle it with crumbs in the same way. Repeat this process with the remaining three sheets of phyllo pastry.

Spoon the asparagus mixture onto the top sheet of phyllo, mounding it in a neat line about 1 inch in from the edge nearest to you, and leaving about 1 inch clear at each side.

Fold the sides of the pastry in, over the asparagus mixture, then loosely roll the pastry to enclose the filling. Place the strudel, with the seam underneath, on the greased baking sheet. Brush the remaining margarine over the top of the pastry.

Bake the strudel until it is golden brown and puffed up—25 to 30 minutes. Serve it sliced, warm or cold.

SUGGESTED ACCOMPANIMENT: *salad of curly endive and red onion rings.*

Spinach and Nappa Cabbage Pie

Serves 6
Working time: about 30 minutes
Total time: about 1 hour and 20 minutes

Calories **170**
Protein **12g.**
Cholesterol **90mg.**
Total fat **10g.**
Saturated fat **5g.**
Sodium **430mg.**

1 lb. Nappa cabbage, leaves separated and washed
1 lb. spinach, washed, stems removed
2 eggs
1 egg white
⅔ cup low-fat cottage cheese
3 tbsp. cut fresh chives
2 tbsp. chopped fresh marjoram or oregano
¼ tsp. salt
freshly ground black pepper
6 sheets phyllo pastry, each about 18 by 12 inches
3 tbsp. unsalted butter, melted

Bring a large saucepan of water to a boil, add the Nappa cabbage leaves, and cook them until they wilt—about one minute. Using a slotted spoon, lift the leaves out of the water into a colander and drain them well. Blanch the spinach leaves in the same water for 20 seconds, then pour them into a colander and refresh them under cold running water. Squeeze the spinach dry in a piece of cheesecloth. Coarsely chop the cabbage and the spinach.

Put the eggs and egg white into a large mixing bowl, and whisk them lightly together. Add the chopped cabbage and spinach, the cottage cheese, chives, marjoram or oregano, salt, and some black pepper. Mix the ingredients together well.

Preheat the oven to 375° F. Grease a 9-by-13-inch ovenproof dish.

Cut the sheets of phyllo pastry in half crosswise. Place one piece of phyllo in the bottom of the prepared dish and brush it with a little melted butter. Add another three pieces of phyllo, brushing each one lightly with melted butter. Pour the cabbage and spinach mixture into the dish, and level the surface. Cover the filling with the remaining eight pieces of phyllo pastry, brushing each piece with melted butter as before. Using a small, sharp knife, mark the top layer of phyllo with a diamond pattern.

Bake the spinach and cabbage pie until the top is golden brown—50 to 55 minutes.

SUGGESTED ACCOMPANIMENT: *mushroom salad with a yogurt and dill dressing.*

Fennel, Endive, and Blue Cheese Triangles

Serves 4
Working (and total) time: about 1 hour and 20 minutes

Calories **180**
Protein **7g.**
Cholesterol **15mg.**
Total fat **11g.**
Saturated fat **4g.**
Sodium **270mg.**

1½ tbsp. safflower oil
14 oz. fennel, stalks discarded, finely chopped
1¾ cups unsalted vegetable stock (recipe, page 9) or water
½ lb. Belgian endive, ends trimmed, thinly sliced
2 oz. Gorgonzola cheese or other blue cheese, cut into small cubes
½ tsp. salt
freshly ground black pepper
6 sheets phyllo pastry, each about 18 by 12 inches
¼ tsp. ground turmeric
1 tsp. anise-flavored liqueur
2 tbsp. plain low-fat yogurt

Heat 1 teaspoon of the oil over medium heat in a heavy-bottomed saucepan. Add slightly less than half

of the fennel and sauté it for five minutes without allowing it to brown. Add ½ cup of the stock or water, increase the heat to high, and cook until the fennel is soft and the liquid has evaporated—about two minutes more. Add the endive, stir lightly, and cook until the endive has wilted—two minutes more. Remove from the heat and allow the mixture to cool. Then add the blue cheese, season with ¼ teaspoon of the salt and some black pepper, and mix lightly.

Preheat the oven to 350° F. Cut the sheets of phyllo pastry in half lengthwise, then fold each piece in half, again lengthwise, to obtain 12 double-thickness strips measuring 18 by 3 inches. Place one strip on a dry work surface, keeping the others covered with a damp cloth to prevent them from drying out.

Brush the phyllo strip very lightly with a little of the oil and place 1 tablespoon of the fennel mixture on the bottom left-hand corner of the strip. Fold this corner of pastry and filling over to form a neat triangle, then fold the stuffed portion away from you, keeping its three-cornered shape. Continue folding—first to the left, then away from you, then to the right, and so on—until you reach the end of the strip. Tuck under the loose end of the phyllo. Fill and fold the remaining phyllo strips in the same way, then brush the bottom of each triangle with a little of the oil and place them on a baking sheet. Brush the tops of the triangles with a little more oil and set them aside.

Heat the rest of the oil—there should be about 1 teaspoon remaining—in a small, heavy-bottomed saucepan. Add the remaining fennel and sauté for two minutes, without browning it. Add the turmeric and the remaining ¼ teaspoon of salt. Pour in the anise-flavored liqueur, and cook over high heat until it has evaporated. Pour in the remaining stock or water, bring it to a boil, then lower the heat so that the liquid simmers. Cover the pan, and cook until the fennel is tender—about 15 minutes more.

Meanwhile, bake the triangles until they are crisp and golden—10 to 15 minutes. As soon as the triangles are cooked, bring the softened fennel to a boil over high heat and boil hard to reduce the liquid to about 2 tablespoons in volume. Remove the fennel from the heat and let it cool slightly before stirring in the yogurt.

Serve the fennel sauce with the triangles, allowing three triangles per serving.

SUGGESTED ACCOMPANIMENTS: *baked potatoes; baby corn.*

Bulgur-Stuffed Phyllo Packages

Serves 4
Working time: about 35 minutes
Total time: about 1 hour and 45 minutes
(includes soaking)

Calories **315**
Protein **10g.**
Cholesterol **0mg.**
Total fat **10g.**
Saturated fat **2g.**
Sodium **115mg.**

⅔ cup bulgur, soaked in 2½ cups hot water for 1 hour
6 oz. carrots (2 medium), grated
6 dried apricots, chopped
1 tbsp. currants
2 oz. unsalted cashew nuts (about ½ cup), coarsely chopped, or 2 oz. pine nuts
½ tsp. ground cumin
½ tsp. ground coriander
2 tbsp. finely chopped parsley
⅛ tsp. salt
freshly ground black pepper
5 sheets phyllo pastry, each about 18 by 12 inches
2 tsp. safflower oil

Preheat the oven to 400° F. Lightly grease a baking sheet. Drain the bulgur well, pressing out as much moisture as possible. Place the bulgur in a large bowl, and add the carrots, apricots, currants, nuts, cumin, coriander, parsley, salt, and some black pepper. Mix all the ingredients together thoroughly.

Lay one sheet of phyllo pastry out on a work surface; keep the other sheets covered by a clean, damp cloth while you work, to prevent them from drying out. Brush a little oil over the sheet on the work surface. Place a quarter of the bulgur mixture near one end of the sheet, halfway between the two longer sides, and flatten it down gently. Fold the shorter edge of the pastry over the filling, fold in the two longer side edges, then roll the stuffed section up to the other end, to form a package. Place the package on the baking sheet, with the seam underneath. Roll up another three phyllo packages in the same way.

Cut the fifth sheet of phyllo into strips. Crumple the strips loosely in your hand and use them to decorate the tops of the packages. Brush the remaining safflower oil or a little skim milk over the phyllo packages, and bake them in the oven until they are golden brown—20 to 25 minutes.

SUGGESTED ACCOMPANIMENT: *mixed bean salad with a vinaigrette dressing.*

Mushrooms and Asparagus in Phyllo Cases

Serves 6
Working (and total) time: about 1 hour

Calories **105**
Protein **5g.**
Cholesterol **0mg.**
Total fat **4g.**
Saturated fat **1g.**
Sodium **90mg.**

4 tsp. safflower oil
6 sheets phyllo pastry, each about 18 by 12 inches
½ lb. asparagus, trimmed and peeled
4 large scallions, trimmed and sliced
1 garlic clove, crushed
¾ lb. mushrooms, wiped clean and sliced
1 cup skim milk
2 tsp. cornstarch
2 large carrots, julienned, parboiled for 5 minutes, and drained
1 tbsp. chopped fresh tarragon
1 tsp. fresh lemon juice
freshly ground black pepper
fresh tarragon sprigs for garnish (optional)

Preheat the oven to 375° F. Brush the bottoms of six ½-cup ramekins or muffin cups with 2 teaspoons of the safflower oil.

Fold each sheet of phyllo pastry in half lengthwise, then in thirds crosswise, to make six 6-inch squares. Trim the three folded edges of each pile of squares, to yield six stacks of pastry, each containing six squares. Take each stack of squares and rearrange the pieces of pastry so that the corners are offset, to resemble the petals of a flower. Place a stack of squares in each ramekin, pressing them into the contours of the dish. Bake the pastry-lined ramekins in the oven until the cases are evenly browned—15 to 20 minutes. Take care not to let the edges burn.

Meanwhile, make the filling. Steam the asparagus in a steamer basket over a saucepan of gently simmering water until it is tender but still crisp—about four minutes. Cut off and reserve twelve 2-inch-long tips for garnish. Coarsely chop the remaining asparagus.

Heat the remaining 2 teaspoons of oil in a small, heavy-bottomed pan, and add the scallions, garlic, and mushrooms. Cook them over medium heat, stirring frequently, until the mushrooms are soft and begin to exude their juices—about three minutes. Add the milk and bring the mixture to a boil. In a small bowl, blend the cornstarch to a smooth paste with 2 tablespoons of water. Add the cornstarch paste to the sauce and bring it back to a boil to thicken it, stirring constantly. Gently mix in the chopped asparagus, carrots, tarragon, lemon juice, and some freshly ground black pepper. Simmer the sauce for one minute, to heat all the ingredients through.

Carefully remove the phyllo cases from the ramekins and place each one on a warmed serving plate. Spoon the vegetable mixture into and around the cases, and garnish each one with two of the reserved asparagus tips and with a sprig of tarragon, if you are using it.

SUGGESTED ACCOMPANIMENTS: *baked tomatoes; new potatoes.*

Baguette and Brie Bake

Serves 4
Working time: about 10 minutes
Total time: about 40 minutes

Calories **220**	3½ oz. Brie or Camembert cheese, chilled
Protein **14g.**	1 small baguette (about 6 oz.)
Cholesterol **80mg.**	1 egg
Total fat **8g.**	2 egg whites
Saturated fat **1g.**	1 scant cup low-fat milk
Sodium **460mg.**	freshly ground black pepper

Preheat the oven to 350° F. Lightly grease a large, shallow ovenproof dish.

Using a sharp knife, slice the cheese lengthwise into ¼-inch-thick slices, then cut each slice into pieces about 1¼ inches wide, to yield 16 small slices. Cut the baguette into sixteen ½-inch slices, and fit the slices of bread and cheese alternately into the prepared dish. Beat the egg and egg whites in a bowl, add the milk and some black pepper, and carefully pour the mixture over the bread and cheese, ensuring that all the bread is thoroughly soaked.

Bake the assembly in the oven until the surface is golden brown and crisp and the custard is just firm in the center—about 30 minutes. Serve at once.

SUGGESTED ACCOMPANIMENTS: *salad of mixed lettuce leaves; tomato, cucumber, and onion salad.*

Salsify and Asparagus Muffins

Serves 4
Working (and total) time: about 30 minutes

Calories **240**
Protein **20g.**
Cholesterol **20mg.**
Total fat **7g.**
Saturated fat **4g.**
Sodium **520mg.**

4 salsify (about ½ lb.), scrubbed well, ends removed
12 asparagus spears, trimmed and peeled
4 whole-wheat English muffins, halved horizontally
4 tsp. plain low-fat yogurt
freshly ground black pepper
1 tbsp. finely chopped mixed fresh herbs, such as tarragon, chervil, dill, parsley
¼ lb. part-skim mozzarella cheese, thinly sliced
1 tsp. paprika
2 tsp. finely cut chives

Cook the salsify in a saucepan of lightly boiling water, covered, until it is tender when pierced with a sharp knife—10 to 15 minutes. Drain the salsify, and using the back of a knife, scrape each root gently under cold running water until all the skin has been removed. Cut each root into three equal pieces.

Meanwhile, steam the asparagus spears in a steamer basket over a saucepan of gently simmering water until they are tender but still crisp—10 to 15 minutes. Remove the asparagus spears from the steamer and dry them on paper towels.

Preheat the broiler and toast the muffins on their uncut sides. Spread the untoasted sides of the warm muffins with the yogurt, and season them with some black pepper and the chopped mixed fresh herbs. Put three asparagus spears on each of four of the halves, and three pieces of salsify on each of the other four halves. Lay the mozzarella slices on top of the vegetables. Place the muffins under the broiler until the mozzarella has melted and is beginning to bubble and slightly brown—three to five minutes. Garnish the salsify muffins with the paprika and the asparagus muffins with the chives. Serve at once.

SUGGESTED ACCOMPANIMENTS: *salad of mixed greens with a vinaigrette dressing; grilled tomatoes.*

Italian Peasant Salad

THIS ADAPTATION OF A TUSCAN PEASANT DISH USES TWO
TYPES OF BREAD: RYE AND WHOLE-WHEAT.

Serves 4
Working time: about 30 minutes
Total time: about 2 hours and 30 minutes
(includes chilling)

Calories **245**
Protein **10g.**
Cholesterol **0mg.**
Total fat **10g.**
Saturated fat **1g.**
Sodium **355mg.**

¼ lb. slightly stale whole-wheat bread (4 to 5 slices), crusts removed
¼ lb. slightly stale black rye or pumpernickel bread (4 to 5 slices), crusts removed
2 medium ripe tomatoes, peeled, seeded (technique, page 14), and diced, seeds and juice reserved
canned or bottled tomato juice
4 small black olives, pitted and finely chopped
½ medium cucumber, cut into 1-inch-long bâtonnets
4 small green olives, pitted and finely chopped
6 large basil leaves, shredded
6 large arugula leaves, shredded, or 16 watercress leaves, shredded
1 tbsp. chopped fresh chervil leaves
1 tbsp. finely chopped fresh tarragon
1 tbsp. finely chopped parsley
2 tbsp. virgin olive oil
2 tbsp. white wine
3 tbsp. red wine
freshly ground black pepper
basil sprigs for garnish

Grate or process the bread to make breadcrumbs, keeping the two types separate. Place the dark and light crumbs in separate mixing bowls. Sieve the reserved seeds and juice from the tomatoes. This should yield about ½ cup of juice; if necessary, make up the quantity with canned or bottled tomato juice. Divide the juice equally between the two bowls of breadcrumbs and mix well.

Add the diced tomatoes and black olives to the whole-wheat breadcrumbs; add the cucumber bâtonnets and green olives to the rye or pumpernickle breadcrumbs. Divide the basil, arugula or watercress, chervil, tarragon, and parsley equally between the two bowls. Pour 1 tablespoon of olive oil into each bowl and mix the ingredients well. Finally, add as much of the wine as the mixture in each bowl will readily absorb, using the white wine with the whole-wheat breadcrumbs and the red wine with the rye breadcrumbs. The rye breadcrumbs will probably absorb more wine than the whole-wheat, and they may require a little additional wine to make a pleasantly moist mixture. Season each bowl with some black pepper. Cover the bowls with damp cloths to prevent the salads from drying out, and place them in the refrigerator for two hours, to allow the flavors to infuse.

Serve the bread salads cool or chilled, garnished with basil sprigs.

SUGGESTED ACCOMPANIMENTS: *Belgian endive; radicchio leaves.*

Bread, Cheese, and Onion Pudding

Serves 8
Working time: about 40 minutes
Total time: about 2 hours and 30 minutes

Calories **300**
Protein **12g.**
Cholesterol **60mg.**
Total fat **14g.**
Saturated fat **4g.**
Sodium **485mg.**

5 tbsp. polyunsaturated margarine
2 large onions, thinly sliced
1 lb. zucchini, julienned
2 tsp. Dijon mustard
2 garlic cloves, crushed
24 thin slices white bread, crusts removed
2 eggs
2 egg whites
2½ cups skim milk
freshly ground black pepper
¾ cup grated Cheddar cheese

Heat 1 tablespoon of the margarine in a large, nonstick skillet over medium heat. Add the sliced onions and cook them until they are soft but not brown—about five minutes. Add the zucchini and cook the vegetables for another six minutes, stirring occasionally. Remove the pan from the heat and allow the onions and zucchini to cool for 15 minutes.

Meanwhile, blend the remaining 4 tablespoons of margarine in a small bowl with the mustard and garlic until smooth. Spread the mixture thinly over the sliced bread. Cut each slice into four triangles.

Put the eggs, egg whites, and milk into a mixing bowl, add some black pepper, and whisk them together lightly.

Grease a 12-by-9-inch ovenproof dish. Layer one-third of the bread triangles in the bottom of the dish, and spread half of the onion and zucchini mixture over the top. Sprinkle with one-third of the grated Cheddar cheese. Add another third of the bread, the rest of the onion and zucchini mixture, and another third of the Cheddar cheese. Arrange the remaining triangles of bread decoratively on the top, overlapping them slightly. Pour the whisked eggs and milk over the bread. Scatter the last third of Cheddar cheese evenly over the top of the assembly. Allow the pudding to stand in a cool place for one hour, to allow the bread to soften and soak up the eggs and milk.

Twenty minutes before cooking the pudding, preheat the oven to 375° F.

Cook the pudding until it is well puffed up, set, and golden brown—45 to 50 minutes. Serve the bread pudding immediately.

SUGGESTED ACCOMPANIMENT: *red-cabbage salad.*

Fennel, Broccoli, and Okra Croustades

Serves 4
Working time: about 40 minutes
Total time: about 1 hour

Calories **270**
Protein **15g.**
Cholesterol **10mg.**
Total fat **11g.**
Saturated fat **4g.**
Sodium **465mg.**

1 loaf unsliced, whole-wheat sandwich bread (minimum 9 inches long)
1 tsp. safflower oil
1 fennel bulb (about ½ lb.) trimmed and chopped
½ lb. broccoli florets (3 to 4 cups)
1½ tbsp. unsalted butter
4 scallions, trimmed and sliced diagonally
2 oz. okra, trimmed and thinly sliced
⅔ cup plain low-fat yogurt
¼ tsp. salt
⅛ tsp. ground allspice
freshly ground black pepper
¼ cup pine nuts, toasted

Prepare four croustade cases from the loaf of whole-wheat bread, brush them with the oil, and bake them *(technique, below)*. While the croustades are baking, prepare the filling.

Place the fennel in a saucepan with water to cover and cook it until it is just tender—two to three minutes. Add the broccoli florets and cook them until they, too, are just tender—two to three minutes more. Drain the vegetables and keep them warm.

Melt the butter in a heavy-bottomed saucepan, and add the scallions and okra. Cook them over medium-low heat until the okra begins to soften and looks slightly sticky—four to five minutes. Add the yogurt, salt, allspice, and some black pepper, and bring the mixture to a boil. Lower the heat and simmer gently until the liquid has thickened a little—two to three minutes. Add the fennel, broccoli, and most of the pine nuts, and heat them through.

Divide the mixture among the croustades, piling it up well in the center. Sprinkle with the remaining pine nuts and serve the croustades immediately.

SUGGESTED ACCOMPANIMENT: *tomato salad.*

EDITOR'S NOTE: *To toast pine nuts, place them in a small, heavy-bottomed skillet over medium-high heat, and cook them, stirring constantly, until they are golden brown and release their aroma—one to two minutes.*

Making Croustades

1 CUTTING THE CASES. Trim the crust. If the bread is soft, put it in the freezer for a few minutes. Cut the bread into 2-inch-thick slices. Using a sharp knife, cut a square in the top of each slice, ¼ inch from each edge; cut to within ¼ inch of the base.

2 LOOSENING THE CENTERS. Insert the knife horizontally ¼ inch above the base of one corner; the knife point should penetrate beyond the square's center. Swivel the knife, withdraw it, then insert it in the diagonally opposite corner, and swivel it to loosen the center.

3 HOLLOWING OUT THE CASES. Use the tip of the knife to lift out the center section of each square. Turn the cases upside down and gently shake out any remaining crumbs. Place the cases on a lightly greased baking sheet.

4 BAKING THE CASES. Put the oil into a bowl. With a pastry brush, apply a thin coat of oil to the surfaces of the bread cases. Bake the cases in a preheated 325° F. oven until crisp and golden—about 40 minutes—turning occasionally so they color evenly.

4 *Red pepper strips and watercress sprigs adorn this reinterpretation of a vegetarian classic—cauliflower cheese (recipe, opposite).*

Microwaving Vegetarian Dishes

A microwave oven offers far more than just a quick and clean alternative to conventional cooking. Meatless meals prepared in a microwave retain all their colors and fresh flavors. More important, few valuable vitamins and minerals are lost in the process, since vegetables cook in their own juices, or at most in a few spoonfuls of added liquid. And because cooking times are generally so short, heat-sensitive vitamins are less likely to be destroyed by microwaving than by traditional techniques. Microwave ovens are ideal for low-fat cooking, too; very little oil is required for the preparation of most vegetarian dishes.

The recipes in this chapter suggest the enticing variety of vegetarian meals a microwave oven can produce. These range in style from a hearty, layered casserole of Jerusalem artichokes and potatoes *(page 126)* to a sophisticated presentation of stuffed grape leaves, bulgur, and warm tomato salad *(page 128)*—a complete meal that takes only about 30 minutes to prepare. Several of the recipes are inspired by far-flung traditional cuisines not normally associated with the advanced technology of microwave cooking. Sweet-and-Sour Tumbled Vegetables *(page 133)*, for example, re-creates the crisp and varied textures of a Chinese stir-fry—but without the stirring.

A few simple techniques help ensure successful results in these and other microwave recipes. When covering a container with plastic wrap, make sure that steam can escape by folding back one corner. Use only wrap that is recommended for microwave cooking; the plasticizer present in ordinary plastic wrap may melt and drip into the food. Stirring the ingredients from time to time and rotating the container encourages even cooking, although if your oven has a turntable, turning the dish is unnecessary. And because food continues to cook after the oven has been switched off, observe any "standing time" called for by a recipe. Rather than risk overdone food, it is advisable to use the shortest cooking time specified in a recipe. If a dish is not entirely cooked after standing, it can be returned to the oven.

All the recipes featured in this section have been tested in 650-watt and 700-watt microwave ovens. Although power settings may vary among different ovens, the recipes use "high" to indicate 100 percent power, "medium" for 50 percent power, and "low" for 10 percent power.

Cauliflower Cheese Mold

Serves 6
Working (and total) time: about 50 minutes

Calories **185**
Protein **11g.**
Cholesterol **100mg.**
Total fat **11g.**
Saturated fat **6g.**
Sodium **270mg.**

2 lb. cauliflower florets
3 tbsp. unsalted butter
6 tbsp. unbleached all-purpose flour
1¼ cups skim milk
½ cup freshly grated Parmesan cheese
2 eggs, beaten
½ tsp. salt
freshly ground black pepper
¼ tsp. freshly grated nutmeg or ground nutmeg
strips of peeled sweet red pepper for garnish
watercress sprigs for garnish

Put the cauliflower florets into a very large bowl, add 6 tablespoons of cold water, then cover the bowl with plastic wrap, pulling it back at one corner. Cook on high, stirring every five minutes, until the cauliflower is cooked but still slightly firm—15 to 20 minutes. Meanwhile, grease an 8-inch round dish. Line the bottom with greased nonstick parchment paper.

Drain any excess water from the cauliflower florets, then process them briefly in a food processor until they are finely broken up but not puréed. Set them aside.

Put the butter into a large bowl and microwave it on high until it melts—about 30 seconds. Mix in the flour, then gradually stir in the milk. Cook on high, stirring every minute with a wire whisk, until the mixture is thick—about four minutes. Remove the mixture from the microwave, and beat in the Parmesan, eggs, salt, some black pepper, nutmeg, and the cauliflower.

Carefully spoon the cauliflower mixture into the prepared dish and level the surface. Cover the dish with plastic wrap, leaving a corner open. Cook on high, giving the dish a quarter turn every three minutes, until the mixture is set—12 to 15 minutes.

Remove the cauliflower mold from the oven and allow it to stand for five minutes, then carefully turn it out onto a flat serving dish. Garnish it with pepper strips and watercress sprigs. Serve it cut into wedges.

SUGGESTED ACCOMPANIMENTS: *new potatoes; mixed salad.*

EDITOR'S NOTE: *To peel a sweet red pepper using the microwave, prick the pepper several times with a fork or skewer, and place it on a double layer of paper towels in the oven. Microwave on high until it is soft, turning once—about five minutes. Transfer the pepper to a bowl and cover it with plastic wrap. Let it stand for 5 to 10 minutes, then peel it. Alternatively, follow the instructions on page 21.*

Zucchini and Tomato Clafoutis

CLAFOUTIS, TRADITIONALLY BLACK CHERRIES BAKED IN A SWEET PANCAKE BATTER, IS A SPECIALTY OF THE LIMOUSIN DISTRICT OF FRANCE. IN THIS SAVORY ADAPTATION, VEGETABLES AND HERBS REPLACE THE FRUIT.

Serves 4
Working (and total) time: about 45 minutes

Calories **120**
Protein **9g.**
Cholesterol **110mg.**
Total fat **4g.**
Saturated fat **1g.**
Sodium **270mg.**

2 eggs
¼ cup whole-wheat flour
¼ cup unbleached all-purpose flour
2 tbsp. wheat germ
1¼ cups skim milk
½ tsp. salt
½ lb. cherry tomatoes, pierced with a fine skewer
½ lb. zucchini, sliced into ½-inch rounds
2 sprigs fresh thyme, leaves only, chopped if large
8 large basil leaves, torn into strips
½ tsp. canned or bottled green peppercorns, drained and rinsed
freshly ground green pepper (optional)

In a bowl, combine the eggs with the whole-wheat and all-purpose flours and 1 tablespoon of the wheat germ, and whisk in the milk and salt. Set the batter aside to rest for 20 to 30 minutes.

Brush the bottom and sides of a 10-inch round, shallow microwave dish with a little olive oil, and sprinkle it evenly with the remaining wheat germ. Arrange the tomatoes and zucchini in the dish.

Stir the batter well, then stir in the herbs and peppercorns, and pour the mixture over the vegetables. Cover the dish with plastic wrap, leaving one corner open. Microwave the dish on medium, stirring the contents from time to time, until the edges of the batter begin to set—three to five minutes. Then microwave it for 10 minutes more, giving the dish a quarter turn every three minutes. Remove the plastic wrap, place a layer of absorbent paper towels lightly over the surface of the *clafoutis,* and cover it with a fresh piece of plastic wrap. Allow the *clafoutis* to stand, covered, for three minutes.

The *clafoutis* should now be set in the center. If not, microwave it for two to three minutes more on medium, and allow it to rest for two minutes more.

Serve the *clafoutis* warm, cut into wedges. Grind a little green pepper over each portion, if you like.

SUGGESTED ACCOMPANIMENTS: *sourdough rye bread; lamb's lettuce.*

Mixed Vegetable Pipérade

PIPÉRADE, A SPECIALTY OF THE BASQUE COUNTRY, IS A SAVORY DISH OF VEGETABLES AND SCRAMBLED EGGS. HERE, BROCCOLI AND POTATO ARE INCLUDED IN ADDITION TO THE TRADITIONAL SWEET PEPPERS.

Serves 4
Working (and total) time: about 20 minutes

Calories **120**
Protein **5g.**
Cholesterol **110mg.**
Total fat **7g.**
Saturated fat **1g.**
Sodium **250mg.**

1 tbsp. virgin olive oil
1 garlic clove, halved
¼ tsp. cayenne pepper
¼ lb. potatoes, cut into ½-inch cubes
¼ lb. broccoli, cut into small florets, stems peeled and finely sliced (about 1½ cups)
1 sweet yellow pepper, seeded, deribbed, and cut into 1-inch squares
1 sweet red pepper, seeded, deribbed, and cut into 1-inch squares
½ tsp. cornstarch, mixed with 1 tsp. cold water
½ tsp. salt
2 eggs, beaten
hot red-pepper flakes, crushed (optional)

Place the oil and garlic in a wide, shallow dish. Microwave them on medium until the oil is hot and infused with garlic—about one and a half minutes. Discard the garlic and sprinkle the cayenne into the oil.

Add the potato cubes, stir to coat them in the oil and spice mixture, then cook them on high, covered with plastic wrap pulled back at one corner, for one minute.

Stir the potato cubes again, add the broccoli and the yellow and red peppers, cover the dish as before, and microwave it on high for five minutes. Stir twice during this time, replacing the plastic wrap each time. After cooking, stir the vegetables once more and allow them to rest for two minutes; covered.

Stir the cornstarch mixture and the salt into the eggs, and pour the egg mixture over the vegetables. Stir the contents of the dish, then microwave on medium for three minutes. Keep the dish covered during cooking as before, but stir the contents after every minute. The egg mixture and juices should be almost set at the end of this stage.

Remove the dish from the oven and let it rest, covered, for one minute more. Serve the pipérade sprinkled with red-pepper flakes, if you are using them.

SUGGESTED ACCOMPANIMENT: *warm poppy-seed rolls.*

Jerusalem Artichoke Gratin

Serves 4
Working (and total) time: about 30 minutes

Calories **200**
Protein **9g.**
Cholesterol **20mg.**
Total fat **5g.**
Saturated fat **3g.**
Sodium **410mg.**

1 lb. new potatoes, scrubbed
1 lb. firm Jerusalem artichokes, scrubbed
1 tbsp. fresh lemon juice
1 tbsp. cornstarch
2 tbsp. dry white wine
½ to 1 tbsp. Dijon mustard
2 tbsp. sour cream
2 tbsp. plain low-fat yogurt
½ tsp. salt
2 medium tomatoes, sliced, slices halved
freshly ground black pepper (optional)
freshly grated nutmeg or ground nutmeg
½ cup finely grated Gruyère cheese
1 tbsp. finely chopped parsley

Halve the potatoes and place them in a shallow dish with 3 tablespoons of cold water. Cover them with plastic wrap, leaving a corner open, and microwave them on high for eight minutes, stirring once or twice during this time. Let the potatoes rest, covered, for two minutes more, then immediately drain and peel them, and slice them into thin rounds.

Halve the artichokes, or quarter them if they are large, then place them in a shallow dish with the lemon juice and 2 tablespoons of cold water. Cover them with plastic wrap, leaving a corner open, and cook the artichokes on high for about six minutes, stirring three or four times during cooking. Let the artichokes rest, covered, for two minutes, then immediately drain and peel them, and slice them into rounds a little thicker than the potatoes. (Any artichokes that are too soft to slice can be placed under slices, or piled into the center, when you assemble the gratin.)

In a bowl, mix together the cornstarch and white wine, then stir in the mustard, sour cream, yogurt, and ¼ teaspoon of the salt. Place the bowl in the microwave and cook on low, stirring every 30 seconds, until the sauce thickens—about one and a half minutes. Remove the bowl from the oven, whisk the sauce vigorously, and set it aside.

In a 9-inch round gratin dish, arrange concentric rings of slices of potato, artichoke, and tomato, then arrange a few more artichoke slices in the center. Sprinkle the tomato with the remaining ¼ teaspoon of salt, and with some black pepper, if desired. Pour the mustard sauce over the artichokes and sprinkle with some nutmeg. Scatter the cheese over the potato slices, and the parsley over the top of the gratin.

Loosely cover the dish, then microwave the gratin on high, turning the dish once or twice, until it is hot in the center—7 to 10 minutes. Let it rest for two to three minutes before serving.

SUGGESTED ACCOMPANIMENT: *crisp green salad with a few toasted, sliced almonds, or steamed broccoli.*

Salad-Filled Potato Pie

Serves 6
Working time: about 30 minutes
Total time: about 40 minutes

Calories **190**	2 lb. large potatoes, scrubbed
Protein **5g.**	1 tbsp. cornstarch
Cholesterol **45mg.**	2 tbsp. skim milk
Total fat **4g.**	1 egg
Saturated fat **1g.**	2 tbsp. plain low-fat yogurt
Sodium **230mg.**	2 tbsp. sour cream
	2 tbsp. finely chopped fresh dill
	¾ tsp. salt
	freshly grated nutmeg or ground nutmeg
	1 tsp. safflower oil
	1 cup loosely packed watercress leaves, coarsely chopped
	¼ lb. cucumber, peeled and cut into 1-inch-long bâtonnets
	2 medium tomatoes, peeled, seeded, and chopped
	freshly ground black pepper
	½ tsp. paprika

Pierce each of the potatoes with a skewer and arrange them in a circle on a double layer of paper towels in the microwave. Microwave them on high, rotating the paper every three minutes, until the potatoes are cooked through—12 to 15 minutes. Allow the potatoes to rest for about three minutes more, then peel and mash them.

In a bowl, blend the cornstarch with the milk, then beat in the egg, yogurt, sour cream, dill, ½ teaspoon of the salt, and some nutmeg. Beat this mixture into the mashed potatoes.

Brush an 11-by-7-inch baking dish with the safflower oil. Spread half of the potato mixture over the bottom and sides of the dish. Scatter the watercress over the potato to within ½ inch of the sides. Arrange the cucumber and the chopped tomatoes on top of the watercress. Sprinkle the filling with the remaining ¼ teaspoon of salt and a generous amount of freshly ground black pepper.

Carefully spread the remaining potato mixture over the filling to enclose it completely. Score the surface with a fork and sprinkle the paprika evenly over the top of the potato pie.

Cover the dish with plastic wrap, leaving two opposite corners open. Microwave the pie on high, giving the dish a quarter turn every two minutes, until it is heated through—7 to 10 minutes. Remove the pie from the oven and allow it to rest for three minutes more. Serve the pie cut into squares.

SUGGESTED ACCOMPANIMENT: *salad of curly endive, red-leaf lettuce, and cherry tomatoes, with a yogurt and mustard dressing.*

EDITOR'S NOTE: *To peel tomatoes using the microwave, pierce the skin once or twice, then microwave the tomatoes on high until the skin starts to peel away—about 45 seconds. Alternatively, follow the instructions on page 14.*

Stuffed Grape Leaves with Bulgur and Tomatoes

Serves 4
Working (and total) time: about 30 minutes

Calories **290**	1 cup bulgur, rinsed and drained
Protein **15g.**	2 cups unsalted vegetable stock (recipe, page 9)
Cholesterol **25mg.**	12 grape leaves, fresh or canned, stems removed
Total fat **7g.**	1 tsp. cumin seeds
Saturated fat **1g.**	2 tbsp. finely chopped fresh mint
Sodium **350mg.**	½ tsp. ground cinnamon
	2½ oz. feta cheese, cubed and rinsed
	½ cup fresh breadcrumbs
	⅓ cup plain low-fat yogurt
	½ to 1 tbsp. lemon juice
	½ tsp. virgin olive oil
	2 large tomatoes, sliced
	12 large basil leaves, torn
	freshly ground black pepper

Place the bulgur in a 1-quart bowl. Bring the stock to a boil and pour it over the bulgur. Stir the bulgur, cover it with plastic wrap, and set it aside while you prepare the grape leaves.

Rinse the leaves and place them in a bowl; if you are using canned leaves, rinse them very thoroughly. Cover the leaves with a generous quantity of boiling water, cover the bowl with plastic wrap, leaving a corner open, and microwave the leaves on high for five minutes to soften them. Drain them in a colander, refresh them under cold running water, and spread them out on paper towels or a dishtowel to dry.

Place the cumin seeds in a small dish, cover them, and microwave them on high until they are warm and aromatic—about two minutes.

Set the bowl containing the bulgur in the microwave oven, pull back a corner of the plastic wrap, and microwave the bulgur on high for five minutes. Stir in the mint and cinnamon, cover the bowl completely, and set it aside until the rest of the meal is ready to serve, by which time all the stock will have been absorbed.

Mash the cheese with a fork, and blend it with the breadcrumbs, yogurt, lemon juice, and cumin seeds. Place a grape leaf, veined side up, on the work surface. Place a heaped teaspoon of the cheese mixture above the base of the leaf, fold the stalk end over the stuffing, then fold both long edges over to enclose the stuffing completely. Gently roll the mound of stuffing toward the leaf tip, tucking in the edges if they loosen, to form a compact roll. Stuff the remaining grape leaves in the same manner.

Arrange the stuffed leaves in a round dish to resemble the spokes of a wheel. Brush the leaves with the olive oil, cover the dish with plastic wrap, again leaving one corner open, and microwave it on high until the stuffed leaves are heated through—three to four minutes; rotate the dish once or twice during this time. Remove the stuffed grape leaves from the oven and let them rest in their dish for two minutes while you warm the tomatoes.

Arrange the tomatoes evenly over the bottom of a wide, shallow dish, overlapping the slices slightly if necessary. Sprinkle them with the torn basil leaves and some black pepper, cover the dish loosely, and heat the tomatoes on high until they are hot and aromatic—about two minutes.

Fluff up the bulgur with a fork, and arrange it on four warmed individual plates, together with three stuffed grape leaves per serving and a portion of the hot tomato salad.

Warm Camembert and Fruit Salad

Serves 4
Working (and total) time: about 20 minutes

Calories **150**
Protein **5g.**
Cholesterol **10mg.**
Total fat **12g.**
Saturated fat **12g.**
Sodium **380mg.**

2 oz. Camembert, rind removed, cut into 12 cubes
1 tsp. crushed mixed white, black, green, and pink peppercorns
3½ oz. broccoli, cut into tiny florets, the stalks peeled and finely sliced
½ tbsp. sesame oil
½ tbsp. safflower oil
1 garlic clove, lightly crushed
1-inch piece fresh ginger, sliced
1 large ripe peach, peeled, halved, pitted, and sliced, slices halved if too large
½ avocado, (about 2½ oz.), pitted, flesh cut into cubes
1 tbsp. balsamic vinegar, or 2½ tsp. of red wine vinegar mixed with ¼ tsp. of honey
½ tsp. salt
2 oz. radicchio leaves, washed and dried, torn into pieces
mixed lettuce leaves, washed and dried

Roll the cubes of Camembert in the peppercorns, and chill them in the refrigerator while preparing the other salad ingredients.

Place the broccoli in a bowl with 2 tablespoons of cold water, cover it with plastic wrap, leaving a corner open, and microwave it on high until the broccoli is no longer tough but still very crunchy—one and a half to two minutes. Drain the broccoli, return it to the container, and set it aside, covered.

Put the oils in a dish with the garlic and ginger, and cook them on medium for two to three minutes, stirring once or twice during this time. Remove the garlic and ginger with a slotted spoon, and discard them. Place the peach slices in the dish with the flavored oil. Cover the dish as before and microwave it on high for one minute. Stir the peach slices, add the avocado, cover the dish again, and cook on high for one minute. Then add the vinegar, salt, and broccoli. Cover the dish, and microwave on high for one minute more. Finally, toss the radicchio in the dish, stir the ingredients well, cover the dish, and set it aside.

Arrange the lettuce leaves around the edge of a large serving platter or on four individual plates. Arrange the Camembert cubes, evenly spaced, on a plate and microwave them on medium until they are just warm—about 20 seconds. Quickly arrange the warm salad in the center of the lettuce and scatter the Camembert on top. Serve at once.

SUGGESTED ACCOMPANIMENT: *white and whole-wheat bread.*

EDITOR'S NOTE: *A nectarine may be substituted for the peach; there is no need to peel a nectarine before use.*

Potato, Carrot, and Cauliflower Curry

Serves 6
Working time: about 30 minutes
Total time: about 1 hour

Calories **230**
Protein **6g.**
Cholesterol **0mg.**
Total fat **11g.**
Saturated fat **5g.**
Sodium **230mg.**

2 tbsp. virgin olive oil
2 onions, finely chopped
2-inch piece fresh ginger, peeled and grated
3 garlic cloves, crushed
2 fresh hot green chili peppers, seeded and finely chopped (cautionary note, page 25)
2 tsp. paprika
½ tsp. ground turmeric
1 tsp. ground cumin
2 cups unsalted vegetable stock (recipe, page 9)
1 lb. potatoes, cut into ½-inch dice
½ lb. carrots (2 to 3 medium), cut into ½-inch dice
½ lb. cauliflower florets (about 3 cups)
6 oz. French beans or green beans, trimmed and cut into 1-inch lengths (about 1½ cups)
6 oz. fresh or frozen peas (about 1½ cups)
1 cup unsweetened shredded coconut, puréed with ½ cup water
1 tbsp. cornstarch, blended with 3 tbsp. cold water
½ tsp. salt
freshly ground black pepper

Put the olive oil and onions into a large bowl. Leave the bowl uncovered, and microwave them on high, stirring halfway through the cooking time, until the onions are soft—five to six minutes. Stir in the ginger, garlic, chilies, paprika, turmeric, and cumin, and cook them on high, uncovered, for two minutes. Add the stock, potatoes, carrots, and cauliflower, and stir them well, then cover the bowl with plastic wrap, pulling back one corner to allow steam to escape. Cook the vegetables on high for 20 minutes, stirring every five minutes. Then stir in the beans and fresh peas, if you are using them, and cook, covered as before, until the vegetables are tender—about 10 minutes more.

Stir the coconut and cornstarch mixtures into the vegetables, along with the frozen peas, if you are using them, and cook the curry, uncovered, on high for five minutes, stirring halfway through. Season the curry with the salt and some black pepper. Allow the curry to stand for five minutes before serving.

SUGGESTED ACCOMPANIMENTS: *pasta tossed in chopped parsley; lemon wedges; thinly sliced onion rings.*

Spiced Bean Medley

BEANS COOKED IN THE MICROWAVE TAKE ALMOST AS LONG AS WHEN COOKED CONVENTIONALLY, BUT THEY HAVE THE ADVANTAGE OF NOT BECOMING MUSHY, HOWEVER LONG THEY COOK.

Serves 6
Working time: about 20 minutes
Total time: about 2 hours and 30 minutes
(includes soaking)

Calories **200**
Protein **12g.**
Cholesterol **0mg.**
Total fat **4g.**
Saturated fat **0g.**
Sodium **25mg.**

⅔ cup dried red kidney beans, picked over
½ cup dried pinto beans, picked over
⅓ cup dried black beans, picked over
3 tbsp. dried adzuki beans (optional), picked over
1 tbsp. safflower oil
2 garlic cloves, sliced
1 onion, diced
1 small fresh red chili pepper, seeded and finely chopped (cautionary note, page 25)
1 small fresh green chili pepper, seeded and finely chopped (cautionary note, page 25)
1 sweet red pepper, seeded, deribbed, and cut into strips
⅛ tsp. salt
3 medium tomatoes, peeled, seeded, and chopped

Put all the beans into a large casserole, pour in about 2 quarts of boiling water, and microwave them, uncovered, on high for 15 minutes. Stir the beans, then set them aside to soak for one hour.

Put the oil, garlic, onion, chilies, and sweet red pepper into a bowl and microwave, uncovered, on high for three minutes. Stir in the salt and the tomatoes, then set the sauce aside until needed.

After the beans have soaked, drain them, and rinse them well in cold water. Return them to the casserole and cover them with fresh boiling water. Microwave the beans, uncovered, on high for 30 minutes; then cook them on medium for 50 minutes more. At the end of the cooking period, drain the beans, and return them to the casserole along with the sauce. Microwave on high until all the ingredients are thoroughly heated—three to five minutes. Stir before serving.

SUGGESTED ACCOMPANIMENT: *steamed broccoli spears.*

EDITOR'S NOTE: *To peel tomatoes using the microwave, pierce the skin once or twice, then microwave the tomatoes on high until the skin starts to peel away—about 45 seconds. Alternatively, follow the instructions on page 14. This dish may also be served cold, in which case a crisp green salad makes a good accompaniment.*

Oriental Parchment Parcels

Serves 4
Working (and total) time: about 20 minutes

Calories **100**
Protein **5g.**
Cholesterol **0mg.**
Total fat **8g.**
Saturated fat **0g.**
Sodium **10mg.**

4 tsp. sesame oil
7 oz. firm tofu, cut into ¾-inch cubes
3½ oz. fresh shiitake mushrooms, finely sliced
2½ oz. fresh or frozen baby corn, cut into 1-inch lengths
1 small zucchini, sliced
1 medium carrot, cut into thin ribbons with a vegetable peeler
4 tsp. low-sodium soy sauce
2 large garlic cloves, halved, or 4 small garlic cloves
2-inch piece fresh ginger, cut in half

Prepare four sheets of nonstick parchment paper, each about 10 inches square. Brush the centers of the four sheets with 1 teaspoon of the oil.

Divide the tofu cubes and vegetables equally among the four pieces of paper, piling the ingredients onto the oiled section. In a small bowl, mix the remaining oil with the soy sauce. Using a garlic press, crush the garlic and ginger, and add the pulp and juices to the bowl, discarding any coarse fibers that may have been pushed through the press. Sprinkle a quarter of this mixture over each pile of vegetables.

Bring two facing edges of one of the paper sheets together above the vegetables, and make a double fold in the edges, to seal and join them. Then make a double fold in each of the two open ends, to seal the parcel completely. Prepare the other three parcels in the same manner, and place all four in a wide, shallow dish, arranging them toward the outside edges of the dish so that they will cook evenly.

Microwave the parcels on high until the vegetables are tender—four to five minutes—giving the dish a quarter turn after each minute of cooking. Serve as soon as possible, keeping the parcels closed until the moment of serving.

SUGGESTED ACCOMPANIMENT: *Asian noodles sprinkled with finely sliced scallion.*

Sweet-and-Sour Tumbled Vegetables

Serves 4
Working time: about 30 minutes
Total time: about 45 minutes

Calories **150**
Protein **5g.**
Cholesterol **0mg.**
Total fat **5g.**
Saturated fat **0g.**
Sodium **25mg.**

1 tbsp. safflower oil
2 garlic cloves, crushed
1 tbsp. finely chopped fresh ginger
½ lb. zucchini (2 medium), ends trimmed, sliced diagonally into ¼-inch-thick slices
¼ lb. okra, stalk ends trimmed
1 bunch scallions, roots trimmed, all but 2 inches of green top cut off, sliced diagonally into 1-inch lengths
1 sweet red pepper, seeded, deribbed, and cut into strips
1 sweet green pepper, seeded, deribbed, and cut into strips
1 sweet yellow pepper, seeded, deribbed, and cut into strips
1 sweet orange pepper (optional), seeded, deribbed, and cut into strips
¼ lb. bean sprouts, picked over
¼ lb. fresh or frozen (thawed) baby corn, stalks trimmed if necessary
1 tsp. honey
2 tbsp. low-sodium soy sauce
⅔ cup unsweetened pineapple juice
¾ lb. fresh pineapple, diced

Put the oil, garlic, and ginger into a large casserole, and microwave them on high for two minutes. Add all the vegetables (except the corn, if frozen), stirring well. In a small bowl, stir the honey, soy sauce, and pineapple juice together. Pour this sauce over the vegetables and stir in the pineapple.

Cover the casserole with plastic wrap, leaving one corner open. Microwave it on high until the vegetables are cooked but still crisp—10 to 12 minutes; during this time, give the casserole a quarter turn every three minutes, and stir the contents after five minutes. If you are using frozen corn, add it for the last three minutes of cooking only.

Remove the casserole from the oven and allow the vegetables to stand, covered, for five minutes. Then stir them once more, and serve.

SUGGESTED ACCOMPANIMENT: *steamed rice.*

EDITOR'S NOTE: *For best results, select tender, young vegetables for this dish. If older vegetables are used, increase the cooking time by one to two minutes.*

Cabbage Timbale with Tomato Sauce

Serves 4
Working time: about 40 minutes
Total time: about 1 hour and 15 minutes

Calories **380**
Protein **18g.**
Cholesterol **20mg.**
Total fat **12g.**
Saturated fat **5g.**
Sodium **485mg.**

12 large Savoy or other dark green cabbage leaves, protruding ribs trimmed away
1 onion, sliced
1 leek, trimmed, split, washed thoroughly to remove all grit, and sliced
6 oz. carrots, diced (about 1½ cups)
6 oz. shelled fresh fava beans, skins removed, or 6 oz. shelled fresh lima beans (about 1½ cups)
1 tbsp. safflower oil
1 scant cup brown rice
1 cup unsalted vegetable stock (recipe, page 9)
⅛ tsp. salt
2 medium tomatoes, halved
1 tbsp. chopped fresh basil
1 tbsp. Worcestershire sauce
1 cup grated smoked low-fat cheese
freshly ground black pepper
Tomato sauce
6 tomatoes, halved
⅛ tsp. salt
freshly ground black pepper
1 tsp. cornstarch, mixed with 1 tbsp. water
1 tsp. tomato paste

First, make the tomato sauce. Place the tomatoes, cut side down, on a plate and microwave them on high for four to five minutes. Remove the skins as soon as the tomatoes are cool enough to handle. Mash the flesh in a bowl, or press it through a sieve for a smoother sauce, and season the mixture with the salt and some black pepper. Stir in the cornstarch and the tomato paste. Cover the bowl with plastic wrap pulled back at one corner, and microwave the sauce on high until it is thick—two to three minutes. Stir it and set it aside.

Arrange the cabbage leaves in a large casserole, keeping them as flat as possible. Add 6 tablespoons of cold water, cover the casserole with plastic wrap left open at one corner, and microwave it on high for six minutes. Drain the leaves well and set them aside.

Put the onion, leek, carrots, beans, and oil in a large casserole, and microwave them, uncovered, on high for five minutes, stirring halfway through the cooking time. Stir in the rice, stock, and salt, cover the mixture as before, and microwave it on medium until the rice is almost cooked—12 to 15 minutes. Remove the rice mixture from the oven and let it stand for five minutes.

Meanwhile, place the tomatoes cut side down on a plate. Cook them on high for three minutes, then remove and discard the skins and seeds. Coarsely chop the tomato flesh.

Drain off any excess water from the rice mixture, and stir in the tomatoes, basil, Worcestershire sauce, grated cheese, and some black pepper.

Line the bottom and sides of a 7-inch soufflé dish or casserole with eight of the cabbage leaves, overlapping them, and allowing the top part of each leaf to overhang the top of the dish. Pour the rice mixture into the center of the dish. Place the remaining cabbage leaves on top of the filling and bring the overhanging leaves in over the top, pressing down firmly. Cover the dish with plastic wrap, leaving one corner open. Microwave the timbale on high for eight minutes, giving the dish a quarter turn after every two minutes. Remove the timbale from the oven and drain off any excess water.

Reheat the tomato sauce on high for two to three minutes, then stir it, and pour it into a serving bowl. Invert the timbale onto a serving plate, and serve it hot, cut into wedges, accompanied by the tomato sauce.

Mushroom Quiche

Serves 4
Working (and total) time: about 40 minutes

Calories **265**
Protein **10g.**
Cholesterol **30mg.**
Total fat **14g.**
Saturated fat **6g.**
Sodium **120mg.**

1 cup whole-wheat flour
2 tbsp. unsalted peanut butter
2 tbsp. unsalted butter, chilled
Mushroom filling
6 oz. fresh shiitake mushrooms
6 oz. oyster mushrooms
1 tbsp. unsalted butter
2 tbsp. whole-wheat flour
⅔ cup skim milk
1 tbsp. chopped parsley
¼ tsp. salt
freshly ground black pepper

To make the pastry, put the flour into a mixing bowl, and lightly rub in the peanut butter and butter until the mixture resembles fine breadcrumbs. Mixing with a wooden spoon, add enough cold water to the flour to form a fairly firm dough—about 3 to 4 tablespoons. Turn the dough out onto a work surface dusted with a little flour and roll it out to line a 7-inch fluted quiche pan or pie pan. The dough is quite crumbly, so use any trimmings to fill in the cracks. Chill the pastry shell in the refrigerator for five minutes, then line it with a paper towel, pressing the towel gently into the contours of the shell. Microwave the pastry shell on high until it looks dry—four to five minutes.

To make the filling, put the mushrooms into a bowl with 2 tablespoons of cold water. Cover the mushrooms with plastic wrap, leaving one corner open, and microwave on high for two minutes. Remove the bowl from the oven and set it aside. In a separate bowl, heat the butter on high until it melts—15 to 20 seconds. Stir in the flour and then whisk in the milk. Add the parsley and cook on high for three minutes, stirring every minute with a wire whisk. Season the sauce with the salt and some black pepper, then add the mushrooms, and cook the filling on high, covered as before, for three minutes more, stirring after the first minute.

Remove the paper towel from the pastry shell, pour in the mushroom filling, and serve immediately.

SUGGESTED ACCOMPANIMENT: *rice salad or green salad.*

EDITOR'S NOTE: *If shiitake and oyster mushrooms are not available, use button mushrooms.*

Nutritional Charts

The figures refer to ½ cup, unless noted, of raw ingredient.

A dash indicates that no information was available.

tr indicates that a trace is known to be present.

The figures given should be taken as a guide only; the composition of many foods can vary.

*Recommended daily intake

**Contains oxalic acid, which may inhibit absorption of the vegetable's calcium

Fruits and Vegetables

	CALORIES *1800-2900	PROTEIN *44-56g.	CARBOHYDRATES *250-400g.	FOLIC ACID *400mcg.	VITAMIN A *4000-5000 Int'l. Units	VITAMIN C *60mg.	CALCIUM *800-1200mg.	SODIUM *max. 3000mg.	POTASSIUM *min. 1875mg.	FIBER *30-35g.
Apples (with skin)	32	0.10	8.39	1.5	29	3.1	4	0	63	0.42
Apricots	37	1.80	8.61	6.6	2,024	7.7	11	tr	229	0.46
Artichoke (1 medium)	65	3.40	15.28	94.2	237	13.8	61	102	434	1.36
Asparagus	15	2.05	2.47	80.0	601	22.1	14	1	202	0.55
Avocados	185	2.28	8.50	2.4	703	9.1	12	12	689	2.42
Bamboo shoots	21	1.98	3.95	—	7	1.5	10	3	204	0.53
Bananas	103	1.16	26.35	21.5	91	10.2	6	1	445	0.90
Beans, fava	256	19.59	43.73	31.7	40	1.1	77	9	796	2.23
Beans, green	17	1.00	3.92	20.1	368	8.9	21	3	115	0.60
Bean sprouts	16	1.58	3.08	31.6	11	6.8	7	3	77	0.42
Beets	30	1.01	6.80	63.0	14	7.5	11	49	220	0.54
Belgian endive	7	0.45	1.44	—	0	4.5	—	3	82	—
Broccoli	12	1.31	2.31	31.2	678	41.0	21	12	143	0.49
Brussels sprouts	19	1.49	3.94	26.9	389	37.4	18	11	171	0.66
Cabbage, celery and Nappa	6	0.46	1.23	29.9	456	10.3	29	3	90	0.23
Cabbage, green	8	0.42	1.88	19.8	44	16.5	16	6	86	0.28
Cabbage, red	10	0.49	2.14	7.3	14	20.0	18	4	72	0.35
Cabbage, Savoy	10	0.70	2.40	—	350	10.9	12	10	81	0.28
Carrots	24	0.56	5.58	7.7	15,471	5.1	15	19	178	0.57
Cauliflower	12	0.99	2.46	33.1	8	35.8	14	7	178	0.42
Celeriac	31	1.17	7.18	—	0	6.2	34	78	234	1.01
Celery	9	0.40	2.18	5.3	76	3.8	22	53	170	0.41
Corn	66	2.48	14.64	35.3	216	5.3	2	12	208	0.54
Cucumbers	7	0.28	1.51	7.2	23	2.4	7	1	78	0.31
Eggplant	11	0.45	2.56	7.2	29	0.7	15	1	90	0.41
Fennel	49	3.50	9.90	—	—	—	—	—	—	2.30
Garlic (1 clove)	4	0.19	0.99	0.1	0	0.9	5	1	12	0.05
Grape leaves (each)	6	0.46	1.29	—	822	3.2	68	2	24	0.20
Jerusalem artichokes	57	1.50	13.08	—	15	3.0	10	—	—	0.60
Kale	17	1.12	3.40	10.0	3,026	40.8	46	15	152	0.51
Kohlrabi	19	1.19	4.34	—	25	43.4	17	14	245	0.70
Leeks	32	0.78	7.36	33.4	50	6.2	30	10	94	0.78
Lemon (1 medium)	17	0.64	5.41	6.2	17	30.7	15	1	80	0.23

	*1800-2900 CALORIES	*44-56g. PROTEIN	*250-400g. CARBOHYDRATES	*400mcg. FOLIC ACID	*4000-5000 Int'l. Units VITAMIN A	*60mg. VITAMIN C	*800-1200mg. CALCIUM	*max. 3000mg. SODIUM	*min. 1875mg. POTASSIUM	*30-35g. FIBER
Mango	54	0.42	14.00	—	3,212	22.8	9	2	128	0.69
Mushrooms, dried	11	0.34	2.71	—	0	0.1	—	—	—	—
Mushrooms, fresh	9	0.73	1.63	7.4	0	1.2	2	1	130	0.26
Nectarines	34	0.65	8.13	2.6	508	3.7	3	0	146	0.27
Okra	19	1.00	3.81	43.9	330	10.5	41	4	151	0.47
Onions	27	0.94	5.86	15.9	0	6.7	20	2	124	0.35
Oranges	43	0.84	10.57	27.2	184	47.9	36	0	163	0.38
Parsley	10	0.66	2.07	54.9	1,560	27.0	39	12	161	0.36
Parsnips	50	0.80	12.05	44.8	0	11.4	24	7	251	1.34
Peaches	36	0.59	9.43	2.9	455	5.6	4	tr	167	0.54
Pears	48	0.32	12.47	6.0	16	3.3	9	tr	103	1.15
Peas, green	63	4.22	11.28	50.9	499	31.2	19	4	190	1.72
Peas, snow	30	2.02	5.44	—	105	43.2	31	3	144	1.80
Peppers, chili	30	1.50	7.10	17.5	578	181.9	13	5	255	1.35
Peppers, sweet	12	0.43	2.66	8.4	265	64.0	3	2	98	0.60
Pineapple	38	0.30	9.60	8.2	17	11.9	5	tr	88	0.42
Potato (1 medium, with skin)	110	3.30	24.87	20.9	tr	26.4	19	11	765	1.17
Pumpkin	15	0.58	3.77	—	928	5.2	12	1	197	0.64
Radishes	10	0.35	2.08	15.7	4	13.2	12	14	134	0.32
Romaine lettuce	4	0.45	0.66	38.0	728	6.7	10	2	81	0.20
Rutabagas	25	0.84	5.69	14.3	0	17.5	33	14	236	0.77
Salsify	55	2.21	12.46	—	0	5.4	40	13	255	1.21
Scallions	13	0.87	2.78	6.9	2,500	22.5	30	2	128	0.42
Spinach** (raw)	6	0.80	0.98	54.4	1,880	7.9	28	22	156	0.25
Spinach (cooked)	21	2.67	3.38	131.2	7,371	8.9	122	63	419	0.79
Squash, yellow	12	0.61	2.63	14.9	220	5.4	14	1	138	0.36
Sweet potatoes	72	1.12	16.63	9.5	13,743	15.6	16	9	139	0.58
Tomatoes	17	0.80	3.90	8.4	1,019	15.8	6	8	186	0.42
Turnips	18	0.59	4.05	9.5	0	13.7	20	44	124	0.59
Water chestnuts	66	0.87	14.84	—	0	2.5	7	9	362	0.50
Watercress	2	0.39	0.22	—	799	7.3	20	7	56	0.12
Yams (Latin American)	70	1.40	17.00	—	tr	2.1	10	—	—	0.42
Zucchini	9	0.75	1.89	14.4	221	5.9	10	2	161	0.29

The figures refer to the amount indicated of raw ingredient.

A dash indicates that no information was available.

tr indicates that a trace is known to be present.

*Recommended daily intake

	CALORIES *1800-2900	PROTEIN *44-56g.	TOTAL FAT *60-100g.	SATURATED FAT *20-32g.	CARBOHYDRATES *250-400g.	CALCIUM *800-1200mg.	SODIUM *max. 3000mg.	POTASSIUM *min. 1875mg.	IRON *18mg.	FIBER *30-35g.
Grains										
Barley, whole grain (1 cup)	700	16	2	.3	158	32	6	320	4.2	1.0
Buckwheat groats (Kasha) (1 cup)	567	19	4	1.0	123	29	40	525	4.0	2.9
Bulgur (1 cup)	600	19	3	1.2	129	49	2	389	9.5	2.9
Cornmeal (1 cup)	500	11	2	.2	108	8	1	166	5.9	.8
Couscous (1 cup)	692	24	1	.2	142	44	18	305	2.0	1.1
Flour, all-purpose (1 cup)	420	12	1	.2	88	18	2	109	5.1	.3
Flour, whole-wheat (1 cup)	400	16	2	.3	85	49	4	444	5.2	2.8
Millet (1 cup)	490	15	4	1.1	109	30	9	645	10.2	4.8
Rice, brown (1 cup)	666	14	4	1.1	143	59	17	396	3.0	1.7
Rice, white (1 cup)	670	12	1	.2	149	44	9	170	5.4	.6
Rolled oats (1 cup)	311	13	5	.9	54	42	3	284	3.4	.9
Semolina (1 cup)	602	21	2	.3	122	29	2	311	7.3	—
Wheat germ (1 cup)	321	24	10	1.7	41	64	3	732	8.0	2.8
Dried Beans										
Adzuki beans (1 cup)	649	39	1	—	124	130	9	2,470	9.8	10.4
Black-eyed peas (1 cup)	562	39	2	.6	100	183	27	1,858	13.8	7.7
Chickpeas (1 cup)	729	39	12	1.3	121	211	49	1,750	12.5	8.2
Fava beans (1 cup)	511	39	2	.4	87	154	19	1,593	10.0	4.5
Kidney beans, red or black (1 cup)	613	43	2	.2	110	263	44	2,587	15.1	11.5
Lentils (1 cup)	649	54	2	.3	110	99	19	1,738	17.3	10.0
Lima beans (1 cup)	602	38	1	.3	113	144	32	3,070	13.4	11.3
Mung beans (1 cup)	719	49	2	.7	130	273	30	2,579	13.9	10.9
Pinto beans (1 cup)	656	40	2	.5	122	233	19	2,563	11.3	11.6
Soybeans (1 cup)	774	68	37	5.4	56	515	4	3,343	29.2	9.2
White beans (1 cup)	674	47	2	.4	122	486	32	3,626	21.0	12.1
Nuts and Seeds										
Almonds (½ cup)	418	14	37	3.5	14	188	8	520	3.6	1.9
Cashews (½ cup)	394	11	32	6.3	22	31	11	336	4.1	.5
Chestnuts (½ cup)	154	2	2	.3	33	20	2	376	.7	1.2
Hazelnuts (½ cup)	364	8	36	2.6	9	108	2	256	1.9	4.2
Peanuts (½ cup)	414	19	36	5.0	12	43	12	524	2.4	3.6
Pine nuts (½ cup)	340	7	37	5.8	12	4	42	376	1.8	2.8
Pistachio nuts (½ cup)	370	13	31	3.9	16	87	4	700	4.3	1.2
Walnuts (½ cup)	385	9	37	3.4	11	57	6	301	1.5	2.8
Pumpkin seeds (1 tbsp.)	47	2	4	.2	2	4	2	70	1.3	.2
Sesame seeds (1 tbsp.)	52	2	4	.6	2	11	1	42	.6	.4
Sunflower seeds (1 tbsp.)	51	2	4	.5	2	11	tr	62	.6	.4

	*1800-2900 CALORIES	*44-56g. PROTEIN	*60-100g. TOTAL FAT	*20-32g. SATURATED FAT	*max. 300mg. CHOLESTEROL	*250-400g. CARBOHYDRATES	*800-1200mg. CALCIUM	*max. 3000mg. SODIUM	*18mg. IRON
Dairy Products									
Whole milk (½ cup)	75	4.00	4.00	2.50	16	5.50	145	60	.06
Skim milk (½ cup)	45	4.00	.22	.14	2	6.00	151	65	.05
Light cream (1 tbsp.)	44	.32	4.64	2.90	17	.44	10	5	tr
Whipping cream (1 tbsp.)	52	.31	5.50	3.50	21	.42	10	6	tr
Sour cream (1 tbsp.)	26	.38	2.50	1.50	5	.51	14	6	.01
Low-fat yogurt (½ cup)	75	6.00	2.00	1.00	7	8.00	207	80	.09
Brie (1 oz.)	95	6.00	8.00	—	28	.13	52	178	.14
Camembert (1 oz.)	85	6.00	7.00	4.00	20	.13	110	239	.09
Cheddar cheese (1 oz.)	114	7.00	9.00	6.00	30	.36	204	176	.19
Cottage cheese (1% fat) (½ cup)	80	14.00	1.00	1.00	5	3.00	69	460	.16
Edam (1 oz.)	101	7.00	8.00	5.00	25	.40	207	274	.12
Feta cheese (1 oz.)	75	4.00	6.00	4.00	25	1.00	140	316	.18
Gruyère (1 oz.)	117	8.00	9.00	5.00	31	.10	287	95	—
Mozzarella, part-skim (1 oz.)	72	7.00	5.00	3.00	16	.78	183	132	.06
Parmesan cheese (1 oz.)	111	10.00	7.00	5.00	19	.91	336	454	.23
Ricotta, part-skim (½ cup)	170	14.00	10.00	6.00	38	6.00	337	155	.55
Roquefort (½ oz.)	105	6.00	9.00	5.00	26	.57	188	513	.16
Fats and Eggs									
Unsalted butter (1 tbsp.)	100	tr	11.00	7.00	31	0	3	2	tr
Polyunsaturated margarine (1 tbsp.)	100	tr	11.00	2.20	0	tr	4	132	tr
Vegetable shortening (1 tbsp.)	115	0	13.00	3.30	0	0	0	0	0
Safflower oil (1tbsp.)	125	0	14.00	1.30	0	0	0	0	0
Sunflower oil (1 tbsp.)	120	0	13.60	1.40	0	0	0	0	0
Virgin olive oil (1 tbsp.)	119	0	13.50	1.80	0	0	0	0	0
Egg (1 large)	80	6.00	6.00	1.70	272	.60	28	69	1.04
Egg yolk (1)	65	3.00	6.00	1.70	272	.04	26	8	.95
Egg white (1)	15	3.00	tr	0	0	.41	4	50	.01
Miscellaneous									
Bread, white (1 slice)	65	2.00	1.00	.30	0	12.00	32	129	.70
Bread, whole-wheat (1 slice)	65	2.00	1.00	.20	0	12.00	32	138	.90
Pasta, dried (1 oz.)	102	3.70	.50	.05	0	21.00	8	1	1.10
Tofu (½ cup)	183	20.00	11.00	1.60	0	5.00	258	17	13.10
Raisins (½ cup)	214	1.83	.39	.13	0	56.89	20	20	1.82
Golden raisins (½ cup)	218	2.50	.33	.11	0	57.60	38	10	1.29
Honey (1 tbsp.)	65	tr	0	0	0	17.00	1	1	.10
Salt (1 tsp.)	0	0	0	0	0	0	2	2,300	0
Sugar (½ cup)	385	0	0	0	0	100.00	2	5	.05

Glossary

Acidulated water: a dilute solution of lemon juice in water, used to keep certain vegetables from discoloring after they are peeled.

Adzuki beans: beans of somewhat sweet flavor and soft texture, available in Asian markets.

Al dente: an Italian term meaning "to the tooth." It is used to describe perfectly cooked pasta: chewy but with no flavor of flour.

Arugula (also called rocket, rocket cress, *roquette, ruchetta,* and *rugula*): a peppery-flavored salad plant with long, leafy stems, popular in Italy.

Balsamic vinegar: a mild, extremely fragrant wine-based vinegar made in northern Italy. Traditionally, the vinegar is aged for at least seven years in a series of casks made of various woods.

Bamboo shoots: sold canned in the West, the best-quality bamboo shoots, known as winter bamboo, are the first to break through early in the new year. Ordinary bamboo is less tender.

Bâtonnet (also called bâton): a vegetable piece that has been cut in the shape of a stick; bâtonnets are slightly larger than julienne.

Bean curd: see Tofu.

Bean sprouts: the germinated and sprouted seeds of a wide selection of grains, dried beans, and other plants, although mung and soybeans are the most frequently sprouted commercially. Bean sprouts are a good source of protein, iron, and vitamins A, C, E, and those in the B group.

Blanch: to partially cook food by briefly immersing it in boiling water. Blanching makes thin-skinned fruits and vegetables easier to peel; it can also mellow strong flavors.

Bok choy (also called Chinese chard): a sweet-tasting cruciferous vegetable with smooth white stalks and wide, dark green leaves.

Buckwheat: the seed of the flowering buckwheat plant. Buckwheat groats (also called kasha) are hulled, steamed, dried, and sometimes toasted. Buckwheat flour is unrelated to wheat flour and lacks the proteins required to form gluten.

Bulgur: wheat whose kernels are steamed and dried before being crushed.

Calorie (kilocalorie): a measure of the energy food supplies when it is broken down in the body.

Caraway seeds: the pungent seed of the herb caraway, often used to flavor rye bread.

Cardamom: the bittersweet aromatic dried seeds or whole pods of a plant in the ginger family. Often used in curries.

Cayenne pepper: a fiery powder ground from the seeds and pods of various red chili peppers.

Celeriac (also called celery root): the knobby, tuberous root of a plant in the celery family.

Ceps (also called porcini): wild mushrooms with a pungent, earthy flavor that survives drying or long cooking. Dried ceps should be soaked in hot water before they are used.

Chervil: a subtly flavored herb with small, lacy leaves, it tastes like parsley with a hint of anise.

Chili peppers: a variety of hot red or green peppers. Serranos and jalapeños are small fresh green chilies that are very hot. Anchos are dried poblano chilies that are mildly hot and dark red in color. Fresh or dried, chili peppers contain volatile oils that irritate the skin and eyes; they must be handled with care *(cautionary note, page 25).*

Cholesterol: a waxlike substance manufactured in the human body and also found in foods of animal origin. Although a certain amount of cholesterol is necessary for proper body functioning, an excess can accumulate in the arteries, contributing to heart disease. See also Monounsaturated fat; Polyunsaturated fat; Saturated fat.

Cilantro (also called fresh coriander or Chinese parsley): the fresh leaves of the coriander plant; it imparts a lemony, slightly bitter flavor to many Latin-American, Indian, and Asian dishes.

Cloud-ear mushrooms: (also called tree ears, tree fungus, mo-er and wood ears): flavorless fungus used for its crunchy texture and dark color.

Coriander: an herb whose earthy-tasting seeds are a basic ingredient in curries. The leaves are called cilantro.

Coulis: a sieved vegetable or fruit purée.

Couscous: processed semolina, traditionally steamed and served with meat and vegetables in the North African stew of the same name.

Crepe: a paper-thin pancake that can accommodate a variety of savory or sweet fillings.

Cumin: the aromatic seed of an umbelliferous plant similar to fennel, used, whole or powdered, as a spice, especially in Indian and Latin-American dishes. Toasting gives it a nutty flavor.

Dietary fiber: a plant-cell material that is undigested or only partially digested in the body but that promotes the digestion of other food matter.

Dijon mustard: a smooth or grainy mustard once made only in Dijon, France; may be flavored with herbs, green peppercorns, or white wine.

Escarole: a broad-leafed relative of curly endive that shares its cousin's pleasingly bitter flavor. It is best used in combination with sweeter greens.

Fava beans (also called broad beans): a European variety of beans, eaten fresh or dried. They have an assertive, almost bitter flavor and granular texture.

Fennel: (also called anise, *finocchio,* and Florence fennel): a vegetable with feathery green tops and a thick, white bulbous stalk. It has a milky, licorice flavor and can be eaten raw or cooked.

Fenugreek: a plant native to Asia. The seeds are highly aromatic with a bitter aftertaste and are normally used as a flavoring in Indian cuisine.

Feta cheese: a salty Greek and Middle Eastern cheese made from goat's or sheep's milk. The curds are ripened in their own salted whey.

Five-spice powder (also called five heavenly spices and five fragrant spices): a pungent blend of spices, most often fennel seeds, star anise, cloves, cinnamon or cassia, and Sichuan peppercorns; it should be used sparingly. If it is unavailable, substitute equal parts ground Sichuan peppercorns, cloves, cinnamon, and fennel seeds.

Flageolet beans: pale green, dried beans (about the size of white beans), available in gourmet grocery stores.

Garam masala: an aromatic mixture of ground spices used in Indian cuisine. It usually contains coriander, cumin, cloves, ginger, and cinnamon. It is available in Asian markets.

Ginger: the spicy, buff-colored rhizome, or rootlike stem, of the ginger plant, used as a seasoning either fresh or dried and powdered. Dried ginger makes a poor substitute for fresh.

Goat cheese: a pungent soft cheese made with goat's milk.

Grape leaves: the tender, lightly flavored leaves of the grapevine, used in many ethnic cuisines as wrappers for savory mixtures.

Hot red-pepper sauce: a hot, unsweetened chili sauce, such as Tabasco®.

Jerusalem artichoke: neither an artichoke nor from Jerusalem, this vegetable is the tuberous root of a member of the sunflower family. In texture, color, and flavor, it resembles the water chestnut.

Julienne: the French term for vegetables or other food cut into matchstick-size strips.

Kasha: see Buckwheat.

Kohlrabi: a cruciferous vegetable whose major edible part is an enlarged part of the stem, a light green or lavender bulb.

Lemon grass (citronella): a long, woody, lemon-flavored stalk that is shaped like a scallion. Lemon grass is available in Asian markets. To store it, refrigerate it in plastic wrap for up to two weeks; lemon grass may also be frozen for storage.

Mace: the ground aril, or covering, that encases the nutmeg seed.

Mango: a fruit grown throughout the tropics, with sweet, succulent, yellow-orange flesh that is extremely rich in vitamin A. Like papaya, it may cause an allergic reaction in some individuals.

Millet: a nutritious grain with a nutty, mild taste.

Molasses: a thick, dark, strongly flavored sugar syrup, rich in iron and a good source of B vitamins.

Monounsaturated fat: one of the three types of fat found in food. Monounsaturated fats are believed not to raise blood-cholesterol levels.

Nappa cabbage (also called Chinese cabbage): an elongated cabbage with long, broad ribs and crinkled, light green to white leaves.

Nonreactive pan: a cooking vessel whose surface does not chemically react with food. Materials used include stainless steel, enamel, glass, and some alloys. Untreated cast iron and aluminum may react with acids, producing off colors or tastes.

Nori: paperlike dark green or black sheets of dried seaweed, often used in Japanese cuisine as a flavoring or as wrappers for rice and vegetables.

Olive oil: any of various grades of oil extracted from olives. Extra virgin olive oil has a full, fruity flavor and very low acidity. Virgin olive oil is lighter in flavor and slightly higher in acidity. Pure olive oil, a processed blend of olive oils, has the lightest taste and highest acidity. For salad dressings, virgin and extra virgin olive oils are preferred.

Oyster mushroom: a variety of wild mushroom, now cultivated. They are stronger tasting than button mushrooms and are usually pale brown.

Paprika: a slightly sweet, spicy, bright-red powder produced by grinding dried sweet red peppers. The best type of paprika is Hungarian.

Phyllo (also spelled "filo"): a paper-thin pastry popular in Greek and Middle Eastern cuisine. Because frozen phyllo dries out easily, it should be thawed in the refrigerator, and any phyllo sheets not in use should be covered with a damp towel.

Pine nuts (also called *pignoli*): seeds from the cone of the stone pine, a tree native to the Mediterranean. Toasting enhances their buttery flavor.

Pistachio nuts: prized for their flavor and green color, pistachio nuts must be shelled and boiled for a few minutes before their skins can be removed.

Polenta: cooked cornmeal, traditionally eaten in northern Italy.

Polyunsaturated fat: one of the three types of fat found in foods. It exists in abundance in such vegetable oils as safflower, sunflower, corn, and soybean. Polyunsaturated fats lower the level of cholesterol in the blood.

Porcini: see Ceps.

Recommended Dietary Allowance (RDA): the average required daily amount of an essential nutrient as determined for healthy people of various ages by the National Research Council.

Reduce: to boil down a liquid in order to concentrate its flavor or thicken its consistency.

Refresh: to rinse a briefly cooked vegetable under cold water to arrest its cooking and set its color.

Rice wine: wine made from fermented rice. The best imported Chinese rice wine is shao-hsing, but it is difficult to find outside Asian communities. Japanese rice wine, sake, has a different flavor, but it may be substituted for the Chinese variety. If rice wine is unavailable, use dry sherry.

Ricotta cheese: a creamy, white Italian cheese made from whey. In the United States, it is made from whey and milk. One cup of part-skim ricotta cheese contains 19 grams of total fat.

Rosemary: a rich-smelling herb, with an almost piney aroma. The leaves, fresh and dried, are used in seasoning and stay potent through cooking.

Safflower oil: a vegetable oil that contains the highest proportion of polyunsaturated fats.

Saffron: the dried, yellowish-red stigmas (or threads) of the saffron crocus, which yield a powerful yellow color as well as a pungent flavor. Powdered saffron may be substituted for the threads, but it has less flavor.

Salsify: a thin, long, cylindrical root with brown or blackish skin.

Saturated fat: one of the three types of fat present in food. Found in abundance in animal products and coconut and palm oils, saturated fats raise the level of blood cholesterol. Because high blood-cholesterol levels may cause heart disease, saturated fat consumption should be restricted to less than 15 percent of the daily caloric intake.

Sauté: to cook a food quickly in a small amount of oil or butter over high heat.

Savoy cabbage: a variety of head cabbage with a mild flavor and crisp, crinkly leaves.

Semolina: the ground endosperm of kernels of durum wheat. Fine semolina makes a pasta of excellent resilience and body.

Sesame oil: an oil derived from the seed of the sesame plant that has a nutty, smoky aroma. It is used as a flavoring, especially in Asian cooking.

Sesame seeds: small, nutty-tasting seeds used frequently in Middle Eastern and Indian cooking. They are also used to make sesame oil.

Shiitake mushroom: a variety of mushroom, originally grown only in Japan, sold fresh or dried. The dried form should be soaked and stemmed before use.

Simmer: to heat a liquid to just below its boiling point, so that the liquid's surface barely trembles.

Skim milk: milk from which almost all the fat has been removed.

Snow peas: flat, green pea pods, eaten whole with only the stems and strings removed.

Sodium: a nutrient essential to maintaining the proper balance of fluids in the body. In most diets, a major source of the element is table salt, which contains 40 percent sodium. Excess sodium may contribute to high blood pressure, which increases the risk of heart disease. One teaspoon of salt, with about 2,100 milligrams of sodium, contains almost two-thirds of the maximum "safe and adequate" daily intake recommended by the National Research Council.

Soy sauce: a savory, salty brown liquid made from fermented soybeans and available in both light and dark versions. One tablespoon of regular soy sauce contains 1,030 milligrams of sodium; low-sodium types, as used in this book, may contain as little as half that amount.

Steam: to cover food and cook it in the steam created by a boiling liquid.

Stir-fry: to cook thin slices of vegetables, fish, or meat over high heat in a small amount of oil, stirring constantly to ensure even cooking in a short time. The traditional cooking vessel is a wok; a heavy-bottomed skillet may also be used.

Sun-dried tomatoes: tomatoes that have been naturally dried in the sun, then preserved in oil and seasoning, usually including herbs. Available in jars or cans.

Sweet potato: either one of two types of nutritious tuber, one with yellowish, mealy flesh, the other with a moist, sweet, orange flesh. The latter is often sold as yam but should not be confused with the true yam *(below)*.

Tahini (also called sesame paste): a nutty-tasting paste made from ground sesame seeds that are usually roasted.

Tamarind (also called Indian date): the pulp surrounding the seeds of the tamarind plant, yielding a juice considerably more sour than lemon juice. Grown throughout Asia, tamarind is available fresh in pod form, in bricks, or as a paste.

Tarragon: a strong herb with an anise taste. In combination with other herbs—especially rosemary, sage, and thyme—it should be used sparingly. Because heat intensifies tarragon's flavor, cooked dishes require smaller amounts.

Thyme: a versatile herb with a zesty, slightly fruity flavor and strong aroma.

Tofu (also called bean curd): a dense, unfermented soybean product with a mild flavor. Tofu is rich in protein, relatively low in calories, and free of cholesterol *(box, page 85)*.

Total fat: an individual's daily intake of polyunsaturated, monounsaturated, and saturated fats. Nutritionists recommend that fats provide no more than 30 percent of a person's total caloric intake. The term as used in this book refers to the combined fats in a given dish or food.

Turmeric: a yellow spice from a plant related to ginger, used as a coloring agent and occasionally as a substitute for saffron. Turmeric has a musty odor and a slightly bitter flavor.

Virgin olive oil: see Olive oil.

Water chestnut: the walnut-size tuber of an aquatic Asian plant, with rough brown skin and sweet, crisp white flesh. Fresh water chestnuts may be refrigerated for two weeks; they must be peeled before use. To store canned water chestnuts, blanch or rinse them, then refrigerate them for no longer than three weeks in water changed daily.

Wheat germ: the embryo of the wheat kernel, usually separated out in milling. Wheat germ is high in protein and fat. It should be refrigerated after opening to avoid rancidity.

Whole-wheat flour: wheat flour that contains the whole of the wheat grain with nothing added or taken away. It is valuable as a source of dietary fiber and is higher in B vitamins than white flour.

Wild rice: the robustly flavored seeds of a water grass native to the Great Lakes region.

Yam: a number of varieties of hairy tuber, rich in vitamin A and similar in taste, when cooked, to the potato. Also called the Indian potato, it should not be confused with the sweet potato, which is sometimes sold as yam. The yam is less sweet and less widely available than the sweet potato.

Yeast, fast-rising: a recently developed strain of yeast that reduces the time necessary for rising.

Yogurt: a smooth-textured, semisolid cultured milk product made with varying percentages of fat. Yogurt can be substituted for sour cream in cooking or be combined with sour cream to produce a sauce or topping that is lower in fat and calories than sour cream alone.

Zest: the outermost layer of citrus-fruit rind, cut or grated free of the bitter white pith beneath it.

Picture Credits

Butcher. 104: John Elliott. 105, 106: Andrew Whittuck. 107: John Elliott. 108, 109: Simon Butcher. 110: Andrew Whittuck. 111-113: John Elliott. 114: David Johnson. 115: John Elliott. 116: Martin Brigdale. 117, 118: John Elliott. 119: David Johnson. 120: John Elliott. 121: Martin Brigdale—John Elliott. 122-126: John Elliott. 127: David Johnson. 128: Simon Butcher. 129, 130: Chris Knaggs. 131: John Elliott. 132: Simon Butcher. 133: David Johnson. 134, 135: John Elliott.

Props: The editors wish to thank the following outlets and manufacturers; all are based in London unless otherwise stated.
Cover: plate, Inshop. 4: *(top)* plates and cutlery, Mappin & Webb Silversmiths; cloth and napkin, Ewart Liddell; *(left)* platter, Hutschenreuther (UK) Ltd.; cloth, Ewart Liddell. 5: *(left)* china, Rosenthal (London) Ltd.; *(bottom)* plate, Inshop. 14: platter, Villeroy & Boch. 15: oblong platter, Rosenthal (London) Ltd. 17: marble, W. E. Grant & Co. (Marble) Ltd. 20: plate, Hutschenreuther (UK) Ltd. 21: plates and cutlery, Mappin & Webb Silversmiths; cloth and napkin, Ewart Liddell. 24: plate, Hutschenreuther (UK) Ltd. 25: plate, Villeroy & Boch. 28: plate, Inshop. 29: platter, Hutschenreuther (UK) Ltd.; cloth, Ewart Liddell. 30: fork, Mappin & Webb Silversmiths. 31: pie dish, Winchcombe Pottery, The Craftsmen Potters Shop. 32: plate, Royal Worcester,·Worcester. 51: marble, W. E. Grant & Co. (Marble) Ltd. 57: plates, Royal Worcester, Worcester. 59: two dishes, Clive Bowen, The Craftsmen Potters Shop. 66: plate, Royal Worcester, Worcester. 71: china, Hutschenreuther (UK) Ltd. 74: plate, Villeroy & Boch. 75: china, Rosenthal (London) Ltd. 77: platter, John Leach, The Craftsmen Potters Shop. 78: plate, Rosenthal (London) Ltd. 79: plate, Royal Worcester, Worcester. 81: platter, Royal Worcester, Worcester. 84: plate, Hutschenreuther (UK) Ltd. 87: platter, Rosenthal (London) Ltd. 90-91: white marble, W. E. Grant & Co. (Marble) Ltd. 94: plates, Line of Scandinavia. 96: plate, Inshop. 98: marble, W. E. Grant & Co. (Marble) Ltd. 99: plate, Royal Worcester, Worcester. 100: marble, W. E. Grant & Co. (Marble) Ltd. 101: plate, Royal Worcester, Worcester. 102: plate, Villeroy & Boch. 105: napkin, Ewart Liddell. 106: pizza pan, Chicago Pizza Pie Factory. 107: plate, Rosenthal (London) Ltd. 108: plates, Villeroy & Boch. 111: large plate, Line of Scandinavia. 112: marble, W. E. Grant & Co. (Marble) Ltd. 113: plate, Inshop. 116: plate, Hutschenreuther (UK) Ltd.; cutlery, Mappin & Webb Silversmiths. 122: marble, W. E. Grant & Co. (Marble) Ltd. 126: marble, W. E. Grant & Co. (Marble) Ltd. 127: plates, Inshop; platter, Rosenthal (London) Ltd. 129: platter, Royal Copenhagen Porcelain and Georg Jensen Silversmiths Ltd. 132: plate, Rosenthal (London) Ltd. 133: plates, Rosenthal (London) Ltd.

Acknowledgments

The editors wish to thank the following: René Bloom, London; Sara Brown, London; Maureen Burrows, London; Jonathan Driver, London; Neil Fairbairn, Wivenhoe, Essex; Ellen Galford, Edinburgh; Wendy Gibbons, London; Hyams and Cockerton Ltd., London; Bridget Jones, Guildford, Surrey; Perstorp Warerite Ltd., London; Sharp Electronics (UK) Ltd., London; Jane Stevenson, London; Toshiba (UK) Ltd., London.

Index

*A*lmonds, salad of avocado, flageolets, and brown rice, 54
Artichokes:
Basmati and wild rice molds with braised, 56
Chickpea salad in, cups, 78
Jerusalem, gratin, 126
Jerusalem, and walnut soufflés, 42
Preparing, for stuffing, 79
Asparagus, 6
And morel tart, 103
Mousse with goat cheese sauce, 21
Mushrooms and, in phyllo cases, 116
Salsify and, muffins, 118
Strudel, 112
Avocado:
Nut and, dumplings with a citrus sauce, 100
Salad of, flageolets, almonds, and brown rice, 54

*B*aguette and Brie bake, 117
Baked potato with an onion and chive filling, 40
Barley and mushroom broth with smoked tofu, 89
Basil:
Spread, 17
Summer beans with fresh fettuccine and, 99
Basmati and wild rice molds with braised artichokes, 56
Bean curd sauce, 46
Beans, 6, 7, 53. *See also individual names*
Butter, succotash, 75
Chili, with cornbread topping, 67

Gingered black, with saffron rice, 72
Lima, baked with an herbed crust, 74
Salad of avocado, flageolets, almonds, and brown rice, 54
Spiced, medley, 131
Storing, 7
Summer, with fresh fettuccine and basil, 99
Tuscan-style, 73
Beetroot, in Scandinavian salad, 41
Belgian endive:
And pistachio-stuffed tomatoes, 23
Fennel, and blue cheese triangles, 114
Black beans, gingered, with saffron rice, 72
Black-eyed peas, cabbage stuffed with, and mushrooms, 76
Blue cheese: Fennel, Belgian endive and, triangles, 114
Boiling, 8
Bread:
Baguette and Brie bake, 117
Cheese, and onion pudding, 120
In fennel, broccoli, and okra croustades, 121
In Italian peasant salad, 119
Brie, baguette and, bake, 117
Broccoli, 6, 7
Fennel, and okra croustades, 121
Carrot and, tortes, 102
And pecorino turnovers, 109
Brown rice. *See* Rice
Brussels sprouts, chestnuts and, with red cabbage and caraway potatoes, 26
Buckwheat and lentil pilaf, 65
Bulgur:
Chickpea and, kofta, 78
Stuffed grape leaves with, and

tomatoes, 128
Stuffed phyllo packages, 115

*C*abbage, 6, 7. *See also* Nappa cabbage, Red cabbage
Hollowing a whole, for stuffing, 76
In mushroom coulibiac, 108
Spicy mold of leeks, zucchini, and, 25
Stuffed with black-eyed peas and mushrooms, 76
Timbale with tomato sauce, 134
Camembert, warm, and fruit salad, 129
Caper, olive and, sauce, 88
Caraway seeds, toasting, 41
Carbohydrates, 6
Caribbean spiced rice, 55
Carrots, 6
And broccoli tortes, 102
Lentils with spinach and, 81
Potato, and cauliflower curry, 130
Potato, and celeriac rösti, 39
Cauliflower, 6
Cheese mold, 123
Mustard, quiche, 105
Potato, carrot, and, curry, 130
Celeriac:
Potato, carrot, and, rösti, 39
Rolls with mustard sauce, 33
Steamed leek and, pudding, 111
Celery, penne with, and ricotta cheese, 95
Cheese, 6, 7, 9. *See also individual names*
Bread, and onion pudding, 120
Cauliflower, mold, 123
Smoked, gougère with a lemon and fennel filling, 110
Chestnuts:

In basmati and wild rice molds with braised artichokes, 56
And Brussels sprouts with red cabbage and caraway potatoes, 26
In eight treasures in lotus leaves, 62
Peeling, 37
Stuffed sweet potatoes with chili sauce, 36
Chickpeas:
And bulgur kofta, 78
And okra casserole with couscous, 77
Salad in artichoke cups, 78
Chili peppers:
Beans with cornbread topping, 67
Cautionary note, 25
Sauce, 36
Tomato relish, 78
Chives, baked potatoes with an onion and, filling, 40
Cholesterol, 7
Chou-puff dough, 110
Citrus sauce, 100
Clafoutis, zucchini and tomato, 124
Coconut:
Cooking methods, 8-9
Toasting, 43
Vegetable curry with, 49
Coriander:
Dough, 103
Yogurt sauce, 71
Corn, whole-wheat pizza with, and pineapple, 106
Cornbread topping, 67
Couscous, chickpea and okra casserole with, 77
Crepes. *See also* Pancakes
Gâteau of, with wild rice and mushrooms, 56
Spring vegetables in watercress, 20

Croustades:
Fennel, broccoli, and okra, 121
Making, 121
Cumin, lentils with, and onion, 83
Curried rutabaga soup, 43
Curry:
Potato, carrot, and cauliflower, 130
Vegetable, with coconut, 49

Dietary fiber, 6, 7
Dietary guidelines, 8
Dough. See also Pastry
Chou-puff, 110
Coriander, 103
Pizza, 106
Yeast, 104, 108
Dressings:
Mustard, 41
Yogurt, 78
Dumplings:
Nut and avocado, with a citrus sauce, 100
Tofu and vegetable, 86

Eggplant:
Fans, 17
And mozzarella ramekins, 15
Rolls with ricotta-raisin filling, 16
Eggs, 6, 7, 9. See also Omelettes, Soufflés
In mixed vegetable pipérade, 125
Yolks, 6, 7
Eight treasures in lotus leaves, 62

Fennel:
Baked, in Roquefort sauce, 22
Broccoli, and okra croustades, 121
Endive, and blue cheese triangles, 114
Smoked cheese gougère with a lemon and, filling, 110
Fettuccine:
Saffron, with hazelnut and tarragon sauce, 98
Summer beans with fresh, and basil, 99
Fillings:
Lemon and fennel, 110
Onion and chive, 40
Ricotta-raisin, 16
Spinach, 28
Flageolets:
In Provençal casserole, 70
Salad of avocado, almonds, and brown rice, 54
In wild and brown rice pilaf with a mushroom ragout, 58
Fruit. See also individual names
Warm Camembert and, salad, 129

Gâteau of crepes with wild rice and mushrooms, 56
Gingered black beans with saffron rice, 72
Gnocchi, semolina, with julienned vegetables, 66
Goat cheese:
And parsley ravioli, 96
Sauce, 21
Gougère, smoked cheese, with a lemon and fennel filling, 110

Grains, 6, 7
Grape leaves, stuffed, with bulgur and tomatoes, 128
Gruyère sauce, 24

Hazelnut and tarragon sauce, 98
Herbed spring rolls with peanut sauce, 101
Herb pastry, 105
Hot-pepper sauce, 35
Hot-and-sour potato and turnip casserole, 51

Indonesian vegetable stew, 80
Italian peasant salad, 119

Jerusalem artichokes:
Gratin, 126
And walnut soufflés, 42
Julienned vegetables, 66

Kabobs, tofu, zucchini, and mushroom, 88
Kidney beans:
In chili beans with cornbread topping, 67
In gingered black beans with saffron rice, 72
In spiced bean medley, 131
Kofta, chickpea and bulgur, 78
Kohlrabi and zucchini gratin, 31

Lacy pancakes with spinach filling, 28
Lasagna, vegetable, 94
Leeks:
Pastry-wrapped pears stuffed with walnuts, Stilton, and, 107
Spicy mold of, zucchini, and cabbage, 25
Steamed, and celeriac pudding, 111
Stuffed, with Gruyère sauce, 24
Lemon:
Shortcrust pastry, 109
Smoked cheese gougère with a, and fennel filling, 110
Lentils:
Buckwheat and, pilaf, 65
With cumin and onion, 83
And potato cakes with mustard pickle, 82
Soufflés baked in sweet pepper cases, 84
With spinach and carrots, 81
Storing, 7
Lettuce, 6
Lima beans:
Baked with an herbed crust, 74
Succotash, 75
Lohans' feast, 46
Lotus leaves:
Eight treasures in, 62
Shaping a, parcel, 63

Mexican sweet potato stew, 50
Mint yogurt sauce, 92
Molds:
Cauliflower cheese, 123
Spicy, of leeks, zucchini, and cabbage, 25

Morel, asparagus and, tart, 103
Mousse, asparagus, with goat cheese sauce, 21
Mozzarella:
Eggplant and, ramekins, 15
Polenta ring with pine nuts and, 69
Muffins, salsify and asparagus, 118
Mushrooms:
And asparagus in phyllo cases, 116
Barley and, broth with smoked tofu, 89
Cabbage stuffed with black-eyed peas and, 76
Coulibiac, 108
Gâteau of crepes with wild rice and, 56
Pea and, risotto, 61
Quiche, 135
Stuffed, caps, 32
Tofu, zucchini, and, kabobs, 88
Wild and brown rice with, ragout, 58
Mustard:
Cauliflower quiche, 105
Dressing, 41
Pickle, 82
Sauce, 33
Mustard seeds, toasting, 41

Nappa cabbage, spinach and, pie, 113
Noodles, tofu and vegetable stir-fry with, 87
Nutmeg sauce, 94
Nutritional charts, 136-139
Nuts, 6, 7. See also individual names
And avocado dumplings with a citrus sauce, 100
Storing, 7

Okra:
Chickpea and, with couscous, 77
Fennel, broccoli, and, croustades, 121
And sweet pepper stew, 48
Olive and caper sauce, 88
Omelette:
Spaghetti with, strips and stir-fried vegetables, 97
Spanish, 13
Onion:
Bread, cheese, and, pudding, 120
And chive filling, baked potatoes with, 40
Lentils with cumin and, 83
Rice cakes with, relish, 64
Salsify with pepper and, relish, 34
Orange sauce, 44
Oriental parchment parcels, 132

Palm oil, 48
Pancakes. See also Crepes
Lacy, with spinach filling, 28
Paprika sauces, 37
Parsley, goat cheese and, ravioli, 96
Pasta, 91. See also individual names
Dough, 99
Pastry, 91. See also Dough; Phyllo
Herb, 105
Lemon shortcrust, 109
Shortcrust, 91, 107
Whole-wheat, 102
Pastry-wrapped pears stuffed with walnuts, Stilton, and leeks, 107

Patties, tandoori, 71
Peanuts, 6
Sauce, 101
Sichuan tofu with sweet pepper and, 84
Pears, pastry-wrapped, stuffed with walnuts, Stilton, and leeks, 107
Peas, 7
And mushroom risotto, 61
Storing dried, 7
Pecorino:
Broccoli and, turnovers, 109
Pumpkin and, risotto, 60
Penne with celery and ricotta cheese, 95
Pepper. See also Chili peppers; Sweet peppers
Green, 6
Hot, sauce, 35
Phyllo pastry, 91
In asparagus strudel, 112
In bulgur-stuffed packages, 115
In fennel, endive, and blue cheese triangles, 114
Mushrooms and asparagus in, cases, 116
In spinach and Nappa cabbage pie, 113
Pickle, mustard, 82
Pies:
Salad-filled potato, 127
Savory pumpkin, 104
Spinach and Nappa cabbage, 113
Pilaf:
Buckwheat and lentil, 65
Wild and brown rice, with a mushroom ragout, 58
Pineapple, whole-wheat pizza with corn and, 106
Pine nuts:
Polenta ring with, and mozzarella, 69
Spinach and, layered terrine, 30
Toasting, 16
Pinto beans, in Tandoori patties, 71
Pipérade of mixed vegetables, 125
Pistachio nuts:
Skinning, 23
Stuffed tomatoes, 23
Pizza:
Dough, 106
Whole-wheat, with corn and pineapple, 106
Polenta, 68
Polenta:
Pizza, 68
Ring with pine nuts and mozzarella, 69
Potatoes, 6, 7
Baked, with an onion and chive filling, 40
Carrot, and cauliflower curry, 130
Carrot, and celeriac rösti, 39
Chestnuts and Brussels sprouts with red cabbage and caraway, 26
Hot-and-sour, and turnip casserole, 51
In Jerusalem artichoke gratin, 126
Lentil and, cakes with mustard pickle, 82
Saffron and, stew with rouille, 38
Salad-filled, pie, 127
In Scandinavian salad, 41
Protein, 6, 7
Provençal casserole, 70
Puddings:

Bread, cheese, and onion, 120
Steamed leek and celeriac, 111
Pumpkin:
And pecorino risotto, 60
Savory, pie, 104

Quiche. See also Tart
Mushroom, 135
Mustard-cauliflower, 105

Ragout, wild and brown rice with
mushroom, 58
Raisin, eggplant rolls with a ricotta,
filling, 16
Ramekins, eggplant and mozzarella, 15
Ratatouille terrine, 14
Ravioli:
Goat cheese and parsley, 96
Making, 97
Red cabbage:
Chestnuts and Brussels sprouts
with, and caraway potatoes, 26
Spiced, 27
Red-pepper sauce, 30
Relishes. See also Pickle
Chili-tomato, 78
Onion, 64
Pepper and onion, 34
Rice. See also Risotto; Wild rice
Basmati and wild, molds with
braised artichokes, 56
Cakes with onion relish, 64
In Caribbean spiced salad, 55
In eight treasures in lotus leaves, 62
Gingered black beans with saffron,
72
Salad of avocado, flageolets,
almonds, and brown, 54
Wild and brown, pilaf with
mushroom ragout, 58
Ricotta cheese:
Penne with celery and, 95
Raisin filling, 16
And zucchini tortellini with mint
yogurt sauce, 92
Risotto:
Pea and mushroom, 61
Pumpkin and pecorino, 60
Roquefort sauce, 22
Rösti of potato, carrot, and celeriac, 39
Rouille, 38
Roulade, spinach, Stilton, and
tomato, 29
Rutabaga, curried, soup, 43

Saffron:
Fettuccine with hazelnut and
tarragon sauce, 98
And potato stew with rouille, 38
Rice, 72
Salads:
Avocado, flageolets, almonds, and
brown rice, 54
Chickpea, in artichoke cups, 78
Filled potato pie, 127
Italian peasant, 119
Scandinavian, 41
Warm Camembert and fruit, 129
Salsify:
And asparagus muffins, 118
With pepper and onion relish, 34
Sauces. See also Dressings

Bean curd, 46
Chili, 36
Cilantro-yogurt, 71
Citrus, 100
Goat cheese, 21
Gruyère, 24
Hazelnut and tarragon, 98
Hot-pepper, 35
Mint yogurt, 92
Mustard, 33
Nutmeg, 94
Olive and caper, 88
Orange, 44
Paprika, 37
Peanut, 101
Red-pepper, 30
Roquefort, 22
Seasoning, 84
Sweet-pepper, 20
Sweet-and-sour, 45
Tomato, 96, 134
Watercress, 102
Savory pumpkin pie, 104
Scandinavian salad, 41
Seasoning sauce, 84
Seeds, 7
Semolina gnocchi with julienned
vegetables, 66
Shortcrust pastry, 91, 107
Lemon, 109
Sichuan tofu with sweet pepper and
peanuts, 84
Smoked cheese gougère with a
lemon and fennel filling, 110
Soufflés:
Jerusalem artichoke and walnut, 42
Lentil, baked in sweet pepper
cases, 84
Squash, 19
Soup:
Barley and mushroom broth with
smoked tofu, 89
Curried rutabaga, 43
Spaghetti with omelette strips and
stir-fried vegetables, 97
Spanish omelette, 13
Spiced bean medley, 131
Spiced red cabbage, 27
Spicy mold of leeks, zucchini, and
cabbage, 25
Spinach, 6, 7
Lacy pancakes with, filling, 28
Lentils with, and carrots, 81
And Nappa cabbage pie, 113
Pasta dough, 94
And pine nut layered terrine, 30
Stilton, and tomato roulade, 29
Spring rolls, herbed, with peanut
sauce, 101
Spring vegetables in watercress
crepes, 20
Steamed leek and celeriac pudding, 111
Steaming, 8
Stilton:
Pastry-wrapped pears stuffed with
walnuts, and leeks, 107
Spinach, and tomato roulade, 29
Stir-fried vegetables, 8
Spaghetti with omelette strips and, 97
Tofu and, with noodles, 87
In a sweet-and-sour sauce, 45
Stock, 9
Storing ingredients, 7
Strudel, asparagus, 112
Stuffed vegetables:

Baked potatoes with an onion and
chive filling, 40
Belgian endive baked with
pistachio-stuffed tomatoes, 23
Cabbage stuffed with black-eyed
peas and mushrooms, 76
Chestnut-stuffed sweet poatoes
with chili sauce, 36
Chickpea salad in artichoke cups, 78
Hollowing a whole cabbage for
stuffing, 76
Leeks with Gruyère sauce, 24
Lentil soufflés baked in sweet
pepper cases, 84
Mushroom caps, 32
Preparing artichokes for stuffing, 79
Stuffed grape leaves, 128
Succotash, butter bean, 75
Summer beans with fresh fettuccine
and basil, 99
Sweet peppers. See also Chili
peppers; Pepper
Lentil soufflés baked in
cases, 84
Okra and, stew, 48
Peeling, 21
Red, sauce, 30
Salsify with, and onion relish, 34
Sauces, 20
Sichuan tofu with, and
peanuts, 84
In sweet potato timbales with two
paprika sauces, 37
Sweet potatoes:
Chestnut-stuffed, with chili sauce, 36
Mexican, stew, 50
Timbales with two paprika sauces, 37
Sweet-and-sour sauce, 45
Sweet-and-sour tumbled vegetables,
133

Tandoori patties, 71
Tarragon, hazelnut and, sauce, 98
Tart. See also Quiche
Asparagus and morel, 103
Terrines:
Ratatouille, 14
Spinach and pine nut layered, 30
Timbales:
Cabbage, with tomato sauce, 134
Sweet potato, with two paprika
sauces, 37
Tofu:
Barley and mushroom broth with
smoked, 89
Sichuan, with sweet pepper and
peanuts, 84
Storing and draining, 85
And vegetable dumplings, 86
And vegetable stir-fry with noodles,
87
Zucchini, and mushroom kabobs, 88
Tomatoes:
Belgian endive and pistachio-
stuffed, 23
In boiled yam with hot-pepper
sauce, 35
Chili, relish, 78
Coulis, 15
Peeling and seeding, 14
Peeling in a microwave, 131
In polenta pizza, 68
In Provençal casserole, 70
Sauce, 96, 134

Spinach, Stilton, and, roulade, 29
Stuffed grape leaves with bulgur
and, 128
Zucchini and, clafoutis, 124
Topping, cornbread, 67
Tortellini:
Ricotta and zucchini, with mint
yogurt sauce, 92
Shaping, 93
Tortes, carrot and broccoli, 102
Turnip, hot-and-sour potato and,
casserole, 51
Turnovers, broccoli and pecorino, 109
Tuscan-style beans, 73

Vegetable:
Oils, 6
Stock, 9
Vegetables. See also individual names
Buying and storing, 7
Curry with coconut, 49
Indonesian, stew, 80
Lasagna, 94
Mixed root, in orange sauce, 44
Mixed, pipérade, 125
Semolina gnocchi with julienned, 66
Spaghetti with omelette strips and
stir-fried, 97
Spring, in watercress crepes, 20
Stir-fried, in a sweet-and-sour
sauce, 45
Sweet-and-sour tumbled, 133
Tofu and, dumplings, 86
Tofu and, stir-fry with noodles, 87

Walnuts:
Jerusalem artichoke and, soufflés, 42
Pastry-wrapped pears stuffed with,
Stilton, and leeks, 107
Watercress:
Sauce, 102
Spring vegetables in, crepes, 20
Wheat bran, 6
Whole-wheat pastry, 102
Whole-wheat pizza with corn and
pineapple, 106
Wild rice:
Basmati and, molds with braised
artichokes, 56
And brown rice pilaf with
mushroom ragout, 58
Gâteau of crepes with, and
mushrooms, 56

Yam, boiled, with hot-pepper
sauce, 35
Yeast dough, 104, 108
Yogurt:
Cilantro, sauce, 71
Dressing, 78
Mint, sauce, 92

Zucchini:
Kohlrabi and, gratin, 31
In Provençal casserole, 70
Ricotta and, tortellini with mint
yogurt sauce, 92
Spicy mold of, cabbage and leeks, 25
Tian, 12
Tofu, and mushroom kabobs, 88
And tomato clafoutis, 124